"The mark of a good book doesn't solve God and does up. Rather, it grapples with l. his incomprehensibility. It leads us to marvel at both how much and how little we know of him. It goes as far as Scripture goes, but no farther. This is just that kind of book, and on that basis I'm glad to recommend it."

Tim Challies, blogger at challies.com; author of *Visual Theology*

"Perhaps not since R. C. Sproul has there been a treatment of such deep theology with such careful devotion and accessibility. *None Greater* explores the 'adorable mystery' of God with clarity and wisdom. Read this book. And stagger."

Jared Wilson, director of content strategy, Midwestern Baptist Theological Seminary; managing editor, For the Church; author of *The Gospel-Driven Church*

"Recent years have revealed that while evangelical Protestantism has done good work in defending a sound doctrine of Scripture, it has badly neglected the doctrine of God and at many points wandered away from classical Nicene orthodoxy, under the influence of a blunt, historically ill-informed biblicism. There is thankfully a renewed interest in classical theism among Protestant theologians, but the discussion often seems rarefied to the point where many Christians are confused as to why it is important and what is at stake for the church. Matthew Barrett's excellent book bridges the gap between the professional theologian and the pew, laying out in clear, accessible terms what the biblical, historic, ecumenical doctrine of God is, why it matters, and why its abandonment by great swathes of the Protestant world is something that needs correction."

Carl R. Trueman, professor, Grove City College; author of *Grace Alone*

"Way back in 1973, J. I. Packer reminded us in his book *Knowing God* that the greatest need of the evangelical church was to think big thoughts about our Triune God and to know him in all of his perfection, glory, and majesty. Sadly, many in the evangelical church have not heeded Packer's cry to know God, as evangelicals seemingly have become consumed with everything but the glory of God, to the detriment of our spiritual life and health. However, Matthew Barrett has not forgotten Packer's cry to know God. In *None Greater*, Barrett has given us what the church in our day desperately needs more than anything else—to behold the beauty, glory, self-sufficiency, and sheer otherness of our Triune God, who alone is worthy of our worship, faith, obedience, and service. This book is must reading if the church is going to regain her way and put God first once again. It is a wonderful antidote to shallow theological thinking in our day, and it returns us to ponder anew our undomesticated Creator and Redeemer. In one of the most readable books on the attributes of God I have ever read, Barrett calls us to return to Scripture and to stand on the shoulders of previous theologians who thought deeply about the God of the gospel. If you want to stand firm for the gospel today and to avoid all the fads and errors of our age, take up this book and by it be led to what is life eternal: the knowledge of God in the face of our Lord Jesus Christ."

Stephen Wellum, professor of Christian theology, Southern Baptist Theological Seminary; author of *God the Son Incarnate*

"This lively and interesting treatment of the attributes of God will lead readers into a deeper appreciation of the God who alone is worthy of our worship. In a day and age when great confusion reigns as to the nature of God, Barrett brings responsible exegesis together with informed historical awareness of the Great Tradition and wraps the package in a writing style that engages the reader and explains complex matters with a deft touch. This is a fine introduction to the attributes of God that will strengthen faith and help us think more clearly."

Craig Carter, professor of theology, Tyndale University College and Seminary; author of *Interpreting Scripture with the Great Tradition*

"Consistent with the classics of Augustine, Aquinas, and Anselm, this book gets to the heart of the question, 'What is God?' With a simple but never simplistic approach, Matthew Barrett unpacks what the Bible says about the character or even the perfections of God. God is beautifully holy, and Barrett reminds us that there is none greater and no one better to know than God. If knowing God is your desire, take up this book and read."

Anthony Carter, lead pastor, East Point Church; author of *Black and Reformed* and *Blood Work*

"The knowledge of God is the soil in which Christian piety flourishes. I am grateful for the publication of Matthew Barrett's book *None Greater: The Undomesticated Attributes of God* and pray it will be a source of growth in godliness among those captivated by its vision of God's supremacy."

Scott Swain, president and James Woodrow Hassell Professor of Systematic Theology, Reformed Theological Seminary–Orlando; author of *Reformed Catholicity*

"In an age of frivolities and distractions, we need more books like this! Here is the greatest of all subjects, theology proper, addressed with clarity and precision. Matthew Barrett writes in a way that is accessible and engaging as he explores the attributes of our God. No reader will walk away from this book disappointed. I pray many will devour this book, because it will not only inform their theology but lead to doxology. And the God detailed in these pages is worth worshiping!"

Jason Helopoulos, senior pastor, University Reformed Church; author of *The New Pastor's Handbook*

"Matthew Barrett is publishing important and edifying material at an astonishing rate. In his latest book he makes accessible a classical treatment of the attributes of God. It is clearly and engagingly written and yet shows the fruit of a great deal of careful theological research and reasoning. Barrett's commitment to the supreme authority of Scripture as God's written Word is apparent on every page. In an age when Christian people have far too often been satisfied with an anemic portrait of the living God, here is a tonic that is sorely needed. Enlarge your view of God by reading this book."

Mark D. Thompson, principal, Moore Theological College

"Deep and powerful currents flow through Barrett's exploration of the doctrine of God. He writes with exegetical rigor, theological precision, and practical insight, all in conversation with some of the church's greatest minds. This book is well worth the time to study who God is and learn that there truly is none greater."

J. V. Fesko, academic dean and professor of systematic and historical theology, Westminster Seminary California; author of *Justification*

"God created us to know, love, and worship him according to his revelation of himself. One of the greatest challenges to this has always been our idolatrous instinct to reimagine God's character as one we are most comfortable with or that fits best with contemporary sensibilities. This happens when we distort or neglect any attributes of God, and this leads us away from the true, life-giving relationship with our Creator that he intends for us. In *None Greater*, Matthew Barrett has given us a tremendously helpful and biblical presentation of aspects of God's character that often get left out in our thinking, preaching, and worship. I'm confident that this book will help God's people to know, enjoy, and worship our great and loving King in a more fulfilling and honoring way."

Erik Thoennes, professor of theology and chair of the Department of Undergraduate Theological Studies, Talbot School of Theology / Biola University; author of *Godly Jealousy*

"This is an important book. The long-standing classic vision of God is being eroded in the contemporary church. Barrett is not a lone voice of protest (he intentionally points us to the best of Christian theology across the ages), but he presents the issues in an accessible form. His writing is engaging and clear throughout. Still, this book will stretch your conception of God. But then any worthwhile book on the doctrine of God should do that, because as Barrett keeps reminding us, God is he whom none greater can be conceived. Yes, Barrett teaches us about God's attributes as well as how they interrelate. But reading this book is not like taking a class; it is much more like a spiritual exercise, even an encounter with the living God. It is like reading an extended hymn of praise. Few will read it without a growing sense of awe. This is a book to read and reread."

Tim Chester, pastor, Grace Church Boroughbridge, UK; faculty member, Crosslands Training; author of *Enjoying God*

"My sins and fears can all ultimately be traced to an impoverished vision of God. This book is a welcome tonic to me. All the weaknesses and fears of the modern church can be traced to an impoverished vision of God. This book is a necessary tonic. I urge you to read it prayerfully and be confronted with the perfect, infinite, overflowing, trinitarian God, who is love, wisdom, power and grace beyond what we can imagine."

Peter Sanlon, author of *Simply God*; director of training, The Free Church of England

NONE GREATER

THE UNDOMESTICATED ATTRIBUTES OF GOD

MATTHEW BARRETT

FOREWORD BY FRED SANDERS

BakerBooks
a division of Baker Publishing Group
Grand Rapids, Michigan

Published by Baker Books
a division of Baker Publishing Group
PO Box 6287, Grand Rapids, MI 49516-6287
www.bakerbooks.com

Printed in the United States of America

Library of Congress Cataloging-in-Publication Data
Names: Barrett, Matthew, 1982– author.
Title: None greater : the undomesticated attributes of God / Matthew Barrett.
Description: Grand Rapids, MI : Baker Books, a division of Baker Publishing
    Group, [2019] | Includes bibliographical references.
Identifiers: LCCN 2018034320 | ISBN 9780801098741 (paperback)
Subjects: LCSH: God (Christianity)—Attributes.
Classification: LCC BT130 .B37 2019 | DDC 231/.4—dc23
LC record available at https://lccn.loc.gov/2018034320

20 21 22 23 24 25   7 6 5 4

To Georgia.

"But when they rose early on the next morning, behold, Dagon had fallen face downward on the ground before the ark of the LORD, and the head of Dagon and both his hands were lying cut off on the threshold. Only the trunk of Dagon was left to him."

1 SAMUEL 5:4

Contents

Foreword

Usually when theologians find out they were wrong about something, they admit it readily enough. But then they cover their tracks. They revise their views in light of the evidence, adopt the correct views, and from then on simply teach and talk as if they had always held these new, improved views. They may have taken a journey out of confusion to get to the truth, but once they arrive, they only tell about the destination. That's fair enough: what we want from theologians is a description of the land of truth.

The best thing about Matthew Barrett's book *None Greater* is that he doesn't wipe out his own footprints. He retraces them and takes us along for the journey. And it is a strange journey of discovery, because what Barrett discovered was the God he already knew. He had been praising God, trusting God, serving God, studying God in his Word, teaching true things about God, and praying to God all along. But somehow, at some point, it dawned on him that there was something unreal, incomplete, and inadequate in the way he had become accustomed to thinking about God.

This is where Barrett's journey intersects the journeys of so many of us raised in the Christian faith. Focusing on a preselected subset of things we like to remember about God (his mercy, intimacy, concern for us, attention to us, love for us), we let our thoughts about God orbit around that familiar center. We grow comfortable with a certain set of reassuring, familiar, and cozy divine attributes. There are no sheer cliffs, dizzying heights, or fathomless abysses in the doctrine of God we let ourselves settle into. It's as if we have a doctrine of God that gets everything right except that it accidentally leaves out the sheer "godness" of God. But that means it gets everything wrong.

That is the shock that Barrett's book captures: Meeting the God you thought you knew, and being shocked by his sheer godness. God is greater than he thought God was! Extending that moment of shock into a whole book, Barrett explores all the divine attributes that we are so tempted to diminish, downplay, avoid, or ignore. Perfection, aseity, simplicity, immutability, impassibility, eternity, and all of the "omni-" attributes come parading by as we learn to confess a higher, more classical, and more biblical doctrine of God.

The main discovery Barrett records in this book is the discovery that God is greater, but there is another discovery that accompanies it: theology is hard. Theology is hard because once you realize how much greater God is—that than which nothing greater can be conceived, in the Anselmian ways of saying it—you realize how much harder God is to talk about. The problem cannot be overcome simply by studying theology books and learning some new, more technical vocabulary. Most readers will in fact pick up a few helpful new words from this book, since words like "aseity" are not exactly household words, and words like "simplicity" have a special meaning in theology. But picking up those terms, and using them to say more of the right things about God, is not enough. These words and concepts of the classical Christian doctrine of God are just markers along the way to reversing some deep-seated habits of thought. Those habits of thought mostly start out with a sentiment like "If I were God . . ." We are easily lulled into a style of theology that starts from ourselves and imagines some ways in which God must be like that, but bigger and better. I feel sad when I am rejected, so God must feel even more rejected, but without acting out because of it. I need to be loved, so God must need to be loved even more, but also somehow he must be able to accept when he isn't. It's possible to take statements like these and nuance them enough, or hedge them with some biblical principles, or rule out gross errors, so that we end up with a decent theology of a respectable God. But there is an underlying problem that will keep generating errors every time we let down our guard. The underlying problem is a theological style that, even in its reading of Scripture, works up from us to God.

With *None Greater*, Barrett is determined to reverse that direction. He has learned that the proper path of theology is to follow the revelation of God from above to below instead, and he wants to bring readers along with him on this journey. It requires some truly counterintuitive moves, because we really have to get outside of ourselves to hear the message of God's perfection and blessedness. And it requires us to pay more attention to some of the major theological witnesses of the great tradition of Christian thought than we may be accustomed to do. That's because many of these older voices—Athanasius with his shocked reaction to Arianism, Augustine with his autobiographical *Confessions*, Anselm with his book-length meditative prayer—also wrote as pilgrims who had been surprised by the godness of God. So there is plenty of company on the journey that Barrett invites readers to join him on. What matters most, though, is to start the journey. What matters is to join the company of those who are permanently shocked by the sheer godness of the God we thought we knew.

Fred Sanders
Professor of Theology
Torrey Honors Institute
Biola University

Preface

Fill the House

For my own part, I tend to find the doctrinal books often more helpful in devotion than the devotional books, and I rather suspect that the same experience may await many others. I believe that many who find that "nothing happens" when they sit down, or kneel down, to a book of devotion, would find that the heart sings unbidden while they are working their way through a tough bit of theology with a pipe in their teeth and a pencil in their hand.

C. S. Lewis, "On the Reading of Old Books"

I have often lamented that there are very few books on the attributes of God written for those in the church in a style that is clear and accessible yet uncompromising and rigorous. While stacks of books invite the scholarly student to pick up and read, the churchgoer has little opportunity to dive headfirst into the deep things of God. Sadly, they turn to popular devotional literature to feed a spiritual hunger that only theology can satisfy.

Is it any wonder that our churches have a big heart for ministry but look almost anemic when asked about the big God we claim to worship?

To make matters worse, that gaping hole is all too eagerly filled by liberal theologians. The last two centuries have demonstrated that the modern and postmodern person is quick to substitute a God who is like us, a God we can domesticate, for the high view of God affirmed by figures like Augustine, Anselm, and Aquinas. The parable of the unclean spirits applies: when bad theology is cast out by one generation but not replaced with a substitute by the next, the home of Christian theology is left empty. When that bad spirit of theology returns and finds the home empty, it brings with it seven more unclean theologies. The last state is worse than the first (Matt. 12:45). Such is our heritage.

But it can change.

This book is meant to *fill the house* with good theology proper, the type that will keep the demons away for good. That means dispensing with the modern theologian's agenda to create a God in our own image, a God whose immanence has swallowed his transcendence, a God that can be controlled by the creature because he is not that different from the creature. But it also means filling the house with a biblical understanding of God as one who is, as Isaiah said, "high and lifted up" (Isa. 6:1), whose attributes remain undomesticated. He is the God Jeremiah confessed, saying,

> There is none like you, O Lord;
> You are great, and your name is great in might.
> (Jer. 10:6)

There is none greater than this God, not because he is merely a greater version of ourselves but because he is nothing like ourselves. Only a Creator not to be confused with the creature is capable of stooping down to redeem those who have marred his image. Our "situation would surely have been hopeless," exclaims

John Calvin, "had the very majesty of God not descended to us, since it was not in our power to ascend to him."[1]

All that to say, I've written this book not for scholars (though I hope many scholars will read it) but instead for churchgoers, pastors, and those beginning students who have yet to pick up a book that takes them into the classical view of God. Sincerely, I hope this book will be passed around among the people of God so that churches of tomorrow will be fortified against those who might cleverly attempt to fill our theological house with a theology proper foreign to the God of Abraham, Isaac, and Jacob.

To that end, I've tried to write this book in a way that is clear and accessible. I have provided a glossary at the end of the book to help readers understand terms and concepts as they work through the book's arguments. I am a strong believer in divine simplicity, so the attribute discussed in one chapter is always related to the attributes in every other chapter. The glossary will assist the reader with terms and concepts even before they have been fully addressed in any given chapter.

I am, of course, truly grateful to many. I must thank Brian Vos, who first approached me about writing a book on the attributes of God for Baker Books. I will admit, I was unsure at first. Writing a popular-level book in a way that is accessible and clear but on a subject as intimidating as the doctrine of God felt a little like trying to climb Sinai as it quaked and smoked. I have found myself hiding in the cleft of the rock with Moses, humbly seeking to know who God is by means of his mighty works and words but without so arrogantly assuming I can see the glory of his essence. While I was writing this book, R. C. Sproul went to be with the Lord. Brian encouraged me to further study Sproul, one so gifted at articulating the complexity of theology in a way the churchgoer could embrace.

I am also indebted to the sharp editorial eye of James Korsmo, who helped smooth out the rough edges so that the arguments and prose were as lucid as possible. I should also like to thank some of my students—Ronni Kurtz, Sam Parkison, and Joseph Lanier—for reading the book ahead of time.

I am especially grateful to Jason Allen, president of Midwestern Baptist Theological Seminary, and Jason Duesing, provost of MBTS, for their support as my family transitioned to Kansas City. Not only did they ensure I had time to write this book, but their excitement to have me teach theology to students has inspired me to excel in scholarship for the church. It is a joy to be on their team.

As always, my wife, Elizabeth, has been my bulwark. What Katie was to Luther, Elizabeth is to me. In the midst of creating a home life that is full of joy and happiness, she never tires of theological conversations. I struggle at times to imitate the lowliness of Christ, but such humility characterizes Elizabeth's spirit daily. She genuinely loves others as Christ does, and no one knows that more personally than her children.

I dedicate this book to my daughter, Georgia. She is a quiet spirit. When she talks I listen. Her gentleness must have come from her heavenly Father. I pray this book shows you something of his beauty so that you are drawn ever closer to his Son by his Spirit.

Matthew Barrett
Kansas City, 2018

Introduction

Surprised by God

You are clothed with splendor and majesty.

PSALM 104:1

The transcendent, majestic, awesome God of Luther and Calvin
. . . has undergone a softening of demeanor.

MARSHA WITTEN, *All Is Forgiven*

"Aslan is a lion—*the* Lion, the great Lion."
     "Ooh!" said Susan. "I'd thought he was a man. Is he—quite
safe? I shall feel rather nervous about meeting a lion." . . .
     "Safe?" said Mr. Beaver. . . . "Who said anything about safe?
'Course he isn't safe. But he's good. He's the King, I tell you."

C. S. LEWIS, *The Lion, the Witch and the Wardrobe*

An Awakening

I fell in love twice when I was in college. The first time I fell in love was when I met my wife, Elizabeth, as a first-year university student outside the cafeteria in sunny Los Angeles. It's hard to believe, but we've been married thirteen years now, and yet I remember the day we first met as if it were yesterday.

Everything happened backward. Valentine's Day was all too quickly approaching, and she had promised her roommate she would find her a date . . . and fast. Like most freshmen, I was clueless, but apparently Elizabeth had decided that date was me. As my friends later told me, for the next two weeks she stalked me, making sure I was a good fit for her roommate. Finally, one day she worked up the nerve to introduce herself to me for the first time. I had just walked out of the cafeteria and was startled by the sudden "hello" from a terribly pretty freshman girl. For the next hour we talked, but she had decided I was not a good fit for her roommate after all. Instead, I was just the right fit for her! Long story short, her roommate had to get another date, and I showed up with flowers at Elizabeth's door that Valentine's Day.

That same year, however, I fell in love a second time. No, it wasn't with another girl. It was with a book, as nerdy as that sounds. As a new student at a Christian university, Elizabeth was enjoying her theology classes. One day she asked me whether I had read any of the books she was reading. Embarrassed, I coughed up a no. Here was the girl I wanted to impress, and she apparently knew more about theology than I did. Unaware of my humiliation, Elizabeth began sharing how much she had learned about the doctrine of grace, for example, and how she was wrestling with the big questions surrounding the Christian faith, like the mystery between divine sovereignty and free will and the problem of evil.

My curiosity was sparked.

A few days later I stumbled across a beat-up and abandoned copy of John Calvin's *Institutes of the Christian Religion* outside the school cafeteria. For the next several days I couldn't sleep. I was glued to this book. I'd never read anything like it before. Sure, I had grown up in a Christian home. And yes, I had gone to church every week to hear the Bible taught. I had even read many Christian books as a young believer. But this book was different. Why?

Calvin articulated so clearly and profoundly the majesty of God. With eyes freshly peeled, no longer was I "studying" God—as the label "theology" sometimes communicates. No, I was meeting the *living* God. That semester I had embarked on a mission to *know* God himself like I'd never known him before. I may have read my Bible for years and been a devoted Christian, but now a window—a door, really—was swung open wide for me to behold the glory of God like never before.

That year, the more I learned about God, the more I had to admit just how little and insignificant I was next to this big God. While the culture told me that God was just a bigger, better version of ourselves, the God I was discovering was one nothing like humans. Like never before, I resonated with Calvin's confession: "Man is never sufficiently touched and affected by the awareness of his lowly state until he has compared himself with God's majesty."[1] Much like Job, the more I fathomed "God's wisdom, power, and purity," the more overwhelmed I became, especially in light of my own "stupidity, impotence, and corruption."[2] Once I was sobered by God's majesty, his infinite glory, supremacy, and perfection suddenly beamed bright, like the sun's warm rays after a merciless, icy winter. The brightness of his divinity had blinded me, yet ironically, I could now see his beauty better than before.

Little did I know that I would undergo yet a further awakening to God's glory that summer during a memorable camping trip.

A Further Awakening

Camping really is the hallmark family adventure. Sleeping in the great outdoors with the stars staring down. Roasting marshmallows and telling ghost stories at night next to a crackling fire. Catching that giant bass with just a worm on your hook. Camping is where memories are made.

Except in my experience, camping can be a total nightmare. I remember the first time my wife and I went camping after we had been married for several years. The mosquitoes had decided to hold their family reunion on our campsite. The first morning, we woke up ready for a hearty breakfast only to realize we had forgotten the pancakes, syrup, eggs, and bacon. And then came the heat. It was so hot I couldn't sleep. Apparently our one-year-old daughter agreed and decided she would let the entire campground know she was an unhappy camper, disgruntled with Mom and Dad's decision to leave the comforts of home (especially air-conditioning). At 3 a.m., we could take it no longer. We threw everything in the back of the car and headed home, defeated.

Despite my recent history of camping disasters, I do have fond memories from when I was growing up of moving from site to site in our old station wagon. I enjoy the stillness of a lake in the morning mist or the gentle breeze on a mountaintop after a rigorous hike, and there are few moments better to reflect on the character of God.

After leaving home and going to college, I tried to keep up the camping tradition. That first summer, I was invited to join my future in-laws, and it was memorable: French toast in the mornings, followed by waterskiing in the afternoons. Believe it or not, that was not the highlight of the trip, as much as I loved maple syrup and skiing at twenty miles per hour with the wind in my face. The highlight came one quiet morning when I had woken up much earlier than everyone else. I had just been given a copy of Saint Augustine's *Confessions*. It was a little paperback that I had accidentally dropped in a dog's water bowl the day before. The book was swollen up like a blowfish, so I almost threw it away. For some reason I kept it, and that dewy morning I sat down under the light of the sunrise to give Augustine a try. My life would never be the same.

Here was a man who had deep struggles with sin, fighting his flesh until he finally surrendered his life to God and trusted in

AUGUSTINE

Augustine of Hippo (354–430) was steeped in Manichaean philosophy as an unbeliever, and this North African's troubled conscience was restless until he discovered that only Christianity could answer the questions he struggled to untangle. You can read about his conversion in his *Confessions*, perhaps the most famous Christian autobiography in history, though atypical of biographies, grounded as it is in theological prayers that say much about the character of God. Augustine would be embroiled in controversy throughout his career. Against the Pelagians, for example, Augustine defended the doctrine of original sin, demonstrating that humanity's inherent depravity necessitates a grace that will powerfully and effectually grant humans new spiritual life, resulting in conversion. Against the Arians in the West, Augustine defended the full deity of Christ, and he went on to articulate a doctrine of the Trinity that is still discussed and debated today. For our purposes, it is Augustine's reflections on the ever-so-delicate balance between divine transcendence and divine immanence that will prove enlightening.

Christ. Augustine would one day look back and retell the story of his conversion. But *The Confessions* is no mere autobiography; it's a rich portrayal of God, one that comes in the form of countless prayers. As I took in the beauty of the lake's navy blue, I suddenly encountered a prayer that opened my eyes to divine beauty I had never seen before:

> Most high, utterly good, utterly powerful, most omnipotent, most merciful and most just, deeply hidden yet most intimately present, perfection of both beauty and strength, stable and incomprehensible, immutable and yet changing all things, never new, never old, making everything new and "leading" the proud "to be old without their knowledge" (Job 9:5, Old Latin version); always active, always in repose, gathering to yourself but not in need, supporting and filling and protecting, creating and nurturing and

bringing to maturity, searching even though to you nothing is lacking: you love without burning, you are jealous in a way that is free of anxiety, you "repent" (Gen. 6:6) without the pain of regret, you are wrathful and remain tranquil. You will a change without any change in your design. You recover what you find, yet have never lost. Never in any need, you rejoice in your gains (Luke 15:7); you are never avaricious, yet you require interest (Matt. 25:27). We pay you more than you require so as to make you our debtor, yet who has anything which does not belong to you? (1 Cor. 4:7). You pay off debts, though owing nothing to anyone; you cancel debts and incur no loss. But in these words what have I said, my God, my life, my holy sweetness? What has anyone achieved in words when he speaks about you? Yet woe to those who are silent about you because, though loquacious with verbosity, they have nothing to say.[3]

Carefully differentiating between the Creator and the creature, Augustine is like an acrobat walking the tightrope.[4] Yes, God is immanent ("intimately present"), but he remains transcendent and incomprehensible ("deeply hidden"). Yes, he effects change in the world ("changing all things"), but he never changes in himself ("immutable"). Yes, he creates and renews, but he himself is timelessly eternal ("never new, never old"). Yes, he nurtures others, but he is never one in need of nurture. Yes, he brings the world into maturity, but he never matures, nor is he ever in need of reaching his potential or being activated; he is maximally alive, pure act ("always active"), never changing (immutable). Yes, he loves, but always impassibly ("you love without burning"). Yes, he is jealous, but his jealousy, unlike human jealousy, is never desperate or impotent (being "free of anxiety"). Yes, he pours out judgment on the wicked, but never as a capricious God ("[you] remain tranquil"), his judgment always metered by his righteousness. And yes, he redeems, paying our debt, but only because he owes debt to no one, being a God of absolute aseity ("owing nothing to anyone").

Not explicitly stated, but quietly interwoven throughout Augustine's prayer, is a foundational premise: *the attributes sing in harmony.* While simplicity—the belief that God is not made up of parts, but he *is* his attributes (see chap. 5 and the glossary)—is never mentioned in Augustine's prayer, it is infused throughout. Augustine not only balances God in himself with how God relates to his creation, but he never partitions one attribute from another, believing each to illuminate the other. In such illumination, we step back and marvel at the perfection of God's one, undivided essence. "Out of Zion, the perfection of beauty, God shines forth" (Ps. 50:2).

After reading Augustine's prayer again and again, I put down the bloated book, looked out at the peaceful horizon, and felt perplexed. Why had I not learned of *this* God before? He was so . . . big, much bigger than I had been taught. Sure, I knew the basics: God is Creator. God is Lord. God is love. But never had I thought about God's perfections like Augustine had. To be honest, some of them I had never considered before. Part of me felt frustrated, too. How could I be a Christian for so long, have studied the Bible for so many years, and been in church so regularly, and yet never have heard about attributes like simplicity, aseity, impassibility, and others? Nevertheless, I was simultaneously overwhelmed by joy. With Augustine by my side, I reread the Scriptures and saw these attributes on every page of the Bible. How could I have missed them before? They were everywhere. Although I had known God for years, in that moment I was completely caught off guard. I was surprised by God.

In the months ahead, I kept returning to Augustine's prayer. Except, as I did so there was one phrase that I just couldn't escape: God is, Augustine observes, "perfection of both beauty and strength." It's the word "perfection" that especially haunted me. What did it mean? And why would Augustine use it to refer to God's many attributes?

In the years ahead, the haunting would grow louder.

Haunted by the Perfect Being

I was slow to admit it, but the fact that I had been surprised by God in this way meant my life had to change. I took just about every theology class I could when I returned from that unforgettable camping trip. I had to know more about this God that Augustine described, especially that word "perfection."

In the years ahead, the smoke started to clear, until finally it all started to make sense. But this time it wasn't Augustine who opened my eyes; it was Anselm. If Augustine was my first awakening to this God, Anselm was my second. I had read handfuls of popular, contemporary Christian books about God, but none of them took God as seriously as Anselm. He asked questions that no one else was asking. The central question was this: Is God the most perfect being? There it was, that word again: "perfect." Anselm had a way of getting at this concept of perfection by asking whether God is someone than whom none greater can be conceived.[5] If he is, then he must be the most perfect being conceivable. And if he is the most perfect being conceivable, then certain perfect-making attributes—or perfections—have to follow, perfections like infinitude (chap. 3), aseity (chap. 4), simplicity (chap. 5), immutability (chap. 6), impassibility (chap. 7), and timeless eternity (chap. 8), perfections that shield God from being crippled by limitations, perfections that ensure he remains the most perfect, supreme, and glorious being.

That explained everything. The reason I had not come into contact with the type of attributes Augustine had described was that no one ever introduced God to me as the *perfect* being, someone than whom none greater can be conceived. As I reflected on my own journey, it was obvious that God had always been introduced into conversations in a very *experiential* way: love is a common human experience, so God must be a God of love; mercy is a commendable virtue, so God must be a God of mercy; and so on. Thinking about God was always from the bottom up—that is, from my experience to who God is. But with the help of Augustine

ANSELM

An Italian by birth, Anselm (1033–1109) lived his early years as an unbeliever, taking after his father, though his mother was a follower of Christ. When he was converted, Anselm took a monastic vow and eventually traveled to England, where he was appointed archbishop of Canterbury. Over the course of his career, Anselm wrote some of the most important works on theology, books like *Cur Deus Homo* (*Why God Became Man*). For our purposes, Anselm's *Monologion* and *Proslogion* are especially relevant. The latter is his famous argument for the existence of God. Most inspiring is Anselm's belief that God is "something-than-which-nothing-greater-can-be-thought."[a] What many fail to remember is that Anselm's argument for the existence of God was but one part of his contribution. From that basic premise in Latin—*id quo maius cogitari nequit*, or "that than which it is impossible to think anything greater"[b]—Anselm demonstrated, through logical rigor, that certain great-making attributes *must* follow. Even though later thinkers, some as colossal as Thomas Aquinas, took issue with Anselm's ontological argument, nevertheless they too saw an unbreakable chain from God's perfection to the rest of his attributes. Our treatment of the divine attributes will be indebted to Anselm's argument, and our attitude throughout this book will be that of Anselm's, one of humility before the infinite Holy One. It will be an attitude of faith seeking understanding. As Anselm prayed near the start of his *Proslogion*, "I do not try, Lord, to attain Your lofty heights, because my understanding is in no way equal to it. But I do desire to understand Your truth a little, that truth that my heart believes and loves. For I do not seek to understand so that I may believe; but I believe so that I may understand."[c]

[a] Anselm, *Proslogion* 2 (*Major Works*, 87).
[b] Anselm, *Proslogion* 2; the translation is from Hart, *Experience of God*, 117.
[c] Anselm, *Proslogion* 1 (*Major Works*, 87).

and Anselm, that approach now seemed dangerous, always flirting with the possibility of creating a God in our own image, always defining God's attributes according to our own limitations.

What was so different about the God of Augustine and Anselm was that they first thought of God as one who is *not* like us. They started from the top (God) and then worked their way down (to humanity). They moved from the Creator to the creature. And this approach seemed far more aligned with the way the biblical authors approached God. As David says, "For with you is the fountain of life; in your light do we see light" (Ps. 36:9).

Being surprised by God changed my entire perspective and approach to God, and for the better. It is my hope that you will be surprised by God too.

One Core Conviction

This is a book about the attributes of God. But it is probably unlike any book you've read before on the attributes of God. Most books on the subject address one attribute and then another and then another. But it is unclear how these attributes relate to one another and whether they all stem from a foundational belief about God.

This book is different. Not only do I believe each and every attribute is key to each and every other attribute in God, but I am convinced that we can only understand God's attributes in all their glory if such attributes originate from one core conviction: *God is someone than whom none greater can be conceived.*

Today, oddly enough, that core conviction is restricted to apologetics, specifically arguments for the existence for God. Anselm meant it to be far more, a conviction that sets a trajectory for how we understand the attributes of God.[6] With that core conviction in mind, the chapters of this book revolve around this central question: *What must be true of God if he is the most perfect being?*[7] If God is someone than whom none greater can be conceived, then certain great-making perfections *must* follow. His perfections are only truly perfections if they are great-making perfections.

Identifying those great-making perfections is our primary mission. But if your experience is anything like mine, then you will be surprised by God too, shocked to discover attributes central to who God is yet never talked about within the doors of the church.

Ancient Roots: The Undomesticated God of Our Fathers

Many of the great-making perfections mentioned by Augustine above are terribly unpopular in our own day. Modern and contemporary Christian thought has either despised them or neglected them altogether, preferring instead a God who is *like us* rather than distinct from us and above us. As a result, God has been domesticated. Nevertheless, the greatest thinkers in the history of the church affirmed these attributes, understood them to be rooted in Scripture itself, and believed that unless they characterize God, he cannot be the most perfect being, the one to whom we owe all glory, honor, and praise.

That is both good and bad news. It is bad news because it means we will have to embark on a quest that most today are not taking. The road ahead has not been paved in a very long time; clearing brush will be part of the job description. It is good news because though few contemporaries are coming with us, the journey is an ancient one. Like the walnut tree in my front yard, this book has roots deep and wide.

If you've ever read John Bunyan's famous allegory, *The Pilgrim's Progress*, then you know that picking the right friends to travel with can be the difference between reaching the celestial city and not. Friends can corrupt us, or they can lead us home. Over the years I've made a handful of friends who can lead us down the right path to knowing God. They are not perfect by any stretch of the imagination, but they have stood the test of time, proving to be faithful to the revelation God has given in Scripture. They're not only faithful but insightful. Isn't this true with old friends? They tend to ask questions that those in our age neglect.

So who are these old friends who will show us the way forward when dark storms blind us from seeing the way ahead? They will be introduced along the way, but I like to call them the A-team: Augustine, Anselm, and Aquinas. We will add other "greats" to this team—Puritans like Stephen Charnock, and Dutch theologians like Herman Bavinck. But all those additional friends tend to depend on this A-team. Their picture of God has sometimes been referred to as "classical theism." Call it what you want; I am persuaded—and I hope you will be too by the end of this book—that the God of classical theism is simply the God of the Bible.

We will invite the A-team to talk to us, and we will listen as they warn us of ditches on the side of the road and inform us of hidden gardens to enjoy while we refresh. At times, our friends will even talk to each other, complementing each other, even building off each other. The goal (their goal) is not merely to help us see the way ahead but to lead us all the way home, back to the one who is the most perfect being. It's a quest each of them has ventured before us, and the writings they have left behind were written to guide pilgrims, like you and me.

Traveling with friends is always a risk. Will they help us persevere along the way that is hard but leads to life, or will they woo us to the way that is easy but leads to destruction (Matt. 7:13–14)? The risk involved reminds us that any friend is only as good as they are true to Scripture, our final and only infallible authority. For there we hear the voice of the one, true, and living God. Our friends from the past will add their voices of support or caution throughout this book, but the ultimate voice to be heard is the voice of God himself. From beginning to end, therefore, the Scriptures will have pride of place, informing our every move. "Your word is a lamp to my feet and a light to my path" (Ps. 119:105). Our roots will be as ancient as Moses, Isaiah, Jesus, and Paul.

Trinity and Attributes

One last introductory word must be mentioned before we begin our pilgrimage. This is a book about God's attributes, not a book about the Trinity. To incorporate something more than a superficial understanding of the Trinity (which is usually necessary since the Trinity is one of the deepest mysteries of the faith!) would take us beyond the parameters of this book, requiring another book altogether.

Nevertheless, I strongly believe that the attributes and the Trinity are not unrelated. The God whose attributes we are describing is none other than the Triune God. That said, at key points throughout the book we will inevitably connect our discussion of the attributes to the three persons of the Godhead. For the three persons fully and truly share the one, undivided essence, and as we will learn in our chapter on simplicity, the attributes of God are not only synonymous with one another but identical with the essence of God.

So while we cannot indulge in a full treatment of the Trinity (as tempting as that would be), the Triune God will be the fabric of everything we say.

From Theology to Doxology

A. W. Tozer once said, "What comes into our minds when we think about God is the most important thing about us."[8] If Tozer is right, then knowing God, as he has made himself known, is at the very center of our identity. Each and every one of us has been made in God's own image and, as John Calvin liked to say, has a sense of divinity within. In that light, the Christian life really is a quest for the truth about God, a pilgrimage that should lead us into a personal encounter with the living God. Naturally we have a desire, even a hunger, to understand God better, to know what to expect from him, and to conform our thoughts to his will. As

Augustine so famously prayed, "You have made us for yourself, and our heart is restless until it rests in you."[9]

On our pilgrimage together, we will go back to the Scriptures in order to understand who God is. The God of the Bible is a God who is not silent. He has spoken and told us what he is like. In doing so, the Creator and Lord of the universe has invited us to know him and enjoy him forever. Our goal is not to walk away with mere knowledge. Rather, this knowledge of God is meant to lead us into worship. Contrary to popular caricatures, doctrine is always meant to lead to doxology, and nowhere is that truer than when we study the *doctrine of God*. As Paul Helm says, "In the Christian theological tradition metaphysics"—the study of God's being or essence—"is but a prelude to worship."[10] Our aim, ultimately, is to know God's perfections and in so doing learn what it means to actually know God in a saving way. Only then will our affections for God be kindled, as Augustine says.

But I must warn you at the start: I will not be interested in wasting your time with a God who is tame and domesticated, a God whose divinity is humanized. That may be the God of popular culture, but it is not the God of the Bible. The God of biblical revelation is the God Isaiah saw, the one who is high and lifted up (Isa. 6:1), possessing all authority in heaven and on earth (Matt. 28:18), and yet one who is simultaneously with us and for us as our Savior (Matt. 1:21–23).

Let the pilgrimage begin.

1

Can We Know the Essence of God?

Incomprehensibility

He who is the blessed and only Sovereign, the King of kings and Lord of lords, who alone has immortality, who dwells in unapproachable light, whom no one has ever seen or can see. To him be honor and eternal dominion. Amen.

1 TIMOTHY 6:15–16

Truly, Lord, this is the inaccessible light in which You dwell. For truly there is nothing else which can penetrate through it so that it might discover You there. Truly I do not see this light since it is too much for me; and yet whatever I see I see through it, just as an eye that is weak sees what it sees by the light of the sun which it cannot look at in the sun itself. . . . O supreme and inaccessible light.

ANSELM, *Proslogion*

H e must have been petrified.

Most likely in the fetal position, he curled up behind a rock. Knees shaking, palms sweaty, throat dry, he prepared himself to see that which no one had dared to see before.

He must have wondered whether he would live to tell others about it. Perhaps not. No one would believe him even if he did. The man hiding behind the rock was Moses. And he was about to see the back of God.

How could this be? For as Moses knew all too well, God is incomprehensible; no one can know—or see!—the very essence of God and live.

Face-to-Face with the Almighty

If there was anyone who had God's ear, anyone who could sit within God's inner counsel, anyone who could petition God on behalf of his people, anyone who could dare to enter into the innermost council of the Triune God, it was Moses, God's chosen leader and mediator. Few prophets, kings, and priests had God's attention like Moses did.

After liberating Israel from Egypt, Moses delivers the people to Mount Sinai. It is there that God will meet with Moses one-on-one to give him the stone tablets, the law by which Israel is to live. Tragically, Israel commits the most horrific of sins: idolatry. The people create a golden calf and bow down in worship, saying this is the god who has delivered them from Egypt (Exod. 32). Moses has to intercede on their behalf: "You have sinned a great sin. And now I will go up to the LORD; perhaps I can make atonement for your sin" (32:30).

When Moses is told to depart and take the people to the land God swore to Abraham, Isaac, and Jacob, God still promises to drive out Israel's enemies in the land. But there is a catch: no longer will God go with Israel, due to her sin. "Go up to a land flowing with milk and honey; but I will not go up among you, lest I consume you on the way, for you are a stiff-necked people" (33:3). When the people hear "this disastrous word," they mourn (33:4), but Moses intercedes once more. With Moses alone the

Lord speaks "face to face, as a man speaks to his friend" (33:11). These "face to face" conversations take place in the tent of meeting as the pillar of cloud—representing the presence of God—descends on the tent.

Please Show Me Your Glory

In one encounter, Moses expresses his reservation at entering into the land without the Lord. "If your presence will not go with me, do not bring us up from here. For how shall it be known that I have found favor in your sight, I and your people? Is it not in your going with us, so that we are distinct, I and your people, from every other people on the face of the earth?" (Exod. 33:15–16). After listening to Moses, the Lord agrees to go with the people, but he makes it very clear that it is because Moses has "found favor" in his "sight" (33:17). Moses is the one the Lord knows "by name" (33:17). The relationship Moses has with the Lord is more personal and more intimate than that of anyone else in Israel. If anyone knows the Lord, it is Moses.

And yet, even Moses cannot experience the very essence of God. Perhaps it is because Moses speaks "face to face" with the Lord so often that he then feels so bold as to ask the unimaginable: "Please show me your glory" (33:18). God's glory? Seriously? How can Moses be so bold? How can he think seeing God's glory is humanly possible? Does he not know whom he is speaking to?

To his credit, Moses is Israel's covenant mediator. In light of the catastrophe in chapter 32 (i.e., Israel's idolatry), Moses is desperate to see God's presence continue with his people into the land, lest they be destroyed. Perhaps Moses also desires confirmation.[1] Previously, God had confirmed his covenant by manifesting his presence with Moses: "The glory of the LORD dwelt on Mount Sinai" by means of a cloud, and the Lord spoke to Moses "out of the midst of the cloud" (24:16). The Lord's glory had also

appeared in the form of a "devouring fire on the top of the mountain" for all Israel to see (24:17). One might assume Moses is simply asking for a repeat experience. Still, Moses seems to be asking
for something that goes well beyond anything he's ever experienced
before.

The response Moses receives is remarkable. On the one hand,
it is impossible for Moses to see the very glory of God. "You cannot see my face, for man shall not see me and live" (33:20). It is
safe to infer from this sobering statement that no one can know
or see the very essence of God. He is so glorious, and his glory so
infinite, that we would be consumed. He is like the sun. If we look
at the sun straight on, our eyes will burn, and our sight will be
lost. Should we dare to approach the sun, we will be disintegrated
before we can ever lay a foot on its surface. The proper way to
experience the sun is through its effects. Its rays warm us, and its
beams give us light where there is darkness. But look at the sun?
No way. Impossible.

On the other hand, God has promised to go with his people,
rather than merely sending his angel. So it is pivotal that God's
presence is manifested to Moses, Israel's mediator, even if not
directly. So the Lord announces his plan: "I will make all my goodness pass before you and will proclaim before you my name 'The
LORD.' And I will be gracious to whom I will be gracious, and will
show mercy on whom I will show mercy" (33:19). Moses cannot
see the "face" of the Lord and live, so the Lord will tuck Moses
behind a rock as he passes by. "Behold, there is a place by me
where you shall stand on the rock, and while my glory passes by
I will put you in a cleft of the rock, and I will cover you with my
hand until I have passed by. Then I will take away my hand, and
you shall see my back, but my face shall not be seen" (33:21–23).

We know from elsewhere in Scripture that God does not have
a body but is spirit (Deut. 4:12, 15–16; John 4:24). The language
is anthropomorphic, using human features (hands, back, face) to
describe the way the Immortal's passing presence and glory will

be experienced in the eyes of a mortal, like Moses. The language is protective, guarding Moses from God's glory and God's glory from Moses. That Moses is even allowed to be hidden in a nearby rock is a privilege. Yet Moses is given more. He may not be allowed to see the Lord's face, but he may see the Lord's back. Moses is permitted to be hidden in the rock, but it is God who is hidden from Moses. Only the Lord's back will be seen. The Lord will place his hand over the face of Moses, keeping Moses from seeing his face, only to remove his hand to allow Moses to see his back as he passes by. Surely "Moses must have quickly realized that, in knowing God more fully, God had become an even greater mystery (problem) than he was before."[2]

If Moses's encounter teaches us anything, it is this: God's essence is beyond the reach of finite mortals like you and me. Not even Moses could see the divine essence and live. Dead men tell no tales, especially those who've seen the very essence of God. It is incomprehensible in all its glory, perfection, and brilliance.

"To Whom Will You Liken Me?"

Moses learns that day that God is so great he defies comprehensibility. That reality will lead Moses to his knees countless times, fearful of the one who is a consuming fire, dwelling in light inaccessible.

Israel, however, does not fear the Lord as Moses does. Divine incomprehensibility does not leave them awestruck that the Infinite One would stoop down to enter into a covenant with such finite, sinful people. They know they cannot touch the foot of Mount Sinai, lest they die, but instead of bowing in worship, waiting for the words of life, they turn away, settling for gods they can see and touch, gods they can make with their own hands, gods they can control and domesticate.

But God cannot be domesticated. As he says through the prophet Isaiah, "To whom will you liken me and make me equal, and compare me, that we may be alike?" (Isa. 46:5). The answer is obvious: no one! God specifically has in mind the false idols of Babylon that Israel is being tempted to worship. They are made by human hands. Craftsmen melt and mold gold, crafting an image; then they elevate that gold image, prostrate themselves on the floor before it, and worship it as a god.

The picture painted by Isaiah is intentionally ironic: the creator worshiping the creature? But the scene becomes even more humiliating still. The worshiped object is, well, an *object* and no more. It can be seen; it can be touched. It is limited to one place, for it does not move; in fact, it cannot move. Mockingly, God laughs: "They lift it to their shoulders, they carry it, they set it in its place, and it stands there; it cannot move from its place" (46:7a). Could there be a more impotent object? God thinks not.

But let's play along, shall we? Perhaps this newly minted idol can at least listen to the words of its worshipers and then respond accordingly. No, it cannot do that either. "If one cries to it, it does not answer," and if it does not answer, then it cannot save that person from their trouble (46:7b). This is a god you can domesticate.

How different is the God of Israel? Listen to him respond: "I am God, and there is no other; I am God, and there is none like me" (46:9). Earlier in Isaiah, God thunders:

> Who has measured the waters in the hollow of his hand
>   and marked off the heavens with a span,
> enclosed the dust of the earth in a measure
>   and weighed the mountains in scales
>   and the hills in a balance?
> Who has measured the Spirit of the Lord,
>   or what man shows him his counsel?
> Whom did he consult,
>   and who made him understand?
> Who taught him the path of justice,
>   and taught him knowledge,
>   and showed him the way of understanding?

> Behold, the nations are like a drop from a bucket,
>> and are accounted as the dust on the scales;
> behold, he takes up the coastlands like fine dust.
>> (40:12–15)

And then comes one of the most sobering statements of all:

> All the nations are as nothing before him,
>> they are accounted by him as less than nothing and
>> emptiness.
> To whom then will you liken God,
>> or what likeness compare with him? (40:17–18)

An idol perhaps?

> An idol! A craftsman casts it,
>> and a goldsmith overlays it with gold. . . .
> He who is too impoverished for an offering
>> chooses wood that will not rot;
> he seeks out a skillful craftsman
>> to set up an idol that will not move. (40:19–20)

Not so with the Creator. It is he

> who sits above the circle of the earth,
>> and its inhabitants are like grasshoppers;
> who stretches out the heavens like a curtain,
>> and spreads them like a tent to dwell in;
> who brings princes to nothing,
>> and makes the rulers of the earth as emptiness.
>> (40:22–23)

Unlike his creation, the "Lord is the everlasting God, the Creator of the ends of the earth." And he "does not faint or grow weary; his understanding is unsearchable" (40:28).

What is abundantly evident from Isaiah 40 is that this God is not just a greater being than us, as if he were merely different in *degree*, a type of superman. No, this God is different in *kind*. He is a different type of being altogether. He is the Creator, not the created. From this fundamental difference—what theologians have called the Creator-creature distinction—every other difference follows. He is not placed into the hands of the creature, but holds every person—even entire nations!—in the palm of his hand. He is not limited to a specific place, to be put up on a stand, like the idols crafted out of gold, but he transcends any one place and is everywhere at once with his whole being. Even when he "sits," so to speak, he sits on his heavenly throne judging the nations. He is not a god whose ears have been fashioned from melted stone but a God who hears the prayers of his people, knows their every need, and therefore can and will save them from their enemies.

There is no one like this God. He is, as Isaiah 40:28 says, "unsearchable." That word "unsearchable" is key. It's not only true that God is incomparable, but he is also incomprehensible. His power, his knowledge, his presence, and his wisdom are inexhaustible and unfathomable. No one ever has known, and no one ever will know, the depths of his essence, the scope of his might, or the height of his glory. He is, in a word, *infinite*. That we cannot say of anyone else. "I am God, and there is none like me" (Isa. 46:9). "For my thoughts are not your thoughts, neither are your ways my ways, declares the LORD. For as the heavens are higher than the earth, so are my ways higher than your ways and my thoughts than your thoughts" (55:8–9).

No-Man's-Land

If God were not incomprehensible, would anything be compromised? And what would have to be true for God to be comprehensible? The short answer is that if he were not incomprehensible, God himself would change for the worse for a variety of reasons.

To begin with, we, the creature, would have to be God to comprehend God in all his glory.[3] But of course, if we were to become divine to comprehend him who alone is divinity, then God himself would cease to be divine. Listen to Augustine's wisdom: "We are speaking of God. Is it any wonder if you do not comprehend? *For if you comprehend, it is not God you comprehend.* Let it be a pious confession of ignorance rather than a rash profession of knowledge. To attain some slight knowledge of God is a great blessing; to comprehend him, however, is totally impossible."[4]

Thomas Aquinas says something similar: "No created mind can attain the perfect sort of understanding of God's essence that is intrinsically possible." Aquinas then makes a statement that will be echoed by all theologians after him: "The infinite cannot be contained in the finite. God exists infinitely and nothing finite can grasp him infinitely." Aquinas concludes, "It is impossible for a created mind to understand God infinitely; it is impossible, therefore, to comprehend him."[5]

Even the names for God in Scripture—Elohim, El Shaddai, Sabaoth, Yahweh—are not meant to reveal the divine essence in *all its fullness*.[6] They certainly do reveal God *truly*, just never *exhaustively*. Never was this God's intention. "He cannot fully impart himself to creatures."[7] To do so would be to compromise his very own existence.

In the past, God's essence has been referred to as his "quiddity."[8] Quiddity constitutes "the essential nature of something."[9] God's quiddity is unlike our quiddity. Infinite as he is, his quiddity is ineffable.[10] "Ineffable" means something is "incapable of being expressed in words."[11] To say that God's quiddity is ineffable is to say that God's essence is indescribable. It is so infinite, so supreme, so glorious, that its majesty, its beauty, and its perfection transcend our feeble human words. Like God told Moses, if we were to directly encounter God in his very essence, we would surely die. Since God's quiddity is ineffable, we would be right to say it is no-man's-land.

The Role of Humility in the Quest for Majesty

Living two decades into the twenty-first century has its advantages. It gives us a bird's-eye point of view, soaring over centuries past, using the eyes of an eagle to see the missteps of past generations. During the Enlightenment era, for example, many thinkers, Christians included, had an extremely optimistic view of humanity. By reason alone, humans could scale the greatest heights the arts and sciences had to offer. Religion was not exempt either. While different approaches were taken, some believed they could determine who God is simply by means of using their reasoning powers alone. The Bible could be set aside for good; reason was enough.

As time passed, it became evident that the Enlightenment experiment had failed. War, for example, exposed the fact that humanity is not morally neutral but corrupt. The ill use of reason demonstrated that humanity was desperately in need of special revelation after all. Autonomous reason was not so autonomous, as it turned out. In fact, it was idolatrous, attempting to remove God from his throne and replace the Creator's authority with the creature's intellect instead. The follies of the Enlightenment should forever remind us that attempting to scale the ladder of heaven to pull God down is the height of human hubris. It is the tower of Babel all over again.

A much better approach couples the quest for knowledge with humility, a humility that looks to God's revelation of himself for understanding. It is the approach of faith seeking understanding. As Anselm prays, "For I do not seek to understand so that I may believe; but I believe so that I may understand."[12] God's Word, the holy Scripture, opens the door for us to have a true knowledge of God. Yet the more we know, the more we realize we don't know. "The more God reveals who he is and the more we come to a true and authentic knowledge of who he is, the more mysterious he becomes."[13] It's like spending countless hours looking in the microscope at some aquatic creature, only to step back and discover the specimen is a humpback whale.

Two Temptations

God's incomprehensibility is a helpful reminder that whenever we speak of the infinite God, there is a proper, biblical role for mystery. Not agnosticism—*mystery*. The agnostic denies that we can know God or that he even exists. At the heart of agnosticism is an irremovable distrust, a piercing skepticism of the divine.[14] It is one step removed from atheism, and some would argue that atheism is its logical conclusion.[15] It has been labeled the "death of theology" for a reason.[16]

But Scripture never accepts such uncertainty. Instead, the biblical authors confidently declare from Genesis to Revelation that God does exist and that the reason we know he exists is that he is not silent. This speaking God has revealed who he is and what his will is for his people. In the eyes of the world the skeptic is considered the sage; in God's eyes the skeptic is called the fool (Ps. 14:1). God may be incomprehensible, but he is not unknowable. Any doubt is removed the moment God opens his mouth.

Others may not go as far as secular agnosticism. They remain unflinchingly religious (God certainly does exist) but religiously mystical (we cannot know him) in their view of God. God is so high that the Mysterious One is robbed of any definition at all. One is left only with total emptiness. These individuals pride themselves on knowing God by knowing nothing about God, ironic as that may sound. They "attempt to transcend all the limitations of space and time, strip our idea of God of all likeness to a finite creature, and end up with an empty abstract idea devoid of value for religion. . . . The Absolute has been reduced to nothing."[17]

Herman Bavinck calls this tendency an "insoluble antinomy."[18] An "antinomy" is a "fundamental and apparently unresolvable conflict or contradiction."[19] The word "insoluble" refers to something that has "no solution or explanation." In science, something is insoluble if it is "incapable of being dissolved in a liquid and especially water."[20] Think back to your school days in the science lab when your teacher asked you to mix oil with water. The result? The two won't mix. Oil remains undissolved by water.

But why would Bavinck call this second temptation an insoluble antinomy? It is because we have given up any reconciliation between God's transcendence and immanence. "Absoluteness and personality, infinity and causality, immutability and communicability, absolute transcendence and likeness to the creature—all these pairs seem irreconcilable in the concept of God."[21] It is to think that there can only be an "irresolvable contradiction."[22] Yet could this "irresolvable contradiction" actually be an "adorable mystery," we might wonder?[23]

Notice, to claim God is incomprehensible, an adorable mystery, is already to say a whole lot about him, as we discovered in Isaiah 40. Incomprehensibility does not encourage but undermines agnosticism and mysticism.

At the same time, incomprehensibility guards the Christian from thinking that a mere mortal can know God's very essence—know God *per essentiam*, "in terms of his essence."[24] It keeps us finite individuals from the theistic rationalism of the Enlightenment— that is, the aggressive belief that we mortals can, by our own unaided human reason, attain comprehensive knowledge of the divine.

The Most Perfect Way of Seeking God: Knowing God by His Works

Augustine once wrote that whenever we think about God, "we are aware that our thoughts are quite inadequate to their object, and incapable of grasping him as he is." Yet Scripture commands us to "think about the Lord our God always," though we "can never think about him as he deserves." How, then, should we approach him? "Since at all times we should be praising him and blessing him, and yet no words of ours are capable of expressing him, I begin by asking him to help me understand and explain what I have in mind and to pardon any blunders I may make. For I am as keenly aware of my weakness as of my willingness."[25]

That may be one of my favorite passages Augustine ever wrote. Every time he sat down to write about God, he put down his pen, got on his knees, and prayed. He knew he would never exhaust the mystery of the one who is incomprehensible. Augustine also knew that his finite attempt to describe him who is incomprehensible was tainted by Augustine's own weakness. To describe God, Augustine desperately needed God's own help.

Respecting this mystery requires a certain degree of modesty, a recognition of our earthly perspective. It entails an acknowledgment that *we are* the recipients and beneficiaries, not the originators and creators, of divine revelation. If *we know* anything about God, it is because he has chosen to make it known; revelation is a gift. In that light, our task cannot be speculation. Our response to his revelation concerning himself is not to demand knowledge of that which he has chosen to conceal.

Instead, Christian humility requires us to receive with gratitude what he has spoken and to limit ourselves to what he has said and done, rather than pine after what he has not said and those works he has left unperformed. "We know," observes John Calvin, "the most perfect way of seeking God, and the most suitable order, is not for us to attempt with bold curiosity to penetrate to the investigation of his essence, which we ought more to adore than meticulously to search out, but for us to contemplate him in his works whereby he renders himself near and familiar to us, and in some manner communicates himself." Echoing Augustine, Calvin concludes: "Because, disheartened by his greatness, we cannot grasp him, we ought to gaze upon his works, that we may be restored by his goodness."[26]

27

God's works, not his essence, arrest our attention. We may probe the former, but we restrict ourselves to marveling at the latter. For that reason, we can say with Bavinck that our God "is the sole object of all our love, precisely because he is the infinite and incomprehensible One."[27] For that reason we can sing,

> Immortal, invisible, God only wise,
> in light inaccessible hid from our eyes,
> most blessed, most glorious, the Ancient of Days,
> Almighty, victorious, thy great name we praise.[28]

2

Can We Think God's Thoughts after Him?

How the Creature Should (and Should Not) Talk about the Creator

> How precious to me are your thoughts, O God!
> How vast is the sum of them!
> If I would count them, they are more than the sand.
>
> PSALM 139:17–18A

> Stammering, we echo the heights of God as best we can.
>
> GREGORY THE GREAT, *Magna Moralia*

> [God's] infinite perfections are veiled under finite symbols. It is
> only the shadow of them that falls upon the human understanding.
>
> JAMES HENLEY THORNWELL, "THE NATURE
> AND LIMITS OF OUR KNOWLEDGE OF GOD"

The All and the Nothing

There are certain wonders in this world you simply must see for
yourself. The Grand Canyon is one of them. With walls taller than

skyscrapers and valleys that seem as wide as the ocean's floor, its magnitude defies description. One summer, on a road trip, I snagged the opportunity to see the Grand Canyon. With the sun setting, draping orange over a canyon ready to sleep for the night, I stood there on the precipice of this colossal giant in awe of its grandeur. Looking across the canyon was like trying to see the other side of the Milky Way. It's transcendence was belittling in the best way.

Since that day it has occurred to me that the distance between one side of the Grand Canyon and the other is but a very small picture of the crevasse between the finite and infinite, between the creature and the Creator. We are bound by time, but he is the eternal God, outside of time altogether. We are constricted by space, but no space can contain his incorporeal being. We are always changing and becoming, but he is always the same; his perfection never fluctuates. The gap we are describing is one between the "All and the nothing." "However little we know of God," writes Herman Bavinck, "even the faintest notion implies that he is a being who is infinitely exalted above every creature."[1] As the psalmist sings, "Great is the LORD, and greatly to be praised, and his greatness is unsearchable" (Ps. 145:3). If the psalmist is right, then we need this unsearchable God to make himself known to us; we need the Infinite One to accommodate himself to our very finite understanding. And we need the incomprehensible God to tell us how we should and should not talk about who he is and what he has done.

Baby Talk

The All and the nothing makes the opening chapters of the Bible shocking. The Infinite One has stepped across the canyon, picked up the dirt, and formed man and woman according to his own image. As unbelievable as it may seem, the infinite, incomprehensible

JOHN CALVIN

John Calvin (1509–64) was a second-generation, sixteenth-century Reformer in Geneva. As a pastor, Calvin returned the church to the Word of God, not only preaching through the Scriptures expositionally but writing commentaries on books of the Bible. Calvin may be best known today for his *Institutes of the Christian Religion*, which not only instructs Christians in the doctrines of the faith, but does so with an eye to applying doctrine to the Christian life. While many think of Calvin's defense of divine sovereignty and predestination, Calvin's *Institutes* also present a Protestant understanding of biblical authority (*sola scriptura*) and justification (*sola fide*). His *Institutes* have proved one of the greatest classics of Christianity and a foundational text for Reformation theology.

God has made us for the distinct purpose of knowing him, even enjoying him, and reflecting his image to the world around us. But wait, it gets better, much better. After forming humankind in his image, God then spoke. That's right, the infinite, transcendent, incomprehensible God used words, and these words revealed not only who he is but what duty God requires of humans. His words established a covenantal relationship between God and his people.

Theologians have a word for this: "accommodation." The church father Origen, for instance, liked to compare God to a parent talking to his two-year-old, speaking "inarticulately because of the child" since it is impossible for the parent to be understood by the child apart from "condescending to their mode of speech."[2] John Calvin compared God to a nurse caring for an infant. The nurse bends low to speak a language that the infant can understand. Calvin called this "lisping."[3] If you are the proud parents of a newborn, you know what Calvin means. I've been in hospitals and seen men the size of linebackers, with hands as hard as a sledgehammer, cradle their newborn and speak baby talk.

The moment is unforgettable, as that six-pound curly head looks up and cries to be embraced. If that is how far we accommodate ourselves to our own children, how much more so our heavenly Father? Such lisping does "not so much express clearly what God is like as accommodate the knowledge of him to our slight capacity."[4]

Yet that raises a question: What exactly does this baby talk look like?

A Is for Analogical

We discovered in the last chapter that we can know God truly even if not comprehensively. It may be impossible to comprehend God *in his essence*, in all his glory and radiance, but that does not preclude us from knowing God *as he has made himself known to us*. God "cannot be comprehended," but he "can be apprehended."[5] We may not have "absolute knowledge" of God, which no finite creature could possibly have of an infinite being, but we can have "relative knowledge" of an "absolute Being"—that is, knowledge that knows in part something true about an infinite being.[6]

We also learned that knowledge of God is a gift God himself gives. The reason we know God at all and in any way at all is only because our Creator communicates by means of his *words* and *works*.[7] One might object: "Yes, but surely if we have knowledge of God, then God must be less than he is in some way, limited and restricted even, for he is now known to some degree." There are several reasons why our knowledge does not limit God.

1. Our knowledge of God is "grounded in God himself."
2. Our knowledge of God "can only exist through him."
3. Our knowledge of God "has as its object and content God as the infinite One."[8]

In short, it is silly to say that "knowing" limits God when our knowledge itself is completely dependent on the one known.

But now we come to a more pressing issue: What *kind* of knowledge do we possess? As long as we are the creature and he is the Creator, as long as we are finite and he is infinite, there must be a basic distinction between our knowledge and his. Since he is the Creator, his knowledge is *original*, the *archetype*. Our knowledge, by contrast, is the *ectype*, meaning it is derivative and a copy, only a likeness of the original. It is an imitation of his knowledge, which is what one would expect since we are made in his image.

What does this archetype-ectype distinction mean for language? For starters, we cannot speak *univocally*. "Univocal" refers to something having the same meaning as something else. In relation to God, we would know something exactly as God knows it. In relation to his being, it would mean we know God exactly as he is, in his very essence. Univocal knowledge is the road to rationalism. The rationalist claims that his or her reason in and of itself can know who God is in and of himself.

On the other end of the spectrum is *equivocal* knowledge. If univocal knowledge leads to rationalism, then equivocal knowledge results in irrationalism. Its advocate concludes that nothing can be known truly. All knowledge is subjective, inconclusive, and indefinite. For finite creatures who believe God has spoken truthfully and clearly, equivocal knowledge is not an option.[9]

Is there any other category left? There is: *analogical* knowledge. "Analogical" means something shares similarities with something else but is not identical with it. It is not totally the same, nor is it totally different. There may be discontinuity, but there is continuity with what is resembled.[10] For instance, if you have joined me for an ice-cream cone, you might say with a smile, "I've died and gone to heaven." You do not mean to be taken in the most literal sense, of course. That would be an insult to God's heavenly glory, which far surpasses the most delicious ice cream. What you do mean, rather, is that the ice cream is so scrumptious that it must be a small taste (no pun intended) of the joy and pleasure that characterize heaven.

Applied biblically, analogical knowledge makes perfect sense. We are not the Creator, but the finite creature, and yet we've been created in the *image* or *likeness* of God. Our identity, our makeup, is analogical by definition. We image the Creator, though we are not the Creator. We mirror his glory, though we should never be confused with his glory. In relation to our knowledge, it is inconsistent with our identity to know God comprehensively, but it is perfectly right, since we are his image bearers, for our knowledge to resemble his knowledge, imperfect as it may be. So while we may not know him as he is *in himself*, in his essence (univocal knowledge), we may know him as he has made himself known to us by *revelation* (analogical knowledge).[11] Analogical knowledge is why we keep returning to God's self-revelation in the Scriptures; we are striving to think God's thoughts after him. To reverse this order is criminal in God's eyes.

The Dog Who Met God

The Latin language has a beautiful way of stressing the analogical nature of our knowledge and language. If something is *res significata* that means the object being identified is in view. In relation to God, *res significata* refers to the "attribute signified."[12] *Modus significandi*, however, refers to the "way in which the term can be applied to the particular kind of thing in question."[13] Thomas Aquinas argued that the *res significata* does not change in any way, but the *modus significandi* can change.[14]

For instance, consider what it would be like if a dog were to meet God. I don't know what kind of dog you have, but my dog is a miniature Australian shepherd. We adopted him as a puppy in 2017, the year that marked the five-hundredth anniversary of the Reformation. So naturally we named him Calvin, after the Genevan Reformer.

Now suppose I look at my dog Calvin and tell him to sit, which he does (receiving the applause of the whole family), and then I

THOMAS AQUINAS

Beside Anselm, another Italian-born theologian we will look to is Thomas Aquinas (1224/5–74), or the "dumb ox," as he was called by his peers. There was nothing dumb, however, about this ox, a theological force the world has never seen since. The man wrote as he breathed, penning around nine million words before his death. There was no reason to question Aquinas's spiritual devotion either. When Aquinas first decided he would join the Dominican order, his family went ballistic. To dissuade him, his family locked him in his room with a nude prostitute! Thomas raged with anger, chasing the prostitute away with a red-hot brand plucked from the fire. Slamming the brand on the door, Thomas left the sign of the cross forever burned into the wood. Thomas is respected not only for his unflinching, Joseph-like commitment to holiness but for his brilliant theological mind. In his *Summa Theologiae* (1266–73), for instance, Thomas starts each section posing a theological question and entertaining how his opponents might answer it, only to then counter with laser-like biblical, theological, and philosophical precision, dismantling all objections. Nowhere is this style more acute than in his treatment of the divine attributes. Aquinas tells us not only what to believe but why to believe it, teasing out the logic behind our conclusions. Modern treatments so often jettison classical attributes (simplicity; immutability, eternity, etc.), but Aquinas demonstrates that such attributes are essential to a perfect, infinite being. For that reason, he will be one of our greatest allies in this book.

respond, "That dog is good."[15] The next day is Sunday. Calvin is put in his kennel, and off we go to church, where the pastor greets the congregation and reminds them that "God is good." As we drive home from church, our five-year-old asks, "Dad, Mom, is God good in the same way the dog is good?" (Granted, he is a philosophical genius in the making.) Naturally, we laugh. "Of course not!" "But why?" he asks, with some perplexity.

As parents, we often stumble over our words in those moments, wondering why our children are so darn perceptive. Yet if we think about it, the answer is obvious: God is infinite, the dog is not. *Modus significandi* is the key phrase here because we dare not say the dog is good just as God is good. No, God's goodness is infinite in measure, even in ways we will never know. The depths of his goodness are unsearchable, bottomless, and endless. Not so the dog!

As Christian thinker Katherin Rogers has explained, "Because God is infinite and unified, the *modus significandi* of a term applied to God and creatures is different. We cannot possibly comprehend just *how* God is good, and so although we do have an understanding of goodness, there is inevitably a vagueness and inadequacy when we use the term of the perfect being."[16] I would add only that the inadequacy we feel is most felt in worship. As we sing to our God, praising him for who he is and what he's done, we know deep down, in that moment, just how different, how unsearchable, his goodness is compared to that of our dog. To think otherwise is to entertain idolatry.

The Supereminent God

Theology has a word that keeps us from such idolatry. It's the word "supereminent."[17] That's right, super-eminent. If something in God is supereminent, then it must be "more eminent" than that which is in us: "In him [God] all that we are is possessed in a higher, fuller, purer, and limitless way." God is the one who "donates everything that we are to us out of his infinite plenitude of being, consciousness, and bliss."[18]

Take the attribute of wisdom, for example. We may be wise, even reflecting the wisdom of God. There is a correlation between divine and human wisdom (see Proverbs). Such continuity is what classifies wisdom as a *communicable* attribute of God (one that is reflected in us in some way), as opposed to an *incommunicable* attribute of God (one that is not in us in any sense). Nevertheless, we would be mistaken to think that we are wise in the same way God is wise. To apply the word "wisdom" as we know it to God is to do so only supereminently, lest we close the gap between the creature and the Creator and confuse the two. The same applies to other communicable attributes. Beauty, goodness, love, and holiness in the creature may reflect the Creator. However, Augustine clarifies, in "comparison with you [God] they are deficient in beauty and goodness and being."[19]

The infinite difference between the dog's goodness and God's goodness or our wisdom and God's wisdom should not push us into agnosticism, as if we could know nothing for certain. There must be a degree of continuity.[20] To image God, as Genesis 1–2 says we do, must involve some degree of conformity; otherwise the mirror is useless and shatters. Aquinas nudges us in this direction: "In this life we cannot understand God's essence as it is in itself. But we can do so in so far as the perfections of his creatures represent it."[21]

In the history of God-talk, there are what are referred to as cataphatic theology and apophatic theology. *Cataphatic theology* is affirmative by design, occurring whenever we assert what God *is*. Nevertheless, as long as God-talk remains analogical, our cataphatic excitement must be tamed by the wisdom of its older sister, *apophatic theology*, which describes God by what he is not (God is *not x, y,* and *z*). This approach is sometimes referred to as the *via negativa* or *via negationis*, the way of negation, because it is asserting something true about God by denying something false about him.[22] So when we want to say that God is *not* mutable or that he does *not* change, we simply say he is immutable. Essentially, we are identifying all that is creaturely and therefore cannot be in God.

All in all, there is a balance to be struck. We must carefully balance the continuity with the discontinuity, lest we strip God of his infinitude and think that the image is the same as that which it images.[23] Hence the importance of recognizing just how analogical our knowledge of God is and must be.

Does God Have Eyes and Ears ... and Wings?

If knowledge of an infinite God is analogical, then language used to describe God is as well. Like knowledge, human language is dependent and indirect, not original and direct.[24] We cannot grasp God in all his fullness or in his invisible essence by any one word or concept.[25] So metaphors, similes, and other figures of speech are entirely appropriate, even necessary. We need words that paint a picture, for the essence of God is not ours to see. As we paint, our imagination can stretch only so far, and so we describe God according to the images of our finite world.

C. S. Lewis once wrote that before he ever saw Oxford, he had a mental picture of the college in his imagination. It was, of course, "very different from the reality in physical details." Did this mean that his mental picture was a "delusion," he asks? Not at all. The picture "had inevitably accompanied my thinking" but had "never been what I was chiefly interested in, and much of my thinking had been correct in spite of [my mental pictures]." Lewis concludes, "What you think is one thing; what you imagine while you are thinking is another."[26]

Likewise, the biblical authors use mental pictures to describe he who is indescribable. For example, throughout Scripture they use *anthropomorphic* language, which occurs whenever God is described with human characteristics. In fact, says Lewis, "all language about things other than physical objects is necessarily metaphorical," and God is not a physical object.[27] This is why Scripture is saturated with anthropomorphic descriptions of God.[28] Consider, for example, the way Scripture speaks about God's omnipotence, omniscience, and omnipresence. The biblical authors talk of God as one who has eyes; Psalm 11:4 even says he has eyelids. Yet we know, taking all of Scripture into account, that God is not a body but spirit (Deut. 4:12, 15–16; John 4:24). So why would the biblical authors describe God as one who sees? There are many reasons.

Attributing "eyes" to God is a human way of conveying that God knows all things, for he sees all things, and because he sees all things, the wicked will not escape his judgment. Such anthropomorphic imagery asserts not only his omniscience but his omnipotence in executing his justice. In other passages God's "eyes" may convey his covenant love, mercy, and protection. "Keep me as the apple of your eye," prays King David. "Hide me in the shadow of your wings" (Ps. 17:8). Not only eyes but wings (!) are assigned to God, who is like a mother bird hovering over her chicks. Elsewhere David attributes not only eyes but ears to God to highlight such covenant benevolence and safety. "The eyes of the LORD are toward the righteous and his ears toward their cry" (Ps. 34:15). Such a metaphor, explains Aquinas, reveals God's "power of seeing things in an intelligible rather than a sensory manner."[29]

Consider another example: Scripture often says God sits and stands. Sitting visualizes his immutable authority; standing pictures his power, his rule and reign over his enemies.[30] Scripture also refers to God drawing near and leaving, as if he were a body that enters and exits a room. As we will learn in chapter 9, God cannot be restricted by space, for he is omnipresent. Such language is anthropomorphic and loaded with meaning. Picturing God entering and exiting a scene reveals either his covenant blessing (God's presence descending on the tabernacle in Exod. 40:34, or on the apostles at Pentecost in Acts 2:3–4) or his judgment (e.g., the Spirit departing from Saul in 1 Sam. 16:14).[31] You've heard it said that a picture conveys a thousand words. How true. But it's also the case that one word can picture God in a thousand ways. Why? Because he is infinite.

As those who read with modern eyes, we struggle to understand how anything but that which is absolutely literal could be appropriate. We expect the Bible to read like an automotive text-book. Yet the metaphorical communicates truth just as much as the literal, sometimes more so. The point is, we "ascribe to God in an absolute sense all the perfections we observe in creatures."[32] As we do so, however, we must keep in mind that there can be no perfection in the creature in the exact same way that it is in God.[33] It is "palpably absurd of you," says the church father Tertullian, "to be placing human characteristics in God rather than divine ones in man, and clothing God in the likeness of man, instead of man in the image of God."[34]

God Is More Than We Know

In the introduction I quoted A. W. Tozer: "What comes into our minds when we think about God is the most important thing about us."[35] Right as Tozer may be, it is a dangerous thing to assume that the conception of God in our minds pictures God *just as he is* in all his infinite incomprehensibility. Added to Tozer's statement should be that of Stephen Charnock, who advises us that if we think about God, we should say to ourselves: "This is not God; God is more than this: if I could conceive him, he were not God; for God is incomprehensibly above whatsoever I can say, whatsoever I can think and conceive of him."[36] Only then, with such humility, will we begin to truly know God as he has revealed himself to us.

3

Is God the Perfect Being?

Why an Infinite God Has No Limitations

Oh, the depth of the riches and wisdom and knowledge of God!
How unsearchable are his judgments and how inscrutable his
ways!

ROMANS 11:33

[He is the] perfection of both beauty and strength.

AUGUSTINE, The Confessions

Narnia No More

In the eyes of a child, the world is a magical place: a snowflake
falling from the sky onto one's nose, a baby chick overcoming its
shell to embrace the sun for the first time, the insatiable joy of
tasting a fresh blueberry on a hot July day. There is a reason the
Pevensie children could see the world C. S. Lewis called Narnia,

while the adults in the world around them could not. It is not because they were gullible; it is because they believed there was wonder in the universe. As much as children ask why, when it comes to the wonder of the world around them, they do not ask why because they are skeptics, but rather they ask because they believe and thirst to know the world's secrets. The miraculous is everywhere, and children embrace it.

There is something about getting older that turns us off to wonder, making our visits to Narnia less and less common. David Bentley Hart contrasts the way of children with the way of adults: "As we age, however, we lose our sense of the intimate otherness of things; we allow habit to displace awe, inevitability to banish delight; we grow into adulthood and put away childish things." How sad; how tragic. More and more, moments of wonder disappear until they come only once in a very great while. "Thereafter, there are only fleeting instants scattered throughout our lives when all at once, our defenses momentarily relaxed, we find ourselves brought to a pause by a sudden unanticipated sense of the utter uncanniness of the reality we inhabit, the startling fortuity and strangeness of everything familiar: how odd it is, and how unfathomable, that anything at all exists; how disconcerting that the world and one's consciousness of it are simply there, joined in a single ineffable event."[1]

If this is true with the world we see, how much more so—unfortunately—is it true with the God we cannot see? Perhaps this is why, if only in part, Jesus said that the faith that brings one into his Father's kingdom must be a childlike faith. It is a faith filled with wonder and awe as it fathoms the one who is infinite in beauty, steadfast in mercy. It is a faith that refuses to "displace awe" and "banish delight." It is a faith that marvels at the "intimate otherness" of not just things created but the Creator himself. It must follow, then, that this Creator is the one than whom none and nothing greater can possibly be conceived. As we will discover in this chapter, our God is the perfect being. And since there is none greater, he is a being without limitations, a being who is his perfections in infinite measure; he is a boundless ocean of being, as the fathers liked to say. From this one premise will follow all the attributes of God we will discuss in future chapters.

Monopolytheism, California Redwoods, and the Superhero Syndrome

In the nineteenth century a very different picture of God emerged, one that continues to be prevalent today. Those in the culture who still believe in God have created a God after their own likeness. The creature is not made in the image of the Creator, but God, the Creator, in the image of the creature. Rather than looking to the supernatural God of the Bible, who defies the finite realm, they prefer what Brian Davies calls "theistic personalism," or what David Bentley Hart labels "monopolytheism." Monopolytheism sounds like an oxymoron, "monotheism" referring to the belief in one God and "polytheism" the belief in many gods. But that's the point; it is oxymoronic. It is that popular, though contradictory, belief that God is not "conspicuously different from the polytheistic picture of the gods as merely very powerful discrete entities who possess a variety of distinct attributes that lesser entities also possess, if in smaller measure." This view "differs from polytheism," Hart believes, "solely in that it posits the existence of only one such being."[2]

I'm a native Californian, and one of my best memories is our family road trip to see the giant redwoods. *Sequoia sempervirens* is the scientific name for the coast redwood, the tallest type of tree in the world. So wide is the coast redwood that you could drive a car (or a bus!) through its trunk. So tall is the redwood that you can look up but fail to see the top, try as you might. The tallest coast redwoods stand around 378 feet tall. When you stand next to such giants, you feel like an ant. It is humbling to be sure. It can be a worship experience as well, as you reflect on how big the Creator must be to make a tree like that.

However true it may be to say that God is bigger than even the tallest redwood, it would be a mistake to think that is all God is, merely bigger. Even if we discovered some magical redwood whose top could never be found, endless in its starry reach, still that would be incomparable to God. Despite the redwood's magnificent height, comparing God to the redwood is like comparing apples to oranges.

Something (or someone) may be *unlimited in its size*, but that is not the same thing as being *unlimited in essence*. We should not make the mistake of thinking the difference between the Creator and the creature is simply a difference in size. To do so is to assume God can be measured, as if he were merely a bigger version of ourselves. I call this the superhero syndrome. Christians like to think of God as their superhero, like us but with superpowers.

But that is a terribly unbiblical portrayal of God's infinite nature. He is not a God who simply possesses our powers but in endless measure. No, an infinite God transcends our characteristics altogether.[3] He is a different type of being, what some have labeled "beyond being" or the absolute "Being itself."[4] The creation may be great in *size*, but God is unlimited in his very *being*. His greatness is one of *essence*. "To be unlimited in size," Thomas Aquinas clarifies, "is not the same thing as to be unlimited in essence. For even if there existed bodily things of unlimited size (fire or air, say), these would still be limited in essence: limited to a particular species by their form, and to a particular individual of the species by their matter."[5]

It must follow, then, that only God can be infinite in his essence. The creation, by contrast, may be large, but even if it were unlimited in size, it still would not compare to God, who defies the concept of size altogether. He is a different species entirely. Anyway, there is no person or thing in the created order that is unlimited in size, for all created things have some type of body or form.[6] God has no form. Could it not be more evident that God is not merely above us but different from us? As the uncreated

Creator, he is the only one who is infinite, unlimited, and immeasurable. That is what makes him the greatest, most supreme, most perfect being imaginable.

God Is "Something-Than-Which-Nothing-Greater-Can-Be-Thought"

That God is the most perfect, supreme being there is cannot be denied by anybody claiming the Christian faith. It is a statement axiomatic to the biblical witness, which is why this book revolves around that central question: What must be true of God if he is the most perfect being? God is, as Anselm so famously said, "something-than-which-nothing-greater-can-be-thought."[7] That statement does not mean, warns Hart, that God is merely "a being among other beings" or the "greatest possible of beings," in the sense that he is just a more perfect version of his competitors, having a leg up on them for whatever reason. As we've learned already, God is a different *kind* or *type* of being altogether, not in the same class at all. Anselm's phrase conveys that God is "the fullness of Being itself, the absolute plenitude of reality upon which all else depends."[8]

Our mission, in this book, is to determine *what* that perfection entails. What *must* be true of God if he is to be that than which nothing greater can be thought? There must be great or perfect-making properties if God is the perfect being. Already we've discovered that one great-making property is divine transcendence, rendering God's essence incomprehensible and divine accommodation essential. But other great-making perfections must be entailed as well, perfections that guard God from finite limitations, perfections such as infinitude, aseity, simplicity, immutability, impassibility, eternity, immensity, omnipotence, omniscience, and so on. As Augustine explains, "The truest beginning of piety is to think as highly of God as possible; and doing so means that one must believe that he is omnipotent, and not changeable in the smallest respect; that he is the creator of all good things, but is himself more excellent than all of them; that he is the supremely just ruler of everything that he created; and that he was not aided in creating by any other being, as if he were not sufficiently powerful by himself."[9] Each great-making attribute is essential; subtract one and we no longer have a perfect divine being. Nonetheless, while each perfection is key, the *infinite* nature of God cannot be stressed enough. Without it, the other perfections would make little sense. But most significantly, for God to be something than which nothing greater can be thought, he *must* be infinite. Infinitude is the very makeup of a perfect being.

One of the reasons we think children are cute is that they say things that make no sense. When Susy or Johnny sits down to learn math and proudly holds up their paper to say, "Look, Mommy, a round square," or "Look, Daddy, dry water," we naturally laugh. If an adult were to say the same, we might wonder if he or she should get counseling. Contradictions sound cute coming from a four-year-old but insane when coming from a forty-four-year-old. When we talk about God, the same logic applies. Oxymorons are not welcome in God-talk. We would never say, for example, "God is infinitely finite" or "God is a finite infinite being." A finite being is, by definition, limited. An infinite being is, by definition, unlimited. To be infinite is to be unbounded, unlimited, and unrestricted. Put positively, to be infinite means God is his attributes in an absolute sense, since he is the fullness of being.[10]

That very basic premise has enormous consequences for all other attributes of God. If we can think of anything that would *limit* God, then it cannot be true of God. If it is true of God, then he is no longer infinite.[11] Consider a few examples. If God is dependent on the created order, as opposed to being independent, then he cannot be infinite. Why? Because he is a needy God, incomplete, reliant on others for either his existence or fulfillment, or both. A needy God is not a perfect God, for a needy God is not infinite.

Or consider God's simplicity. If God is made up of parts, as opposed to being simple, then he cannot be infinite. Why? A God made up of parts may also be divided by his parts; a God made up of parts is dependent on his parts; a God made up of parts needs someone or something else to compose his parts to make up his very being. Both compromise the unity and independence of God. A divided God is not a perfect God, for a divided God is not infinite.[12]

Last, consider God's immutability. If God changes, as opposed to being immutable, then he cannot be infinite. Why? A God who changes is vulnerable to imperfection, either changing for the better, which assumes he was less than perfect beforehand, or for the worse. Either way, God's perfection is not eternal but always subject to fluctuation.

We could go on, but in each case God is less than perfect because he is less than infinite. So again, it must be stressed that a perfect God is a God who is limitless, unbound by all those confines that characterize our finite, creaturely existence.

Yet infinitude does not merely mean rejecting any quality that would limit God; it also means that God is his perfections in *infinite measure*. Not only must any "quality which is inherently limiting" be "denied of God," says philosopher Katherin Rogers, but "any perfection attributed to God" must be "attributed in an unlimited degree."[13] That is what Anselm meant when he called God the "fullness of Being" and the "absolute plenitude of reality."[14] For a perfection of God to be a "great-making" perfection, such a perfection must characterize God "to the highest degree or infinitely."[15] For example, consider what infinity entails for all that is in God. God's power is an infinite power, which is why we call him omnipotent (all-powerful). God's knowledge is an infinite knowledge, which explains why we title him omniscient (all-knowing). God's wisdom is an infinite wisdom, which justifies praising him as omnisapient (all-wise). God's presence is an infinite presence, which urges us to acknowledge that he is omnipresent (everywhere present). And if infinity "applied to space is omnipresence," then infinity "applied to time is eternity."[16]

The point is, God's essence is unbounded, immeasurable, unfathomable, and inestimable in every way. He cannot be his attributes more than he already is. He is his attributes absolutely. That is what it means to be perfect. "No perfection is wanting to God," Stephen Charnock observes. A "limited one is an imperfection," but an "unbounded essence is a perfection."[17] It is crucial, then, to say that no matter what divine perfection we describe, it is true of God in infinite measure.[18]

Great Is Our Lord beyond Measure

Do we see this marriage between divine infinitude and all other divine perfections in the story of Scripture?

New Year's Day, next to Christmas, is one of the more exciting holidays of the year. The ball drops in New York City, and champagne glasses are raised in the air, toasting to new beginnings. For a Christian, the new year is especially meaningful. It is an opportunity to reflect on the many evidences of God's grace in our lives over the past year. Yet it is also an opportunity to plan for the future. While the world is busy making resolutions to lose weight and start new businesses (neither of which are bad in themselves), the Christian is resolved to live the next year to the glory of God alone (*soli Deo gloria*). That is a tall order, one that needs the daily discipline of Scripture meditation.

Personally, the Psalms are one of my favorite books for my "daily bread." They capture the peaks and valleys of life, teaching us how to pray and trust in the Lord in the midst of great hardship. Many Christians see the Psalms as practical theology. However, one need not read more than two or three psalms to realize that each one is a theology lesson with rich descriptions of the character of God. Repeatedly we hear the psalmist praise

God as the one who is "gracious and merciful, slow to anger and abounding in steadfast love" (Ps. 145:8). Not only are God's love and grace referred to in the psalms, but so is his infinite essence. The psalmists even connect his infinitude to his other attributes.

One of my favorites is Psalm 147, a psalm of healing for those whose spirit is broken. "He heals the brokenhearted and binds up their wounds" (147:3). The brokenhearted are given every confidence that the Lord can heal, for this is the same God who "determines the number of the stars" and "gives to all of them their names" (147:4). And so the psalmist confesses, "Great is our Lord, and abundant in power; his understanding is beyond measure" (147:5). The Lord, says the psalmist, is one whose power knows no limits, whose knowledge and wisdom (i.e., understanding) know no bounds.

Immeasurable Greatness of His Power . . . Even over Dark Magic

If there was ever an apostle who knew how to pray like the psalmists, it was the apostle Paul. In his letter to the saints in Ephesus, Paul begins with a prayer of thanksgiving. He is thankful for the Ephesians because their faith in the Lord and their love for one another are exemplary, evidence that the Holy Spirit is at work in them. Overjoyed, Paul never ceases to give thanks for these brothers and sisters in Christ. Paul prays that they might have their "hearts enlightened" so that they might know the "immeasurable greatness of his power toward us who believe" (Eph. 1:19).

Stop right there. Not only does Paul say that God's power is infinite, but he assumes, even prays, that the believer can and will know, experience, and live a life defined by God's infinite nature. That may seem impossible. After all, how can we know the immeasurable greatness of the Almighty? But Paul is confident we can, if only in part, because Christ is risen. The empty tomb is the reason we can know the one who is infinite. Paul prays that

Christians would know the "immeasurable greatness of his power toward us who believe, according to the working of his great might that he worked in Christ when he raised him from the dead and seated him at his right hand in the heavenly places" (Eph. 1:19–20).

Remarkable.

The same infinite power of the Almighty that raised Jesus from the tomb is at work in us who believe.

Could there be a greater power? That was a relevant question to Christians in Ephesus. Ephesus was a hot spot for those who practiced magic. Ephesians were constantly looking to the power of the dark arts. The book of Acts recounts that Paul spent time in Ephesus and performed "extraordinary miracles" (19:11). Others tried to mimic Paul. Seven sons of Sceva, a high priest, attempted to cast out an evil spirit, for example. To their surprise, the spirit "leaped on them, mastered all of them and overpowered them, so that they fled out of that house naked and wounded" (19:16). When everyone heard what happened, fear filled Jews and Greeks alike, and "the name of the Lord Jesus was extolled" (19:17).

We then read that those who have converted are "confessing and divulging their practices" and that a "number of those who had practiced magic arts brought their books together and burned them in the sight of all" (19:18–19). These were expensive books. Fifty thousand pieces of silver was their worth, or by today's monetary value six million dollars.[19] These Ephesians were willing to throw millions of dollars into the fire because they believed the power of their dark magic was no match for the infinite power of the Almighty, the God of Abraham, Isaac, and Jacob. It is fitting that the story concludes, "So the word of the Lord continued to increase and prevail mightily" (19:20). God's infinite power is invincible. So when Paul later prayed that these Ephesians would know the "immeasurable greatness" of God's power (Eph. 1:19), these Ephesians knew that the same power that raised Christ from the dead was at work in them.

Who Can Atone for Sin against an Infinite God?

Evangelism is tough. Sometimes sharing Christ with a non-Christian is met with genuine interest, but many times it is met with indifference or outright hostility. Have you ever tried to share the gospel only to be on the receiving end of a piercing question, like "Hell? Seriously, you're telling me that my sin deserves an eternity of punishment?"

Responding is hard, not least because the unbeliever does not grasp the sinfulness of sin. More fundamentally, they have no category for *who* they have sinned against: an *infinite* God. They have spit in the face of a God whose holiness is inestimable, whose glory is unfathomable, and whose perfection is of infinite measure.

Blinded by sin, we struggle to understand the magnitude of our offense, because we look at our sin and think it is of little significance. We make light of our sin, but that is because we judge it over against other sinners, thinking, "Well at least I'm not as bad as that guy." It's not until we stand in the heavenly courtroom, as Isaiah has done, beholding the infinite holiness of God, that we cry out, "Woe is me!" God does not hold up our sin against the sins of others but against the blinding light of his infinite perfection.

Understanding we have sinned against the one who is infinite in his perfections is not only scary but can lead us to total despair. For it is painfully obvious there is no one who can make atonement. Such a person would have to be infinite himself to atone for a sin against an infinite God, to pay sins that deserve a penalty that has no end. In our finite, fallen world, clearly there is no one like this to be found. It's at that moment—a moment of utter despair—that the gospel shines in all its brilliance. We are like those shepherds sitting in the field, in the darkness of night, when suddenly "the glory of the Lord shone around them" and they heard those too-good-to-be-true words: "Fear not, for behold, I bring you good news of great joy that will be for all the people.

For unto you is born this day in the city of David a Savior, who is Christ the Lord" (Luke 2:9–11). Then the entire heavens burst open in praise:

> Glory to God in the highest,
>> and on earth peace among those with whom he is
>> pleased! (2:14)

Peace? Have we not sinned against an infinite God? Yes, but the Infinite One himself has stepped out of the heavens to pay for your sin, something he alone can do. The eternal Son of God took the "form of a servant" (Phil. 2:7); the "image of the invisible God," by whom "all things were created" and in whom "all the fullness of God was pleased to dwell," has reconciled "to himself all things . . . making peace by the blood of his cross" (Col. 1:15–20).

Sin against an infinite God cannot be atoned for by a Savior who has emptied himself of his divine attributes. No, it is his divine attributes that qualify him to make atonement in the first place. Sin against an infinite God can be met only by a Savior who is himself deity—and all the perfections identical with that deity—in infinite measure.

Immeasurable Riches of His Grace . . . Even over Rotting Corpses

In light of our need for an infinite Savior, Paul transitions from the immeasurable greatness of God's power in Ephesians 1 to the immeasurable riches of God's grace in Ephesians 2. The two are related. The infinite power of God that is displayed in the raising of his Son from the dead is equally manifested in the raising of our spiritually dead souls to new life. Although "you were dead in the trespasses and sins in which you once walked, . . . following the prince of the power of the air, . . . God, being rich in mercy . . . raised us up with him and seated us with him in the heavenly places in Christ Jesus" (Eph. 2:1–2, 4, 6).

I've been a Christian as long as I can remember, but I know others who distinctly remember when they were saved. If that's you, then you really feel the weight of what Paul says. You were enslaved not only to the world but to the "power of the air"—Satan himself. Satan's power, however, is not infinite. It is no match for the immeasurable power of God. At God's command, those spiritually lifeless souls, six feet under, suddenly stand to attention and walk out of their tombs—much as Lazarus did. Though we were dead, God "made us alive together with Christ" (Eph. 2:5). What Paul describes, theologians call "regeneration." It is God's work alone, for only he has the infinite power capable of raising spiritually dead souls.

Yet not only have we been raised to new life, and not only have we been raised up and seated with Christ in the heavenly places, but God has performed such a miracle "so that in the coming ages he might show the immeasurable riches of his grace in kindness toward us in Christ Jesus" (Eph. 2:7). Not only is God infinite in power, but he is infinite in mercy, infinite in grace, and infinite in kindness. As the psalmist exclaims:

> The LORD is merciful and gracious,
>   slow to anger and abounding in steadfast love.
> He will not always chide,
>   nor will he keep his anger forever.
> He does not deal with us according to our sins,
>   nor repay us according to our iniquities.
> For as high as the heavens are above the earth,
>   so great is his steadfast love toward those who fear him;
> as far as the east is from the west,
>   so far does he remove our transgressions from us.
>   (Ps. 103:8–12)

There is no word in Hebrew for "infinity," yet the concept is present when the psalmist announces that God has removed our transgressions as far as the east is from the west and that his steadfast love is as high as the heavens.[20] What the psalms express through metaphor, Paul says more directly: God's grace is infinite, and our union with the risen Christ is the guarantee that we will one day enjoy his infinite grace without end and in its most perfect form.

Only a Supreme Being Is Worthy of Worship

With Ephesians 1 and 2 in mind, is it any surprise that Christians down through the centuries have used the word "supreme" to refer to God? "Supremacy" captures the perfection of God's infinite nature. Listen to our friend Anselm: "And clearly any good thing that the supreme nature is, it is that thing supremely. It is, therefore, supreme essence, supreme life, supreme reason, supreme health, supreme justice, supreme wisdom, supreme truth, supreme goodness, supreme greatness, supreme beauty, supreme immortality, supreme incorruptibility, supreme immutability, supreme happiness, supreme eternity, supreme power, supreme unity."[21] Each and every attribute deserves to be called "supreme"; for that reason alone our God is one who deserves our worship. Our finitude constantly reminds us that we owe our lives to the one who is infinite. He has no limitations. He is his attributes in infinite measure. Therefore, he is the most perfect being, "something-than-which-nothing-greater-can-be-thought." He is, without qualification, without reservation, the supreme being, the fullness of Being itself.

Practically, this means that we "must define God as the best possible, otherwise we are imagining a finite being woefully limited by our own imperfections and hence undeserving of our worship."[22] May we not imagine God in our own image, but bow to the ground, like Moses before the burning bush, as finite creatures before the supremacy of the perfectly infinite God.

4

Does God Depend on You?

Aseity

Who has first given to me, that I should repay him?
Whatever is under the whole heaven is mine.

JOB 41:11; CF. ROM. 11:35

God has all life, glory, goodness, blessedness, in and of Himself;
and is alone in and unto Himself all-sufficient, not standing
in need of any creatures which He has made, nor deriving any
glory in, by, unto, and upon them.

THE WESTMINSTER CONFESSION OF FAITH

What was God doing before he created the world? Perhaps he was lonely. And being lonely, he needed to fill that empty hole in his heart. So he decided to create the world—that way he could have fellowship with others. Now that the world is here, God is not so lonely anymore. Because of us, he feels fulfilled and whole.

This answer is not uncommon. It can be heard in many churches today by well-meaning Christians. Please brace yourself, because I have something shocking to say: God does *not* need you. He doesn't need you, he doesn't need me, and he doesn't need anyone or anything in this world. In fact, he doesn't need the world at all. Period.

God is *not* a needy God. It's not as if he was bored, twiddling his thumbs, desperately lonely prior to creating the world. God is *not* dependent on the world for his existence, nor is he dependent on the world for his happiness and self-fulfillment. Instead, he possesses life in and of himself. More precisely, he *is* the fullness of life in and of himself.

What we are describing is the attribute of *aseity—a se* being Latin, meaning "from himself." Depending on what you've been taught in church, it is likely you've never even heard about God's aseity before. But we will discover that this attribute is assumed and taught everywhere in Scripture and proves to be the key that unlocks God's attributes.

Life in and of Himself

To affirm God's aseity is to say, first and foremost, that he is life in and of himself, and on that basis he must be self-existent and self-sufficient.[1] It is because God is life in and of himself that there can be no sense in which he is caused by another.[2] For that reason, one might just as well refer to God's "*in*seity" as his "*a*seity."[3]

There is, most fundamentally, a difference in nature between the Creator and the creature, the former having life in and of himself, the latter deriving life from the one who is life. We are born into this world totally dependent, finite in every way. Our existence is derived from our mother and father. If we are to continue living, the God of the universe must sustain us. We are dependent on not only our earthly father but our heavenly Father too. Our nature, our very existence, is contingent in every way.

Not so with God. His nature is not at all like our nature. He is incommensurable, incapable of being measured by the same standards of our human existence. Unlike everything in this world, his existence is not grounded in, derived from, or contingent on something or someone else. No one brought him into being, nor is he dependent on something or someone else to continue being. He is underived from and unconditioned by that which is finite, contingent, limited, and changeable. That much is evident in how he created the world. He did not depend upon some preexisting matter to create the universe, but he created *ex nihilo*, out of nothing. Furthermore, only one who has no beginning or cause to his own existence can bring the world into existence out of nothing (an unmoved mover). Uncaused, his existence is grounded *in himself alone*. That means not that he created himself or caused himself to be but that he alone, as Anselm says, "has of himself all that he has, while other things have nothing of themselves. And other things, having nothing of themselves, have their only reality from him."[4]

That phrase "has of himself all that he has" handsomely summarizes aseity. The same cannot be said of objects in the created order. Placed next to God, observes Augustine, "they are deficient in beauty and goodness and being."[5] But there is no such deficiency in God's being. Aseity defines God as a *perfect* being.

The Happy Life of the Triune God

If God "has of himself all that he has," then aseity must also mean God is perfectly *fulfilled* and *happy* in and of himself. "God is infinitely happy in the enjoyment of himself," says Jonathan Edwards, "in perfectly beholding and infinitely loving, and rejoicing in, his own essence and perfections."[6] Notice what this entails: if God had never chosen to create the world—and it is important to remember that he did not *have to* create the world—he would have remained perfectly satisfied and content in and of himself. This also means that God's choice to voluntarily create the world was *not* because he felt a hole within him, as if he were in need of us to somehow fill up the joy otherwise lacking or give meaning to his otherwise meaningless existence. He was and continues to be self-sufficient as the one who *is* life in the most absolute sense of that word.

We have said before that the aseity of God is due to the fact that God is a different *type of being* in comparison with our being, different not merely in quantity but in quality. To elaborate, that difference in being has everything to do with God as Trinity. As the orthodox creeds have confessed, God is one in essence, three in person. These three are to be identified in eternity by certain *eternal relations of origin* or *personal modes of subsisting*: paternity, filiation, and spiration.[7] The Son is eternally generated from the Father (filiation), and the Holy Spirit eternally proceeds from the Father and the Son (spiration). God apart from creation exists as an immanent Trinity; the one essence of God subsists in these three persons eternally, independent of the created order. We will return to this mystery in chapter 5.

Eternal Relations of Origin in the Trinity

Paternity	The Father is eternally unbegotten.
Filiation	The Son is eternally begotten by the Father.
Spiration	The Spirit is eternally spirated by the Father and the Son.

What that truth entails for the Creator-creature distinction should not be missed. Before our Triune God ever created the universe, the Father, Son, and Spirit had perfect communion (to borrow an old Puritan word) with one another as the one, undivided

Godhead. The three persons of the Trinity enjoyed an impeccable fellowship before any stars or planets came into orbit. Hence Jesus can appeal, just prior to the cross, to the glory he experienced with the Father in eternity: "Father, glorify me in your own presence with the glory that I had with you before the world existed" (John 17:5). Jesus goes on to pray for his disciples, "I desire that they . . . may . . . see my glory that you have given me because you loved me before the foundation of the world" (17:24). The three persons of the Trinity expressed love toward one another, in this case the Father loving the Son, even before the world came to be. Glory, love—these characterize the fellowship of our Triune God from all eternity. Yet it's not just glory and love that characterize the three; it's *life* as well. As Jesus says in John 5:26, "For as the Father has life in himself, so he has granted the Son also to have life in himself."

We need not digress into all the nuances of what that life means for each person of the Trinity, but we should say, at the very least, that the implications for the Christian life are not insignificant.[8] Should the Father not be life in himself, and should he not grant the Son to have life in himself, then the Son would have no life to give to those he came to redeem, which is basic to his entire mission (John 3:16, 36; 4:14; 5:24; 6:40, 47, 54). Yet Jesus dismantles such a possibility when he says that an "hour is coming, and is now here, when the dead will hear the voice of the Son of God, and those who hear will live" (5:25). Certainly, then, the "life which the Son receives and has in himself is that which he in turn bestows upon creatures."[9]

The Lord Who Owns All and Gives to All

In the Old Testament the aseity of God is assumed and affirmed everywhere. To begin with, we see God's aseity when we reflect on God as *Creator*. The Old Testament repeatedly asserts that

God, as Creator, is the owner of all things. The opening chapters of Genesis put his ownership on display, for he is the God who made everything, from the jellyfish in the sea to the grasshopper on the tree. Naturally David can exclaim,

> The earth is the LORD's and the fullness thereof,
>   the world and those who dwell therein,
> for he has founded it upon the seas
>   and established it upon the rivers.
>   (Ps. 24:1–2; cf. Neh. 9:6)

God's aseity is wrapped up in not only his identity as Creator but his role as Israel's *covenant Lord and Savior*. When God enters into a covenant relationship with Abraham and later on with Israel, he does so as the God who is independent. His independence entails his possession of (rather than his dependence on) all things. As the God who is sovereign over all things, he can give to Abraham and Israel a great and prosperous land and make them a nation that will bless all nations.

For example, consider the encounter between Melchizedek and Abraham in Genesis 14, an encounter that takes place shortly after God appears to Abraham and commands him to depart for a new land Abraham has yet to see (Gen. 12:1–2). Melchizedek is an extraordinary and mysterious king-priest figure who blesses Abraham just after Abraham has won a mighty battle over his enemies. In his blessing Melchizedek begins by addressing "God Most High" as "Possessor of heaven and earth." Here we see a subtle hint at God's aseity. Then Melchizedek praises God for delivering Abraham's enemies into his hand (14:19–20). Since God owns the whole earth, he is able to hand over Abraham's enemies, protecting his original promise to one day give Abraham a land and make him into a great nation (12:1–2). God's covenant promises to Abraham rest on the solid foundation of divine aseity. It is because God is self-sufficient, not needing anything, being the owner of all things, that he is able to bless Abraham and his offspring with a global inheritance, one that is ultimately fulfilled in the coming of Jesus Christ, whom Hebrews calls the "guarantor of a better covenant" (Heb. 7:22).

Or consider God's covenant relations with rebellious Israel. Psalm 50 begins with the Lord, the "Mighty One," summoning the earth (50:1). When the Lord speaks and summons, he expects to be heard. He calls all humankind, and Israel in particular, to listen up as he has something important to say. God's people, Israel, are a people in covenant with the Lord, and this covenant has been established by "sacrifice" (50:5). But here's the problem, and it's a big one: Israel thinks that God *needs* her sacrifices and therefore she can use her sacrifices to bribe God! Notice how the Creator of the universe responds to his covenant people:

> I will not accept a bull from your house
> or goats from your folds.
> For every beast of the forest is mine,
> the cattle on a thousand hills.
> I know all the birds of the hills,
> and all that moves in the field is mine.
> If I were hungry, I would not tell you,
> for the world and its fullness are mine.
> (Ps. 50:9–12; cf. 146:5–7)

The point is clear: the Creator needs nothing, for he owns everything. And it is this affirmation of divine aseity that sets the tone for Israel's relationship with him. The people are not to approach their covenant Lord as they would a god they have made, one they can manipulate and bribe with their sacrifices. Instead, Israel is to approach her Creator and covenant Lord by offering a "sacrifice of thanksgiving" (50:14), calling on him in "the day of trouble" (50:15). He is not a God who needs Israel; Israel is a people who needs God. Israel was made to glorify him, and this people is completely dependent on him for deliverance (50:15).

Not Served by Human Hands

Not only is God's aseity seen in Old Testament language concerning creation and covenant, but it is carried into the New Testament as God's covenant promises are fulfilled in the coming of Jesus Christ. As the gospel is proclaimed to all people, it is paramount that those hearing this good news understand who exactly this saving God is to begin with.

The apostle Paul turns to God's aseity as the basis for his evangelism to the Athenians. In Acts 17:16–34 Paul is in Athens—famous for a philosophical tradition including thinkers like Socrates, Plato, and Aristotle—and he encounters the city's philosophers in the marketplace. As Paul walks through the city, his spirit is "provoked within him." Now why would this be? As Paul walks, he sees that the city is full of idols (17:16). Such idolatry motivates Paul to preach Jesus and his resurrection, a teaching that is new to his Athenian hearers.

Curious as to what this new teaching is all about, these philosophers invite Paul, who is labeled a "preacher of foreign divinities" (17:18), into the Areopagus. The approach Paul takes is striking. He acknowledges how "religious" his audience is, given the many gods they worship (17:22). But Paul is strategic, turning this moment into an opportunity to compare the gods they worship with the one, true, and living God. Pointing to an altar dedicated to "the unknown god," Paul says what they worship as "unknown" he will now make known (17:23). "The God who made the world and everything in it, being Lord of heaven and earth, does not live in temples made by man, nor is he served by human hands, as though he needed anything, since he himself gives to all mankind life and breath and everything" (17:24–25).

Keep in mind, included among those listening are Stoic philosophers, philosophers who believe that nature is divine, that everything in nature (humans included!) has a spark of divinity within. For the Stoics, the divine is absolutely dependent on the created order, so much so that the divine is identified with the created order. Today, worldviews like pantheism (God is the world, and the world is God) and panentheism (the world is within God) share similarities to this Stoic outlook. God and the world are mutually dependent. Such worldviews, however, imprison God's freedom, making the world necessary, and compromise his essence, making his existence dependent on the world.[10]

Notice what Paul says by contrast. God is the *Creator*, which means the whole world owes its existence to him. As Lord of heaven and earth, he does not need humans, nor is he served by human hands. If he were, then creation would be Lord instead of him. As the giver of life and all things, God is not in need of anything. It's not as if he lived in a temple (as the gods in Athens do), depending on others to feed him and serve him. The God Paul preaches is self-sufficient, self-existent, and independent of the world. He does not need humans, nor is he to be confused with the created order. He is not one with the created order but Lord over the created order, for he is the Creator of the universe. Here we see our attribute in focus: God is *by nature* independent, or *a se*.

Setting the Record Straight

But wait a minute. Isn't it true that Scripture also says we *serve* God and *give* to God? Yes, it does. And yet, we give to God only what he has first given to us.

In Luke 16:1–13, the parable of the dishonest manager, Jesus teaches us that we are stewards of God. As stewards, we will each be held accountable for what we have done with all that he has given to us (cf. Luke 12:42; Titus 1:7). Similarly, in Luke 17 Jesus is clear that even when we obey God, doing what he has asked, we have only done what is required of us. We should not think that God is somehow obligated to repay us, as if he owed us back. Our response should simply be, "We are unworthy servants; we have only done what was our duty" (17:10).

This is a lesson Job learns the hard way. Through his intense suffering, which we learn at the start of the book is ordained by God, Job is tempted (no thanks to his friends and his wife) to curse God. At the end of the book, after a very long silence, God answers Job, explaining that he owes an explanation, apology, and debt to no one. Job is not in a position to be God's advisor. "Who has first given to me, that I should repay him? Whatever is under the whole heaven is mine" (Job 41:11). No doubt Job finds these words sobering. And so does the apostle Paul. In Romans 11:34–36, Paul quotes Job 41:11 to make a very similar point: "'For who has known the mind of the Lord, or who has been his counselor?' 'Or who has given a gift to him that he might be repaid?' For from him and through him and to him are all things."

My wife and I have four children. Sometimes one of them will start fighting with a big brother or sister, saying something like, "This is *my* room. Get out!" Or when Mom asks one of them to share dessert with a little brother, Mom sometimes gets the entitled response, "But this is *my* ice-cream sandwich." In these moments, we remind our children that, actually, they do not own anything. Everything they have was first given to them. So when children give or share, they are giving or sharing that which was first given to or shared with them.

Few classics can compare to the family dynamic of the Huxtables in *The Cosby Show*. In one episode, Vanessa comes home from school upset, announcing that she was in a fight. Cliff naturally asks, "Did you win?" As Vanessa sits down with Cliff and Claire, she explains how two girls at school called her a stuck-up rich girl. Vanessa rolled up her sleeves, and the next thing you know the girls were rolling around on the floor. Cliff interrupts: "You took both of them on!" Vanessa explains how Mr. Morris pulled them all apart and made everyone apologize. Once more, Cliff cannot help himself: "If Mr. Morris hadn't stopped you, you think you would have beat both of them?"—a comment that provokes a glare from Claire. But then Vanessa says something that invites a glare from both Cliff and Claire: "None of this would have happened if we weren't so rich." After a baffled silence, Cliff sits up, folds his hands, and says, "Let me get something straight, okay? Your mother and I are rich. You have *nothing*. You can tell your friends and your enemies that, okay?" Cliff smiles.

Hilarious. But so true. If this is true with our kids, how much more so in relation to our Creator? Yes, we serve him and give to him—whether it be our time or finances. But we need to remember—much like Vanessa—that as sons of Adam and daughters of Eve, all that we have is from the Lord in the first place. Not one breath we take, not one minute of time, and not one single dollar is truly ours. It all belongs to the Lord, and he can take it away in an instant (as Job learns by firsthand experience). Therefore, when we serve God and when we give to him, we should do so out of thanksgiving, remembering that all of this is his to begin with.

The Key That Unlocks God's Attributes

Now that we're clear on just how dependent we are and just how independent God is, it is critical to understand how aseity relates to the other attributes of God. If God is life in and of himself, what other great-making attributes must follow?[11]

To begin with, if God is self-sufficient, then so also is he *self-divine*, for a God who is self-existent cannot receive his deity from anything or anyone outside himself. If God is self-sufficient, then he is also *self-wise*, for if others could inform God of what is wise or what wise choices he should make, then he would be less than perfect in his wisdom, growing in the wisdom he receives from others. Moreover, if God is self-sufficient, then he must be *self-virtuous*, for if he received his virtue from another, then he could

65

not be perfectly moral; he who increases in virtue cannot be the very standard of morality.

Similarly, if God is self-sufficient, then so also must he be *self-attesting*, since he is the very criterion for truth, just as he is for morality. God does not merely possess the truth, know the truth, and speak the truth; he *is* the truth. To know the truth, everyone must look to him because he is the very standard of truth. He is truth in and of himself, independent of any other. The same applies to his justice; he is *self-justifying*. As Isaiah asks rhetorically, "Whom did he consult, and who made him understand? Who taught him the path of justice, and taught him knowledge, and showed him the way of understanding?" (40:14). To echo Anselm, God not only is just, but he is just through himself.[12]

If God is self-sufficient, then God must be *self-empowering*; otherwise he is less than all-powerful, others having to help him when his power fails. If God is self-sufficient, then he must be *self-knowing*, meaning he does not depend on any creature to know what has happened or what will happen. That would entail that his knowledge is incomplete and he must rely on the knowledge of others to help him plan the future.

Last, if God is self-sufficient, he must be *self-excellent*, for if there were another being more excellent, more glorious, more majestic than God, then he would be dependent on that being for the very excellency that characterizes who he is and what he does.

Self-Excellency

That last point is extremely important and deserves further attention. We have been arguing throughout this book that God is the most perfect, supreme, and infinite being. And we've been asking what great-making attributes must follow if such a statement is true. Here that question is just as relevant. If God is the perfect being, then he must have life in and of himself. If he were dependent on someone/something else, he would forfeit his perfection, giving it to another. As Anselm reminds us, "For anything that is great through something else is less than that through which it is great." God's perfection must be an *independent* perfection. His excellency must be *self*-excellent. His nature, observes Anselm, must be "superior to others in such a way that it is inferior to none." Only that "which exists through itself and through which all other things exist is the being that is of all beings supreme."[13] Apart from aseity, God cannot be the *supreme* being.

Christians in past generations, like Anselm, have conveyed such self-excellency by the word "absolute." God is the "absolute being," for nothing and no one compares to him; nothing and no one is like him; nothing and no one makes him who he is. The absolute God, then, is the God of absolute power, absolute knowledge, absolute wisdom, absolute divinity, absolute glory, absolute excellence, and so on. In Latin there are several words that convey this truth:

esse	God is the supreme *being*.
verum	God is the supreme *truth*.
pulchrum	God is the supreme *beauty*.

Source: Bavinck, *Reformed Dogmatics*, 2:151.

If each of God's attributes is characterized by such supremacy, then Anselm is right: God is something than which nothing greater can be conceived. Inevitably, "all being is contained in him." He is "a boundless ocean of being."[14]

The Good without Which There Is No Good

If we are right, that God is the self-excellent, perfect, supreme, absolute being, then the implications for the rest of the world are massive. God's supremacy means that all else is dependent for any and all good upon the one who alone is independent. Applying to the one, true, and living God what the Greek philosopher Epimenides of Crete said of Zeus, Paul writes, "In him we live and move and have our being" (Acts 17:28). His supreme nature, says Anselm, "is the good without which there is no good."[15]

If we return to the distinction between God's incommunicable and communicable attributes, God's aseity means he is the source of each communicable quality in his creatures. Not only is he the "good without which there is no good," but he is the beauty without which there is no beauty, the wisdom without which there is no wisdom, the righteousness without which there is no righteousness, and so on. That said, he is not only the source but the cause of every good quality we witness in this world. "Not only does he sustain this universe (as he once founded it) by his boundless might, regulate it by his wisdom, preserve it by his goodness, and especially rule mankind by his righteousness and judgment, bear with it in his mercy, watch over it by his protection," observes John Calvin, but "no drop will be found either of wisdom and light, or of righteousness or power or rectitude, or of genuine truth, which does not flow from him, and of which he is not the cause."[16]

In the end, aseity is the key that unlocks all other attributes. Without it, every other attribute cannot be what it is. With it, we see why God is who he is. We see why his perfection is, well, so perfect. Yet it is also the very reason why God's communicable attributes are manifested in the world. As the one who is not dependent on anyone, he is the supreme source from which all else has its being, "With the exception of the supreme essence itself," concludes Anselm, "nothing exists that is not made by the supreme essence."[17]

The Gospel Depends on a God Who Does Not Depend on You

In Isaiah 40 and 44 we learn that God is not like the pagan gods of the surrounding nations. These gods are fashioned by humans

(40:19–20). Using satire, Isaiah explains that the wood humans use to keep warm and cook their food by the fire is the same wood they use to form a god so that they can bow down to it in worship, praying, "Deliver me, for you are my god!" (44:17). Notice how irrational such people are: they think their god can save, but this god is something made by human hands (and out of everyday stuff). This god cannot save. Fittingly, God mocks these man-made gods, as well as those who worship them. This is not a god who saves but a god you must save.

In contrast, Paul describes the Lord in Acts 17:24–30 not as a creature but as the Creator. Paul is emphatic: God is not worshiped by us "as though he needed anything." Biblical worship is due to God not because he needs us but because we need him. When we lift up our voices, God receives our worship, yet we should never think that in doing so we somehow give to God what he otherwise would lack, as if he needed us to make him complete. Consider the words of the twenty-four elders who fall down before the throne of God, worshiping him, casting their crowns before him, saying, "Worthy are you, our Lord and God, to receive glory and honor and power, for you created all things, and by your will they existed and were created" (Rev. 4:11).

If God were not life in and of himself, if he were not independent of us, then he would not be worthy, qualified, or able to save us, let alone worthy to receive worship and praise. If God were not *a se*, then he would be weak and pathetic, for he would be needy and dependent too. He would need saving, just as we do. He would be a God like us but not a God other than us. He would be a God in our world but not a God distinct from our world. "We might pray *for* this God, but definitely not *to* him."[18]

To conclude, it is precisely because God is free from creation that he is able to save lost sinners like you and me (Eph. 1:7–8). If God were a needy God, he would need our help just as much as we need his. What good news it is, then, that the gospel depends on a God who does not depend on us.

5

Is God Made Up of Parts?

Simplicity

Hear, O Israel: The LORD our God, the LORD is one.

DEUTERONOMY 6:4

The nature of God is simple and immutable and undisturbed,
nor is he himself one thing and what he is and has another thing.

AUGUSTINE, *On the Trinity*

God, . . . being light, is not pieced together from things that are
darkness.

HILARY OF POITIERS, *On the Trinity*

A denial of divine simplicity is tantamount to atheism.

DAVID BENTLEY HART, *The Experience of God*

Dutch Apple Caramel Pie

Back during my seminary days, our family lived in Louisville,
Kentucky. One of the advantages of living in Louisville was the

occasional trip to Homemade Pie and Ice Cream, which had the most scrumptious pies in town. Each year people from all over the country, even the world, travel to Louisville for the famous Kentucky Derby. Before the race, the festivities are not only marked by flamboyant hats and mint juleps, but most bakeries will sell out of their Derby pie, a mouthwatering chocolate and walnut tart pie no one can resist. I enjoy a classic Derby pie, but there is one pie I enjoy even more: the award-winning Dutch apple caramel pie. As you can tell, I like the Dutch; there will be no shortage of quotes in this book from the Dutch Reformed theologian Herman Bavinck. I don't know if Bavinck ate a Dutch apple caramel pie in his day, but (humor me) I can think of nothing better than sitting next to a garden of tulips, with Bavinck's *Reformed Dogmatics* in one hand and a piece of Dutch apple caramel pie in the other. I know, I know—the things theologians dream about.

Truth be told, the caramel on the pie is so thick (too thick for the taste buds of some) that you need a butcher's knife to cut through it. But let's say you've found your knife and you begin dividing up the pie: a fairly large piece for me, thank you, and perhaps smaller pieces for everyone else. It kills me to admit this, because a theologian is always looking for an insightful illustration wherever he can find one, but Dutch apple caramel pie is a poor illustration for what God is like. That's right, a really bad one. And yet it's how many people think about God's attributes. In fact, it's what makes me nervous about writing one chapter after another on different attributes of God, as if we're slicing up the pie called "God."

The perfections of God are not like a pie, as if we sliced up the pie into different pieces, love being 10 percent, holiness 15 percent, omnipotence 7 percent, and so on. Unfortunately, this is how many Christians talk about God today, as if love, holiness, and omnipotence were all different parts of God, God being evenly divided among his various attributes. Some even go further, believing some attributes to be more important than others. This happens most

HERMAN BAVINCK

It was during my first year in seminary that I received the complete set of Herman Bavinck's (1854–1921) *Reformed Dogmatics*. I had read this giant thinker before, but at the time I was too poor to afford his *magnum opus*. To this day, it is one of the best Christmas gifts I have ever received. No one so smoothly synthesizes every discipline—biblical studies, historical theology, philosophy, psychology, science—into a single presentation of Christian theology. Bavinck is, says J. I. Packer, "solid but lucid, demanding but satisfying, broad and deep and sharp and stabilizing."[a] Bavinck was the successor to Abraham Kuyper, the Dutch statesman, at the Free University in Amsterdam. In a day when Bavinck witnessed the heavy pull of liberalism in his own denomination, the Dutch theologian became revered for his steadfast faithfulness to the Scriptures. His treatment of the doctrine of God has become well established as one of the best, holding the line against the many trends of his modern era that had abandoned a biblical portrait of God.

[a] Endorsement of Bavinck, *Reformed Dogmatics*, back cover.

with divine love, which some say is the most important attribute (the biggest piece of the pie).

Such an approach is deeply problematic, turning God into a collection of attributes. It even sounds as if God were one thing and his attributes another, something added onto him, attached to who he is. Not only does this approach divide up the essence of God, but it potentially risks setting one part of God against another (for example, might his love ever oppose his justice?). Sometimes this error is understandable; it unintentionally slips into our God-talk. We might say, "God has love" or "God possesses all power." We all understand what is being communicated, but the language can be misleading. It would be far better to say, "God *is* love" or "God *is* all-powerful." By tweaking our language, we are protecting the unity of God's essence. To do so is to guard the "simplicity" of God.

A Pub, a Suntan, and the A-Team

Simplicity may be a new concept to your theological vocabulary, but it is one that has been affirmed by the majority of our Christian forebears over the past two thousand years of church history, even by some of the earliest church fathers. And for good reason, too. Let's consult our A-team once again.

Apparently, I am not the only one who has appealed to an illustration to demonstrate what God is *not* like. In the fifth century, the church father Augustine did the same, though it wasn't Dutch apple caramel pie. Instead, Augustine appealed to liquor, the human body, and sunshine. The nature of the Trinity is called simple, because "it cannot lose any attribute it possesses" and because "there is no difference between what it *is* and what it *has*, as there is, for example, between a vessel [cup] and the liquid it contains, a body and its colour, the atmosphere and its light or heat, the soul and its wisdom." Augustine concludes, "None of these *is* what it contains."[1] A cup and liquid, a body and its color, the atmosphere and its light or heat, the soul and its wisdom— what do these all have in common? Answer: division.

I was born in Los Angeles, the City of Angels. Southern Californians are known for their suntans. Whether it's Huntington Beach, Newport Beach, or Laguna Beach (which has the best milk shakes, by the way), they all have one thing in common: sunbathers. Sporting swimwear, sunbathers lie on the beach all day long, soaking up the sun until their skin looks like bronze. But you don't want to see sunbathers indoors on one of those rare So Cal rainy days. They look awful. Clearly, their bronze color is not natural, and when it fades, it looks like a pumpkin two weeks after Halloween.

In our experience, it appears as though skin color changes, and it morphs into different shades depending on the amount of sunshine it receives. A body and its color at the beach, a cup and its liquor at the pub—though related, they remain entirely separate entities from one another. Not only are they distinct, but the one (color, liquor) adds to the other (the body, the cup) something that was not there before. They are accidental, inessential, and optional. Not so, however, with God and his attributes.

God's attributes are not external to his essence, as if they added a quality to him that he would not otherwise possess. It's not as if there were attributes that were accidental to God, capable of being added or subtracted, lost and then found, as if they did not even have to exist in the first place. Rather, God *is* his attributes. Instead of addition and division, there is absolute unity. His essence is his attributes, and his attributes, his essence. Or as Augustine says, "God has no properties but is pure essence. . . . They neither differ from his essence nor do they differ materially from each other."[2]

Augustine is not alone. If we draw from the wisdom of the A-team (Augustine, Anselm, Aquinas), we discover a consensus. Take Anselm, for example. If something is "composed of parts," he remarks, then it cannot be "altogether one." Whenever there is a plurality of parts, that which is made up of those parts is vulnerable to being dissolved. How disastrous this would be for God! By contrast, God is "truly a unitary being," one who is "identical with" himself and "indivisible." "Life and wisdom and the other [attributes], then, are not parts of You, but all are one and each one of them is wholly what You are and what all the others are."[3]

Or consider Thomas Aquinas. Since God does not have a body (like us), he "is not composed of extended parts," as if he were composed of "form and matter." It's not as if God were something different from "his own nature." Nor is it the case that his nature is one thing and his existence another thing. We shouldn't suppose, either, that God is some type of substance, one that has accidents, traits that can be disposed of or cease to exist. "God is in no way composite. Rather, he is entirely simple."[4]

While Aquinas uses the words "composite" and "composition" to explain what God is *not*, the church father Irenaeus uses the word "compound" to explain what God is *not*. If something is compounded, it means it has more than one part to it, each part being separate from the other. By contrast, God, being simple, is an "uncompounded Being," not having different "members." He is totally "equal to himself." Perhaps it's appropriate, then, to put the word "wholly" in front of each of his attributes to emphasize this very point. "God is not as men are," explains Irenaeus. "For the Father of all is at a vast distance from those affections and passions which operate among men. He is a *simple, uncompounded* Being, without diverse members, and altogether like, and equal to Himself, since he is *wholly* understanding, and *wholly* spirit, and *wholly* thought, and *wholly* intelligence, and *wholly* reason, . . . *wholly* light, and the *whole* source of all that is good."[5]

With the A-team by our side it is appropriate to conclude that simplicity is not merely a negative statement—God is without parts—but a positive one as well: God is identical with all that he is in and of himself.[6] In the purest sense, God is one; he is singular perfection. In Scripture, this cannot be said of the gods made by humans, gods composed of parts. Given how unique God is, then, it is only right that God's people confess together, as does Israel, that "the Lord our God, the Lord is one" (Deut. 6:4).

The One Symphony Whose Composer Is without Composition

But is simplicity really such a big deal? After all, what would be so wrong with a "composite" God—that is, a God who possesses different parts?

One of the more artistic buildings in the country is the Kauffman Center for the Performing Arts in Kansas City, Missouri. Its architecture takes the form of two giant waves, but with layers like an onion or an artichoke. On the descending side of these waves is an all-glass entrance the length of the entire building. Driving by on the freeway, you can see directly into this architectural masterpiece.

The inside of the building is just as impressive. The seats curve around the symphony, whose music bounces off the wood beams hanging overhead. Listening to the music the symphony performs gives the phrase "music to my ears" a whole new meaning. One leaves inspired by the bellowing of the cello and wooed by the commanding presence of the double bass. How odd it would be, I must admit, to leave wondering whether there were a composer. Of course there is. The violin, the French horn, and the tuba all play different parts that make up the symphony, and these parts must be put together by a composer to construct a piece of music. The parts—and how well they are played—can make or break a composer. A composer is only as good as the musical parts that constitute a piece of music, and for that reason the composer is dependent on them in order to receive a standing ovation at the end of the hour.

But here is what is so unique about God: he is *without parts*. And as a God without parts, he has no composer. The world, on the other hand, does have parts and must be composed. It is neither self-existent nor self-sufficient. It has not life in and of itself. Only the one who is life in and of himself, the one and only one who is without composition, has the ability to act as its composer. In short, it is because God has no composer that he can be the composer of the natural symphony we see around us. It is, miraculous as this may be, the only symphony whose composer is without composition.

The Marriage of Aseity and Simplicity in a Perfect, Infinite Being

Dangerous consequences would follow if God did have a composer. For starters, his *perfection* and *supremacy* would be called into question. If Aquinas is right that "every composition" truly "needs some composer,"[7] then Anselm, too, must be right when he says that one who is composite "just is not supreme."[8] Think of it this way: Who is greater, a God who depends on someone or something else to make him what he is, or a God who is composed by no one but simply is?

Certainly, it must be the latter. If it were the former, then would not God's perfection be in doubt?[9] What would stop one of his parts from being more advanced than another? What a strange situation that would be for God. He would be at odds with himself, one part fully developed but another part still awaiting its full potential. Yet that is the nature of anything that has parts that make up the whole. And so it would be with God.[10]

Such logic is one compelling reason why discussing simplicity after a chapter on aseity makes sense.[11] If God is composite, made up of parts, then not only are his perfection and supremacy compromised but so is his *aseity*. If God is life in and of himself, being self-existent and self-sufficient, then it follows that he is not a God made up of various parts, for if he were, then he would *depend* on those parts, which would violate his aseity. To make matters worse, not only would he depend on those parts, but those parts would even *precede* him. "Everything composite," Aquinas remarks, "is subsequent to its components and dependent on them." A God made up of parts cannot be "the first of all beings."[12]

In one of the greatest definitions of simplicity, Stephen Charnock stresses this very point: "God is the most simple being; for that which is first in nature, having nothing beyond it, cannot by any means be thought to be compounded." Charnock then tells us why: "For whatsoever is so, depends upon the parts whereof it is compounded, and so is not the first being." But remember, the being of God is "infinitely simple, hath nothing in himself which is not himself, and therefore cannot will any change in himself, he being his own essence and existence."[13]

The difference, then, between a simple being (God) and a composite being (everything else) comes down to aseity. In the physical world, says David Bentley Hart, "nothing has its actuality entirely in itself, fully enjoyed in some impregnable present instant, but

> ### STEPHEN CHARNOCK
>
> Stephen Charnock (1628–80) ministered in what J. I. Packer calls seventeenth-century "nominally Christian Britain."[a] He was not only gifted in the pulpit, as his preaching career in Ireland demonstrates, but he had an ability to communicate the most complicated doctrines with clarity and profundity, as is evident in his work *The Cross of Christ*. He attempted to write a systematico-practical theology but died before he could finish. Nevertheless, we possess the start of it, which is six hundred thousand words on the existence and attributes of God. Charnock is instrumental for our purposes because he not only expounds each attribute in unparalleled depth but is always eager to show us the relevance of such attributes for the Christian life.
>
> [a] J. I. Packer, *Puritan Portraits*, 47.

must always receive itself from beyond itself, and then only by losing itself at the same time. Nothing within the cosmos contains the ground of its own being." That is what makes God so astoundingly, unbelievably unique: he does contain the ground of his own being in and of himself. We are one thing today and another thing tomorrow, "wavering between existence and nonexistence."[14] But there is no wavering with God. As the one who is life in and of himself, he remains eternally indivisible and therefore constantly reliable, the one "with whom there is no variation or shadow due to change" (James 1:17).

A Dark Thought: Destructibility, Corruptibility, and the Will of God

It is a scary thought to even consider a God who is without simplicity, mostly because such a God would, to put it bluntly, *self-destruct*. As we learned in chapter 3, a perfect being is an infinite being. If God is that being than which none greater can be conceived, then he must be a being who is without limitation. Yet if God were made up of parts—a composite, complex, and compound being—then he would be a limited being if for no other reason than that parts make God divisible.[15]

But here's where everything gets quite dark: *If God is divisible, then he is also destructible.*[16] That's right, destructible. Remember, anything that is physical in this universe is composite and therefore must be transient, impermanent, reducible, mutable, fragile, incomplete, and, therefore, dissolvable.[17] Moreover, if something is divisible, then it is capable of being *corrupted* as well. If something can be dismantled, taken apart, whether physically or intellectually, then such parts must be capable of decomposition.[18] Breakdown ensues since divine unity itself has disintegrated. In the end, simplicity is essential to a God immune to division and corruption.

Such corruptibility takes on many forms, but the most startling is the way a divisible, corruptible God's good will is affected. Ask yourself that question that often entertained the brightest minds of the late medieval era: Is something good because God wills it to be good, or does God will something because it is good? This famous conundrum is the ultimate puzzle, situating God between a rock and a hard place. If we say something is good because God wills it to be good, then God sounds arbitrary. Nothing is inherently good, but God simply decides what he wants to be good. On the other hand, if God wills something because it is good, then is God not subservient to whatever is good? A standard of goodness exists external to God himself.

The paradox is far less problematic if we take into consideration divine simplicity. How so? "God neither obeys the moral order, nor does He invent it," says Katherin Rogers. "He is Goodness Itself, and all else that is good is good in imitation of God's nature."[19] The same applies to other perfections. Is something true because God says it is true, or does God declare something true because it is true? The question betrays God's simplicity. God does not bow to some external norm for truth, nor does he invent truth *ex nihilo*. God *is* truthfulness itself. All truth is truth because it mimics the very nature of God, who is truth.

Each example should buffet any reversal of the Creator-creature distinction. If God is a simple God, then he *is* his perfections eternally. Any sign of his perfections in the created order finds its origin in God. As "absolute source God is indeed Wisdom and Justice and Goodness *per se*, and other things possess these qualities through participation in the divine."[20]

Simplicity, Refraction, and Baseball

Admittedly, simplicity can be a hard concept to wrap our minds around. You may be inclined to object: "If we affirm simplicity, then all of God's attributes are the same. We cannot distinguish properly between any of them."

What I love best about traveling is seeing old churches. Churches that are several hundred years old typically have stained glass. Back then, churches would hire a craftsman to fashion biblical scenes using the colorful glass. Stepping back from the glass, one could see the entire story of the Bible pictured. The beauty of stained glass is seen most when one sunbeam hits the glass and several different colors are portrayed on the inside of the glass—yellow, red, blue, and so on. That imagery pictures simplicity in a way. God is one, and his attributes are identical with one another. Yet when God's undivided essence is revealed to humanity, it shines in various ways. Nevertheless, it is the same, single ray of light that radiates. God's attributes, says the Puritan George Swinnock, "are all one and the same; as when the sunbeams shine through a yellow glass they are yellow, a green glass they are green, a red glass they are red, and yet all the while the beams are the same."[21] Long before Swinnock, Augustine called this God's "simple multiplicity" and "manifold simplicity."[22] "Although this light is of one kind, nevertheless it suffuses the objects with a luster that varies in accordance with their different qualities."[23]

Or consider how light works when it enters a prism. A "ray of sunlight is composed of many wavelengths that in combination appear to be colourless." What happens if that ray enters a prism made of glass? "The different refractions of the various wavelengths spread them apart as in a rainbow."[24] In physics, this is called refraction. Though every illustration is imperfect, refraction does illustrate simplicity.[25]

We could also say that the prism symbolizes the revelation of God, not in his essence but according to his works. As the one, simple God is manifested to his creatures through human words and mighty acts, that one, undivided essence is displayed in a variety of ways. Or as James Dolezal has said, "In God's effects the perfection of His undivided essence is shown forth in a vast array of creaturely perfections. Accordingly, what is a simple unity in God is presented to the human knower under the form of creaturely multiplicity."[26] Such refraction does not eliminate the possibility of the creature knowing the Creator, but it eliminates the possibility of knowing him in his infinite simplicity. "This refraction of His simple glory into so many beams of finite perfection does not mean that multi-farious beams speak no truth about His simple nature. They just do not speak that truth under the incomprehensible simple form of that nature."[27]

It was said in chapter 3 that no one name can describe the fullness of an infinite God. The reason is that God is infinite, while we are finite. As finite creatures with finite minds, we can never comprehend the fullness of his infinite majesty or the inestimable splendor of his glory. The only way we could comprehend God's essence all at once, in all its immeasurable perfection, would be if we were infinite too. That not being the case, a plurality of names is essential.[28] Given our finitude, each name serves a unique purpose, enabling us to understand yet another aspect of God's one, undivided essence. God is not a composite, made up of many good things, but is "one good thing" that is "signified by many names," says Anselm.[29] Whether Scripture refers to his mercy or righteousness, his jealousy or love, such naming is a way of addressing the God who is one, the "single undifferentiated divine reality."[30]

Compare it to season tickets for watching your favorite baseball team. Whether you sit in the bleachers or behind home plate, you are watching the same baseball game, looking at the same baseball field. But as anyone who has sat behind home plate will tell you, you leave the game with an entirely different point of view. Aquinas never played baseball (I have no idea what sports entertained twelfth-century medieval monks), but he understood this to be true: "The different and complex concepts that we have in mind correspond to something altogether simple which they enable us imperfectly to understand. Thus the words we use for the perfections we attribute to God, though they signify what is one, are not synonymous, for they signify it from many different points of view."[31]

The Boy Who Tried to Buy a Thousand Dollars with Fifty Cents

Winters can be brutally cold if you live in the Midwest or on the East Coast of America. Our family likes to take indoor field trips around the city when it's too cold to be outside. We are fortunate enough to have one of the only twelve Federal Reserve Banks in our own backyard. So when the temperature drops below freezing, we jump in the van and enjoy a day looking at, literally, billions of dollars. Suppose you too took a trip to a Federal Reserve Bank and overhear a conversation like the following between a father and son.[32]

"Dad," says five-year-old Tommy, "I want to buy that gold coin in the glass case." Tommy quickly empties the change from his pockets.

Starting to chuckle, Dad says, "Tommy, I don't think you have enough coins to buy it."

Perplexed, Tommy responds, "But why not? I've got ten coins in my pocket. Isn't that more than enough to buy just that one coin?" Tommy looks down at what seems like a handful of riches, not realizing his many coins only make up fifty cents, not nearly enough to buy a coin worth a thousand dollars.

As Tommy receives a boring lecture from Dad on monetary value, you cannot help but notice just how applicable this scenario is to divine simplicity. As you return home to your warm fireplace and library, you remember a passage in Bavinck: "Just as a child cannot picture the worth of a coin of great value but only gains some sense of it when it is counted out in a number of smaller coins, so we too cannot possibly form a picture of the infinite fullness of God's essence unless it is displayed to us now in one relationship, then in another, and now from one angle, then from another."[33]

Whether it's a prism, baseball, or the Federal Reserve, we must always bear in mind how human language works whenever it speaks of the one who is above and beyond us. We are attempting to describe the one who is without composition, but as finite creatures we can do so only by using composite objects in the physical world to somehow portray the one who is incomprehensible.[34]

Simplicity and Trinity: Friends or Foes?

With all our talk about simplicity, we have yet to address the elephant in the room. How can God be simple, without parts, without composition, if he is triune? Are there not three in God: Father, Son, and Spirit? And do we not distinguish between them? It would seem that the Trinity rules out simplicity, and it would appear that we have a contradiction on our hands.[35]

Actually, simplicity is not only compatible with the Trinity, but it is essential to the Trinity, having even assisted Christians of the past in avoiding certain trinitarian heresies. For instance, when a non-Christian (a Muslim, for example) is presented with the

Trinity, they are likely to object, "If God is Father, Son, and Spirit, do Christians not worship three gods instead of one?" Tritheism is a serious accusation, one that the church has denied for many reasons. One of them is this: if tritheism does follow, then the divinity of God is divided between three gods.

Historically, simplicity has been the answer to this dilemma, reassuring Christians that tritheism is untenable, a misconception of the Christian God. The Trinity is not made up of three *parts* called Father, Son, and Spirit, but the Trinity is three *persons.* Each person does not possess part of the divinity (one-third each), nor does each person make up a part of God, as if you must add up the persons to end up with the total essence of God. Instead, each person equally and fully shares the one, undivided essence and the one divine essence wholly subsists in each of the three persons.[36] And since God's essence and attributes are identical (God *is* his attributes), each person wholly shares every attribute.[37]

To elaborate, each person being *fully, wholly* God, not *partially* God, means that God remains indivisible in his essence. The one essence is not split into three things (i.e., tritheism) but wholly and personally subsists in three distinguishable yet inseparable persons.[38] As we saw in chapter 4, these persons are distinguishable from one another by what the creeds and confessions of the church down through the ages call *eternal relations of origin* or *personal modes of subsistence*: paternity, filiation, and spiration. The Father eternally generates the Son (paternity and filiation), and the Spirit eternally proceeds from the Father and the Son (spiration). These three relations of origin have allowed the church to distinguish between the three without aborting the unity of the three as one in essence.[39] "Simplicity in respect to essence, but Trinity in respect to persons," says Francis Turretin.[40]

Such unity in the very being or essence of the Triune God (the immanent Trinity) is further manifested in how God acts toward the world (the economic Trinity).[41] For instance, when we refer to the three persons bringing about our redemption, we should always be careful to add that they do so inseparably from one another. This is called "inseparable operations" in theology, made famous by fathers like Gregory of Nyssa.[42] One particular person of the Trinity may take on a special or focal role (e.g., the Son becomes incarnate; the Spirit descends at Pentecost). That is called the doctrine of divine "appropriations," because a specific work or action is appropriated to a particular person of the Trinity.[43] Nevertheless, every external work of the Trinity remains undivided (*opera Trinitatis ad extra sunt indivisa*), so that in any work of creation, providence, and redemption the three persons work inseparably (i.e., inseparable operations).[44] For example, it is the Son of God who becomes incarnate and dies on the cross; nevertheless, his mission is from the Father (John 3:31–36; 5:19–23), and he goes to the cross by the eternal Spirit (Heb. 9:14). In every redemptive activity the three persons work indivisibly.

The External Works of the Trinity

Inseparable Operations	The external works of the Trinity are undivided (*opera Trinitatis ad extra sunt indivisa*), so that in any work of creation, providence, and redemption the three persons work inseparably. This unity in their missions stems from the unity—the simplicity—of the divine essence eternally.
Divine Appropriation	One person of the Trinity takes on a special or focal role in any external work of the Trinity (examples: the Son becomes incarnate; the Spirit descends at Pentecost). Such an appropriation reflects the distinctions between the three persons in eternity (i.e., eternal relations of origin).

Inseparable operations have much to do with simplicity. Yes, there are three persons, but since each person is not a *part* of God but *wholly* God, there can be only one will and intellect in God. Will and intellect are to be identified with the one, undivided, and shared divine essence (not the three persons). Just as one essence means there is but one goodness, one love, one power, and so on, in God, so too does it mean there is one will and one intellect.[45] If there were three wills and intellects in God, rather than one will and intellect, then simplicity would be compromised, and it would be far more difficult to avoid tritheism (as each person would have a different will than the other two). Such a view is called social trinitarianism, and it fails to preserve the simple nature of the Triune God.

There is also a heretical danger on the other end of the spectrum from tritheism: modalism (also called Sabellianism or modalistic monarchianism), the belief that the one God is not three *distinct persons* but merely three *impersonal modes* or phases in God's existence. The one God is Father, and then he decides to become Son, and at another time Holy Spirit. He merely wears different masks when appropriate; he is not three persons but one person manifested in three ways.

Simplicity is key to avoiding this trinitarian heresy as well. If God's essence is his attributes and his attributes are his essence, then when we refer to Father, Son, and Spirit, we do not have in mind merely three *impersonal* "modes of subsisting" but "*personal* modes of subsisting."[46] Simplicity protects the three persons from becoming impersonal altogether. The one divine essence does not merely take on different forms or wear different masks that we call Father, Son, and Spirit. Rather, the one, undivided divine essence (i.e., simplicity) wholly subsists in three *persons* (Father, Son, and Holy Spirit), each of which is distinct from the other due to their eternal relations of origin (paternity, filiation, and spiration).

The church father Augustine is exemplary in the way he articulates simplicity and Trinity, all the while avoiding heresies like modalism (Sabellianism). First, Augustine explains why simplicity does not preclude distinct persons: "The Trinity is one God; the fact that it is a Trinity does not mean that it is not simple. For when we speak of this [God] as being by nature simple, we do not mean that it consists solely of the Father, or solely of the Son, or solely of the Holy Spirit, or that there is really only a nominal Trinity, without subsistent Persons; that is the notion of the Sabellian heretics." Yet Augustine simultaneously demonstrates how the one, simple divine essence wholly subsists in all three persons. "What is meant by 'simple' is that its being is identical with its attributes, apart from the relation in which each person is said to stand to each other. For the Father of course has the Son; and yet he himself is not the Son; and the Son has the Father; and yet he himself is not the Father. But when each is regarded in himself, not in relation to the other, his being is identical with his attributes. Thus each in himself is said to be living, because he *has* life; and at the same time he himself *is* life."[47]

Simplicity, then, is critical to guarding Christianity from the accusation of modalism, and is equally instrumental in protecting its commitment to monotheism (the belief in one God) over against tritheism.[48] On the one hand, the essence is not composed of parts as if these parts are then added up, one on another, to make up each person in the Trinity. On the other hand, neither do the persons themselves act as parts, as if each were a slice of the divine pie we call God.[49]

How Serious Is a Denial of Simplicity?

The denial of simplicity is serious. So serious that Hart says it is "tantamount to atheism."[50] That sounds extreme. Yet Hart reminds us that up until the nineteenth century, most would have agreed. Back in chapter 3, we discussed that view known as monopolytheism (or theistic personalism)—that is, the belief that there is one God but he looks a lot like the gods of mythology, possessing human attributes, only in greater measure. If monopolytheism were true, however, then God not only would be made up of various parts or properties but would be "logically dependent on some more comprehensive reality embracing both him and other beings."[51] And if God were dependent on something or someone else, then he would have given up his deity altogether, for whatever he would be dependent on would have to be something than which nothing greater can be conceived, something more comprehensive than himself.

That is serious.

6

Does God Change?

Immutability

With [God] there is no variation or shadow due to change.

JAMES 1:17

It is instinctual for every rational creature to think that there is an altogether unchangeable and incorruptible God.

AUGUSTINE, *The Literal Meaning of Genesis*

We blossom and flourish as leaves on the tree,
and wither and perish, but naught changeth Thee.

WALTER SMITH, "IMMORTAL, INVISIBLE"

Rock of Ages, Cleft for Me

One of our family's most memorable vacations was a two-week stay in Wales. Among the highlights were medieval castles that injected one with sudden chivalry, sandy beaches just under the soaring heights of green-pastured cliffs, and bridges suspended above real-life versions of Monet's *Water Lilies*. Wales truly is God's country.

My favorite memory has to do with a site well off the beaten path in Pembrokeshire. Sandwiched between two giant rocks, sitting halfway down a threatening limestone cliff, rests a chapel built into the cleft of the rock. The chapel is named after Saint Govan, a sixth-century monk who lived in a cave. Legends surround this saint, making it difficult to decipher fact from fiction. As one legend has it, the monk was on the run from pirates when the cliff swallowed him up into safety until the pirates passed by. Govan remained on that cliff the rest of his life as a hermit, assisting those who lived nearby by his readiness to warn others of the pirates should they come back one day. Regardless of whether this story is true, what we do know is that in the eleventh century a chapel was built on the site of Govan's cave, and some say his bones are buried beneath the altar.

As I descended the fifty-two steps lodged between the two towering cliffs, I tried to imagine what it must have been like for Saint Govan to escape those deadly pirates that day. As he ran for his life, this cleft in the rock acted as a fortress. Not only did it hide him from plain sight, but it protected him from the winds and waves of the sea, which would have crushed any pirate ship that dared approach. Never would Saint Govan have simultaneously felt so afraid and yet so safe. And here I was, hundreds of years later, as the same rock secured my footing.

As I stood there nestled in the arms of the rock, the opening line of Augustus Toplady's hymn "Rock of Ages" buzzed in my ear:

> Rock of Ages, cleft for me,
> Let me hide myself in thee.

The imagery of a rock conveys many things, but most vivid of all is its immutable nature. Wars come and go, countries rise and fall, and all the world changes from one century to the next. But not the rock. It is not thwarted, it does not vacillate. It is the same yesterday, today, and forever.

In but a small way, that rock is like God; he does not change. Come what may, this God remains the same. He is firm and secure, always there, never fluctuating, incapable of defeat, and forever steadfast as a fortress to those in trouble.

Who Is a Rock, except Our God?

Long before Saint Govan fled from pirates, David fled from King Saul. Filled with envy, Saul tracked David relentlessly, like an assassin on a mission to eliminate his target. Fleeing for his life, David turned time and time again to caves, hidden deep in the heart of a rock, because he found them to be impenetrable. On one occasion, David praises the Lord for delivering him from his enemies, Saul included, and he sings,

> The LORD is my rock and my fortress and my deliverer,
>   my God, my rock, in whom I take refuge.
>   (2 Sam. 22:2–3)

> For who is God, but the LORD?
>   And who is a rock, except our God? (22:32)[1]

Repeatedly in the Psalms, David addresses God as his rock, a title that identifies where the source and assurance of his salvation are to be found:

> He alone is my rock and my salvation,
>   my fortress; I shall not be greatly shaken. (Ps. 62:2)

> On God rests my salvation and my glory;
>   my mighty rock, my refuge is God. (62:7)

"Rock" even is used as a proper name for God, as David begins and ends his prayers, exclaiming, "O LORD, my rock and my redeemer" (19:14).[2]

David sees an inseparable connection between God's character and real life. God's immutable essence or being is the very foundation of David's trust in God for salvation, both physical and spiritual. If God is not unchanging, like a rock, then he cannot act as David's fortress in times of turmoil. But if God is a God who does not change, then David has every reassurance that he can run to God when the whole earth has given way under his feet.

"For I the LORD Do Not Change"

David is not the only one who connects these theological dots between God's immutable nature and the Christian life. Consider the prophet Malachi. Malachi has a tough task. Through Malachi (whose name means "messenger"), the Lord sternly rebukes his people. Israel deserves it for a whole slew of reasons. The priests, for example, profane worship, bringing polluted offerings before the Lord. They come into God's presence offering animals that are blind, sick, and handicapped, rather than offering up to God their best. That says volumes about what they think about God.

Word has gotten out among neighboring nations, too. These priests dragged God's name through the mud for all to see. God will not stand for this evil: "My name will be great among the nations" (Mal. 1:11). "Behold, I will rebuke your offspring, and spread dung on your faces" (2:3). Now that is a punishment!

Throughout the book of Malachi, what stands out is the contrast between God and Israel. While Israel keeps sliding into unfaithfulness and covenant disinterest, God remains steadfast, never wavering. Israel has grown complacent, and Malachi is calling the people to repent and renew their covenant with God, to trust once again in his covenant promises, rather than entertaining unbelief, indifference, and ethical compromise.

In view of such sin, Israel surely deserves to be extinguished. Time and time again Israel has failed to trust God, be faithful to the covenant, and exhibit love for God by obedience. It seems as if there is no hope left. But then God says something remarkable: "For I the LORD do not change; therefore you, O children of Jacob, are not consumed" (3:6). God's faithfulness stems from his nature. It is because he is immutable in *essence* that his *works* operate immutably as well. He does not change in who he is (his essence); therefore he does not change in what he says and does (his will). He will not go back on his covenant promises to Abraham, Isaac, and Jacob. Yes, Israel has been unfaithful to the covenant, but the Lord has been and will remain faithful. His immutability, we cannot fail to stress, results in mercy, inviting his people to return to him; and the Lord promises that when they return to him, he will renew the covenant once more.

The God without a Shadow

The immutability of God was not foreign to the followers of Jesus either. Consider James, who is writing to Christians experiencing all kinds of trials. James reminds them, "the testing of your faith produces steadfastness. And let steadfastness have its full effect, that you may be perfect and complete, lacking in nothing" (James 1:3–4). James also reminds these suffering Christians of the great reward that awaits them should they not give up: "Blessed is the man who remains steadfast under trial, for when he has stood the test he will receive the crown of life, which God has promised to those who love him" (1:12). God has ordained such trials, as painful as they may be, to conform James's readers (and us) more and more into the image of his Son, which is why James can so boldly say, "Count it all joy . . . when you meet trials of various kinds" (1:2).

However, we should never jump to the faulty conclusion that God is tempting us to sin. "God cannot be tempted with evil, and he himself tempts no one" (1:13). Rather, we are being enticed by our own sinful desires. God is good, and the gifts he gives are good. "Every good gift and every perfect gift is from above, coming down from the Father of lights" (1:17). James calls him the "Father of lights" because, according to Genesis 1 and Psalms 74 and 136, God is the Creator of the lights in the heavens (sun, moon, stars). Such lights showcase just how good God is to his creation.

Yet how can one be sure God will remain good? What if he were to change, and with such change no longer act in such a good way? The answer comes in what James says next: With the "Father of lights . . . there is no variation or shadow due to change" (1:17). With the sun and the moon come variation. During the day it is sunny, but then night falls and, with it, darkness. In the middle of the day, your shadow is very small, for the sun's rays shine from directly overhead. Then as the sun moves toward the horizon, your shadow grows in size. If you were to stand next to a tall building, your shadow might stand as tall as a twenty-foot wall. Your shadow has changed.

God, however, has no shadow. Nor is he like a shadow, subject to change. He always remains the same. On that basis, James concludes, you can trust God to remain good, and you can trust that this God always has your good in mind and will always act in a way that reflects his perfect goodness, even in the midst of the trials he has ordained for you.

A Perfect Being Must Be Immutable

What would happen if God were subject to change, like a shadow? Variation in God would spell the death of his own perfection. No longer would he be someone than whom none greater could be conceived.

If he were to change for the better, that would imply that he was less than perfect beforehand. There was some type of deficiency and imperfection to his being. If he were to change for the worse, that would imply that he *was* perfect but no longer *is* perfect. An imperfection has been added to him or a perfection in him has been lost. So, he must change either from better to worse or from worse to better. In either option God ceases to be *eternally good*. A God who is not eternally good is not eternally perfect either. And a God who is not eternally perfect cannot be God in the end. Immutability, we are impelled to conclude, is essential and necessary to God's identity as the perfect, supreme being.[3]

Additionally, if God changed from good to better, we would have to ask what perfection was lacking.[4] His wisdom? His power? His knowledge? His love? We might also ask whether God is at the mercy of such a change or if such a change is voluntary. If he were at the mercy of such a change, then God would be impotent, vulnerable to the will of another, no longer the most sovereign being, no longer the most supreme being.

On the other hand, if such a change were voluntary, God would be at odds with himself. For he would have willed change in his being even though his perfections defy any change, at least as long as they are to remain *perfections*. In other words, he would have willed that his perfections become less than perfect. For example, if God is the most omnipotent being but then wills that he no longer be the most omnipotent being, then God has changed not only his power but the perfection of his power. No longer is his power supreme, and a power that is not supreme in the divine being cannot be a perfect power, for it is now susceptible to the power and will of another.[5] Whatever the attribute in view, each must be characterized by immutability if it is to remain what it is and perfectly so.

I claimed in chapter 3 that a perfect being is a being without limitations. Put positively, a perfect being is an *infinite* being. Since change introduces something new in God (implying some perfection was lacking that has now been gained), change must be a limitation.[6] "But since God is infinite," Thomas Aquinas pushes back, "comprehending in Himself all the plenitude of the perfection of all being, He cannot acquire anything new."[7] An infinite, perfect being cannot be "the receiver of some new perfection" but must always be the "source of all perfection."[8] If God were the receiver, rather than the source, then he would be dependent on something outside himself for his completion and fulfillment.

Pure Act: Über Weird but über Helpful

If God is not a God who is becoming, but remains the same, then he is not a God who has *potential*. Potential, by definition, assumes someone has yet to reach a state of fulfillment. Potential implies deficiency in some way.[9] But God is not a being in need of perfecting. He is not perfectible. He is eternally and immutably the perfect being, and he is the perfect being in infinite measure. He is, as we've learned from Anselm, the fullness of Being. As an eternally, immutably infinite perfect being, he is not someone who has potential. Potential would mean he needs to grow in his perfection, and growth like this would imply he is not yet perfect but hopes to become so. He hopes to one day reach his potential. By contrast, God is "perfect not because he has perfected all his potential, but . . . he is perfection itself."[10]

In order to avoid the idea of God having potential, rather than perfection, older theologians like Aquinas liked to call God "pure act" (*actus purus* in Latin) or "pure actuality" (*purus actua*). "God is simply act" or "Pure Act," they said.[11] The intent of phrases like these is to guard God from any type of "passive potency."[12] Passive potency means there is something in need of being activated and fulfilled in God. Yet nothing need be activated in God, as if he were in need of becoming something more than he already is. No, he is pure act itself, being life in the most absolute sense, in and of himself.

Denying that there is any "passive potency" in God is also a fancy way to keep the Creator distinct from the creature. He is not a God whose parts must be activated, as if their full potential were still to be reached. Potential would imply not only incompleteness but the ability to be affected by something external.[13] In God's case, he would be affected, changed, even hurt by his creation. But the God of the Bible is no weak, vulnerable God to be pitied, which is why it is wise to call him "pure act," a phrase meant to convey that God is *not acted on* but is the one who *acts on others*.[14]

Pure Act	Passive Potency
The Creator	The creature
God has the power to effect change in others; God can move others to reach their potential and perfection. However, God himself has no potential, undergoes no change, and is in no need of becoming more perfect than he already is eternally. He is pure act.	The creature changes and is moved by others; the creature has potential due to his/her imperfection. It is proper to predicate passive potency to the creature, but never to God.

If God is not acted on, then it is right to call him, as Aquinas does, the first and only *unmoved mover*.[15] Everything in our world is mutable, and so it is moved by something else. If we were to trace back as far as possible every action and event in your life, we would discover that there never was a moment when you were not moved by something or someone else. The point is, our ever-changing universe is full of movers always being moved.

But where did that chain of moved movers begin? Better question yet: *How* did it begin? The chain cannot be infinite, for if it were, then we would not be able to explain movement at all. "There has to be an end to this regress of causes," says Aquinas, "otherwise there will be no first cause of change, and, as a result, no subsequent causes of change." He concludes, "So, we are bound to arrive at some first cause of change that is not itself changed by anything."[16] Notice, the first mover must be unmoved himself. He must be immutable, the only one who is not put in motion by another. But if God is not pure act, then he cannot be that first unmoved mover, and if he is not the unmoved mover, then the motion that defines this world has no ultimate explanation. God must be the "sufficient causal reason for all movement."[17]

Calling God "pure act" (or pure actuality or pure active potency) may sound weird, über philosophical perhaps. Point taken. But we need not be afraid of such phrases; they are über helpful, as it turns out. Such phrases communicate, says Aquinas, that God "cannot acquire anything new."[18] His perfection does not increase or decrease. He never needs to become more perfect than he is.[19] He is a "being without becoming."[20] The God who is pure act has in and of himself "all the plenitude of perfection of all being."[21]

The Glory and Enamel of All Attributes

Immutability is not only central to a correct understanding of a perfect, supreme being, but it also proves indispensable to all other attributes. Stephen Charnock calls immutability the "glory" that belongs to "all the attributes of God" because it is the "centre wherein they all unite." Or we might compare it to "enamel" because apart from immutability the rest would come undone.[22] To see why, consider seven entailments of immutability.

1. It is because God does not change that he is a God of aseity. If God did change, then it would mean that he needs something, depends on something, and adds something to himself, all of which defy God's aseity and imply that he is less than fully perfect. A needy God cannot be an immutable God, for such a God must change to become complete. Such a God is like matter; matter changes and is in motion, but it does not have being in and of itself. It is incomplete. God, on the other hand, has the power of being in and of himself.[23]

Mention of God's aseity takes us back to his identity as Creator as well. To be truly independent is to be the Creator rather than the creature. Yet such independence as the Creator is compromised if this Creator can and does change. A God who is "becoming" is a God who has forfeited his "being." As Herman Bavinck explains, "All that is creaturely is in process of becoming. It is changeable, constantly striving, in search of rest and satisfaction, and finds this rest only in him who is pure being without becoming."[24] If God changes, then he is now subject to a creaturely limitation, disqualifying himself from being the Creator.

2. *It is because God does not change that he remains simple.* If God did change, then he would be a God made up of parts. Remember, parts change by their very nature, and change assumes parts are involved. One part of God would have to adjust or alter to adapt to another part of God, or worse, to something or someone outside of God. God's very essence would be divided. On the other hand, a God who does not change is a God whose very essence is perfectly united, for every one of his attributes "is identical with his essence."[25]

Plus, change also means subtraction or addition has occurred. Change in God would result in (a) "separating something from him" or (b) "adding something to him." If something has been separated from God, then God is now a compounded being, and the thing that is now separate is "distinct from himself." But if a part of God's being has been separated, then how can God be all that is in him, and how can he be who he is in all his glory? He is no longer wholly God, but part of God has been subtracted from him. His being has experienced a loss.[26] The situation is no better if something is added to God instead, for that, too, means he is capable of being compounded, in this case growing greater in quantity and quality. It makes us wonder, as well, whether what has been added is essential to God's being or merely accidental. If essential, then how did God exist without it?

Here is the bottom line: if God is not simple, then he is made up of parts, and to consist of parts is to be divisible, by having those parts subtracted or new parts added. Either way, God's being changes in the process. Immutability is key to preserving God's simplicity.

3. It is because God does not change that he is all-knowing and all-wise. If God were to change in what he knows, then there would be a time when he did not know all things. If there was a time when he did not know all things, then his knowledge is, or was, flawed, inaccurate, or at the very least partial, whereas now it is exact and complete. Immutability is the bedrock of omniscience. If his immutability forbids deficiency in knowledge, then any alteration to his wisdom is precluded as well. For God to be infinitely wise, he must not be ignorant of anything, nor can he ever be mistaken in what he knows to be true.[27] To know something today that he did not know yesterday would imply not only that his knowledge has improved but that his wisdom was lacking as well. Ignorance, in other words, is an indication that wisdom has yet to reach its full maturity. If God has learned something today he did not know yesterday, then we have little reason to think his decision yesterday was just as good as his decision today. Such a God is susceptible to error, a feature that is antithetical to a perfect being.

4. It is because God does not change that he is not restricted by time and space. Being created, finite, and physical beings, you and I are bound by time and space. God, our Creator, is an infinite, incorporeal (nonphysical) being, and therefore he cannot be restricted by the limitations of time and space. He is timelessly eternal, for example. While we will consider these attributes in depth in chapters 8 and 9, let's briefly explore how they relate to immutability here.

First, to come into existence or to be constrained by the limitations of time would imply change for a variety of reasons. Time, by definition, involves a succession of moments. For example, it's 1:05 p.m. now, but in a minute it will be 1:06 p.m. Once 1:06 arrives, 1:05 will be no more. With the passing of time, we age, and there is nothing we can do about it. As we experience one moment to the next, we change with time, becoming something more or less than we were before. The key principle is this: a succession of moments always involves change.

But God is not a temporal being; he is timeless. He never had a beginning, nor will he have an end. He just is. God transcends the notion of time altogether (Ps. 102:26; Isa. 40:8).[28] Being eternal, then, is key to God being immutable. Yet we could also say being immutable is key to God being eternal. Because he is a being without change, he cannot be restricted to a succession of moments, for that would change who he is. It's not as if one minute he were one thing but the next minute he would become something he was not a minute ago.

God's immutability must also mean this God is not spatially limited as we are. To occupy one space at a time, as we do, assumes not only that we are limited to that space but that we must change to occupy another space at another time. Not having a body, God, on the other hand, is not bound by space but is ubiquitous, filling all places with his whole being simultaneously. God transcends space as he does time, so that he is immutably all-present, or omnipresent, in all places simultaneously.

5. *It is because God does not change that he is omnipotent.* Our God is not impotent, changing in his power, as if he must increase in strength to achieve omnipotence. Nor is he a God who has been omnipotent but now faces the danger of losing control over the world. He is not like Sampson, whose power turns ineffective the moment he receives a haircut. God does not have a secret Achilles' heel. Our God is eternally and immutably powerful, never becoming more powerful, since he is always the most powerful he could be. Nor does he decrease in power because he has fallen prey to the power of another. "How feeble his power, if it were capable to be sickly and languish!"[29] His supremacy remains constant, insusceptible to his enemies. He is "immutable in his essence, therefore irresistible in his power."[30]

6. *It is because God does not change that he remains holy and just.* A God mutable in holiness may be the scariest thought of all. Holiness is the dividing line between God and the devil. If holiness can be or not be in God, we no longer know for certain if the God we worship will do that which is right.

For instance, consider how horrifying it would be if God's just character vacillated. A God who changes in his justice is liable to prosecution. In our human court system, a judge who does not rule justly, according to the law, is considered either corrupt or negligent. Either one can result in such a judge being placed behind bars. If this is true of our human and fallible court system, how much more is it true of God? Should he change in his justice, his own holiness would be suspect. Imagine if he punished the wicked one day, only to turn a blind eye to their criminal actions and approve of their wickedness the next. By contrast, Moses sings that God, our "Rock, his work is perfect; for all his ways are justice. A God of faithfulness and without iniquity, just and upright is he" (Deut. 32:4).

It is noteworthy that when immutability and justice collide, other attributes do as well.[31] If God's justice is immutable, then so is his knowledge, for an immutable justice demands that God never forget the sins of the wicked (Hos. 7:2).[32] Similarly, an immutable justice requires immutable goodness and love. "Goodness," says Charnock, is always the "object of his love," and wickedness is always "the object of his hatred." His "aversion to sin" never changes or grows lax.[33]

7. It is because God does not change that he is love. Jonathan Edwards tells us that it is because God is "an infinite being" as well as an "all-sufficient being" that he must be "an infinite fountain of love." But it is also because he is an unchangeable, eternal being that he is an "eternal fountain of love."[34]

It is critical to clarify, however, that God is an eternal fountain of love, but such love reflects the character of his own love for himself.[35] It is because God loves himself without change that his love for us is a love that does not change. Should his love *for himself* fluctuate, there would be little assurance that his love *for us* would remain steadfast.

Can you imagine if God's love were not immutable? Salvation would be the first doctrine to go. What assurance would we have in his gracious, benevolent election of us before the foundation of the world (Eph. 1:4)? It is only because God's love is an immutable love that we can rest assured that the God who chose us prior to creation will not only turn us into new creatures but guard us from the evil one so that one day we will enjoy the new creation. It is because his love is eternally immutable that we sing, "Oh give thanks to the LORD, for he is good; for his steadfast love endures forever!" (1 Chron. 16:34), a phrase sung by the psalmists countless times (e.g., Ps. 107:1).

We no doubt waver in our experience of God's love, one day not *feeling* it as much as the day before. Thankfully, our assurance is not based on our feelings. Rather, it rests in a love that never changes. The Father's love for us is as unchanging as his love for his Son, Jesus Christ.

To sum up, immutability is the enamel of all that is in God. "Those who predicate any change whatsoever of God," warns Bavinck, "whether with respect to his essence, knowledge, or will, diminish all his attributes: independence, simplicity, eternity, omniscience, and omnipotence. This robs God of his divine nature, and religion of its firm foundation and assured comfort."[36]

Is God Rigidly Immobile?

Despite the case we've made for immutability, there are two common objections. First, if God is immutable, then he must be inert, static, immobile, and dead. Such an assumption became widely popular in the twentieth century.[37]

Such an objection, however, falls short. To begin with, a misunderstanding has occurred, creating a caricature. Advocates of immutability do not mean God is static; they never have. They recognize that the metaphor of a rock can only be pushed so far. Furthermore, immutability and a being who is alive are not contradictory concepts. Remember the phrase "pure act"? That phrase stresses that there is nothing to be activated in God, as if he must become something he is not. But that does not mean God is lifeless. Rather, to deny that anything needs to be activated in God is to simultaneously confess that any change in God would compromise his perfectly active life. Already he is life in its fullness, in all its plenitude. Thomas Weinandy captures this very point: "God is unchangeable not because he is inert or static like a rock, but for just the opposite reason. He is so dynamic, so active that no change can make him more active. He is act pure and simple."[38]

Vitality, vibrancy, dynamism—these are all characteristic of God but can be so only if God does not change.[39] Perhaps it appears counterintuitive, but only an immutable God can be supremely alive, active, and vibrant. Should he change, we would have no assurance that his vitality would continue or that his vibrancy would remain pure and perfect. Immutability "should not be confused with monotonous sameness or rigid immobility."[40]

Such confusion even betrays our human experience. Suppose you are an artist inspired by the sounds and smells of the city. One day you stare intently at a bustling marketplace. Enthralled, you write a poem capturing what you see. The next day, however, your imagination is expressed not through the production of poetry but this time in the vivid colors of a pastel painting. (You are an artist of many talents!) How silly it would be to assume that because you are the same person, the same artist, depicting the same city, the way you communicate or relay your art must be static and monotonous.[41] The point is, immutability does not automatically preclude vitality and vibrancy.

Does God Change His Mind?

A second objection is that Scripture uses language that seems to communicate that God does change. When humanity's corruption pervades the earth and God responds by flooding the whole earth, God is said to regret having made humans (Gen. 6:6). After King Saul continually disobeys the Lord, God says he regrets having made Saul king (1 Sam. 15:11). There are also a host of places where the Lord says he will do one thing, but then he relents, pulling back from what he said he would do. For example, after Israel creates a golden calf and worships it, the Lord tells Moses to step aside because he will destroy this people. After Moses pleads and begs, God relents from the disaster he has threatened (Exod. 32:10–14). Or when Jonah (reluctantly) arrives in Nineveh, he says they have but forty days until Nineveh is overthrown. After the people repent, however, God relents and does not destroy them (Jon. 3:4–10).[42]

What are we to make of these passages? I remember taking my first class in hermeneutics in college. (Hermeneutics is the study of how to interpret the Bible.) That first day my professor drilled one thing into our heads: "Context! Context! Context!" He knew that unless we learned to read any single verse within its wider context, we would carelessly misunderstand its meaning. That is never truer than when we deal with passages like these.

When we read that God "relents," we should keep the context of each passage in mind. Although in that moment it appears as if God had changed his mind, if we have a bird's-eye view we see that God is doing what he has promised or intended all along. This is why, for instance, Jonah is so frustrated with God. When Nineveh repents and God "relents," the text says Jonah becomes very angry. Shaking his fist at God, Jonah says, "O LORD, . . . I knew that you are a gracious God and merciful, slow to anger and abounding in steadfast love, and relenting from disaster" (Jon. 4:2). Could this have been God's plan all along? Jonah sure thinks so. God sent him to threaten Nineveh with annihilation for their wickedness, and God intended such a threat itself to be the means by which this people would receive God's mercy. What appeared to be an unconditional, absolute statement on the surface ("Yet forty days, and Nineveh shall be overthrown!"; 3:4) was a conditional threat, consistent with God's declaration throughout the Scriptures that should sinners repent, he will be merciful, something Jonah knows but resents, apparently. God has not changed his mind but fulfilled what he immutably willed from eternity: that Nineveh would be saved! Something very similar is happening when God "relents" from the disaster he spoke against Israel after Moses intercedes on her behalf.

Or consider King Saul. In 1 Samuel 15 Saul fails to put to death King Agag and devote the best spoils of war to destruction as the Lord has commanded him. Seeing this, the Lord says to Samuel, "I regret that I have made Saul king, for he has turned back from following me and has not performed my commandments" (15:11). On the surface, it seems God now realizes he has made a mistake. He thought Saul was the man for the job, but now he's changed his mind after seeing how rebellious Saul can be. Not only would such an interpretation undermine God's perfection (he is a God who makes mistakes), trustworthiness and wisdom (can we trust a God who makes mistakes?), and immutability (he changes his mind), but it does not fit with the context of the story, which directly addresses and refutes such a reading of the text. After refusing to admit he has disobeyed the Lord, Saul finally confesses he has sinned, but only after Samuel tells Saul the Lord "has also rejected [him] from being king" (15:23).

But it's too late. Although Saul asks for pardon and for Samuel to return with him, Samuel says no, reiterating once more that the Lord has rejected Saul as king. Knowing the Lord's blessing is slipping from him, Saul seizes Samuel's robe just as he is leaving, tearing it, to which Samuel responds, "The LORD has torn the kingdom of Israel from you this day and has given it to a neighbor of yours, who is better than you. And also the Glory of Israel will not lie or have regret, for he is not a man, that he should have regret" (15:28–29).[43] The message is loud and clear: God has rejected Saul as king and will not go back on his judgment, for

God is not a human, changing his mind or regretting what he has done. Here is the Creator-creature distinction plainly stated and without qualification. Humans change, lie, and have many regrets in life. Not God. He does not change, he does not lie, and he has no regrets. Both in his nature and in his relations, he remains the same.

So what, then, does God mean when he says he "regrets" making Saul king? His intention is to use an experience humans can relate to in order to communicate his displeasure with the sinfulness of Saul's actions, especially since Saul is to be leading God's people in holiness. The language of "regret" is not meant *literally* but serves as a signal, indicating to the reader not only that God has judged Saul but that God's plan all along has been to raise up a king after his own heart. By declaring his "regret," God is announcing that this new king is on the horizon ("The LORD has torn the kingdom of Israel from you . . . and has given it to a neighbor"). As the next chapter reveals, that neighbor is David, son of Jesse. Rather than witnessing a change *in God*—and an emotional one at that—we are instead witnessing the effects of God's will on his creatures.[44]

As we learned at the start of the book, the biblical authors, and God himself, purposefully use anthropomorphic terms and phrases, communicating something true of God but through categories and images of our finite, human world, and the emotions that define our human experience. "Relenting" and "regretting" is our human way of observing a change from our perspective, one that occurs in the moment. But from a bird's-eye point of view, such accommodated language, interpreted in context, is never meant to undermine God's immutability but highlights how an immutable God's eternal will is received by very mutable, finite creatures, like you and me. The marvel of our God is that he can will change in us, though he himself changes not.[45] Or as Augustine says, our God is "without any change in himself" as he is "making changeable things," yet all the while "undergoing nothing."[46]

The Immutability of God's Promises in Christ

On a Sunday afternoon, I love nothing more than losing myself in a biography. My favorite biographies are about Christians who endured much for the cause of the gospel, not because they were confidently triumphalist but for the exact opposite reason—they were transparent about their absolute dependence on God in the midst of nearly giving up. Often the biographies will point to the little things God used to keep the Christian going—a fellow church member's persistent prayers, a spouse's quiet faithfulness, or the warning of a close friend to keep one from slipping.

The author of Hebrews knew that means like these were key to endurance in the Christian life, which is why the book of Hebrews is filled with warnings against apostasy. The book not only warns but comforts, pointing Christians to the immutable character of a holy God for assurance in times of testing.

If you want to guarantee the truthfulness and reliability of a promise you've made, you will likely swear on the most personal, significant, and valuable object you can conceive. That explains why so many swear on their mother's grave. Human beings are known to lie and change their mind, so if they are to be trusted, they must swear by the character of something or someone else to reassure the other party that they will keep their word.

But not God. He has nothing greater to swear by than himself. Never changing in his holiness, he is the very standard of justice and morality in the universe. In a court of law it used to be the case that one had to place a hand on the Bible, swearing to tell the "truth, the whole truth, and nothing but the truth, so help me God." But if God were to step up to the witness stand, he would have nowhere to place his hand but on his own chest.

In order to reassure the readers that they are children of the promises to Abraham, the author of Hebrews turns to God's own nature and character. "For when God made a promise to Abraham, since he had no one greater by whom to swear, he swore by himself, saying, 'Surely I will bless you and multiply you.' . . . So when God desired to show more convincingly to the heirs of the promise the unchangeable character of his purpose, he guaranteed it with an oath, so that by two unchangeable things, in which it is impossible for God to lie, we who have fled for refuge might have strong encouragement to hold fast to the hope set before us" (6:13–14, 17–18). Whether or not God's oath, on which our salvation depends, is reliable depends entirely on the unchanging nature of his holy character. Whether all the covenant promises will be yours rests not only on God's faithfulness to the covenant but on the unchanging nature of God himself.[47]

Knowing he is an immutably holy God—one who does not change and therefore will not lie—the Christian has every reason to flee to God for refuge in an hour of great trial. And this side of the empty tomb, the soul's "sure and steadfast anchor" is found in no one else but Jesus, the Christ, the one who is "the same yesterday and today and forever" (Heb. 13:8).[48] He stepped into the very presence of God, into the "inner place behind the curtain" of the temple (to use Old Testament imagery; 6:19), offering up an eternal sacrifice for our sins as our eternal high priest (6:20), as our immutable mediator (Ps. 110:4).

At the start of this chapter I told the story of how that famous hymn "Rock of Ages" buzzed in my ear as I stood in the cleft of the rock on those Welsh shores. But I quoted only the first line. In light of Hebrews 6, it now makes sense why the hymn turns our attention to Jesus himself as the Rock of Ages:

> Rock of Ages, cleft for me,
> Let me hide myself in thee;
> Let the water and the blood,
> From thy wounded side which flowed,
> Be of sin the double cure;
> Save from wrath and make me pure.

7

Does God Have Emotions?

Impassibility

The Glory of Israel will not lie or have regret, for he is not a
man, that he should have regret.

1 SAMUEL 15:29

[You] love without burning, you are jealous in a way that is free
of anxiety, you "repent" . . . without the pain of regret, you are
wrathful and remain tranquil.

AUGUSTINE, *The Confessions*

Myself, I find the idea of a God who is made to suffer by us, and
who needs us to be fulfilled, a depressing conception of divinity.

KATHERIN ROGERS, *Perfect Being Theology*

love big cities. For a time, I lived in London, a city made for the
culturally curious. A rare books shop hidden in a small alley,
the smell of Chinese food just around the corner, the bright

lights of the theater just blocks away, a quiet museum displaying priceless art—it's all just a tube ride away (the tube being London's version of a subway).

When I was able to sneak away, you might guess where I headed: the National Gallery. Here hang some of the most exquisite paintings by some of the most famous artists in the world: *The Madonna and Child* by Raphael, *The Head of John the Baptist* by Caravaggio, *Ecce Homo* by Rembrandt. I'm naming my favorites. My wife has her favorites too: *Sunflowers* by Van Gogh and *Whistlejacket* by George Stubbs.

These are the paintings the crowds flock to, but there are other paintings that I find myself particularly drawn to, paintings that do not always draw huge crowds. These are paintings that tell the legends of the Greek gods, stories that are unpredictable and sometimes scandalous. Robert Parker, an expert in Greek religion, explains how the Greek gods "did not eat human food" and "would not age or die." Nevertheless, the "gods had human form; they were born, and they might have sexual contacts."[1] Many believed there used to be a day, long ago, when the gods lived among humans. Some gods even romanced women, creating children in their own likeness (little gods). That day came to an end, and no longer do the gods dwell with humankind.[2]

There are many striking features to these gods. For instance, they often act immorally. "Their behaviour in poem was often scandalous," says Parker. One ancient myth conveys this clearly:

> There might you see the gods in sundry shapes
> Committing heady riots, incest, rapes.[3]

For instance, one disturbing painting by Paolo Veronese is called *The Rape of Europa*.[4] The painting is based on Ovid's story *Metamorphoses*, a title that gives the story away. Depicted is the god Zeus, who undergoes a transformation, becoming a bull, so that Europa, the princess, might be hoisted onto his back and he might ride away to have her for himself. In Veronese's interpretation of the story, Europa is painted with a very confused look on her face, as if she is unsure what is happening. Meanwhile, the bull has already started licking her foot as Cupid decorates his horns with flowers.

It is impossible not to notice Zeus's perversity, as well as the way he fluctuates in form. Like Zeus, the gods changed in their identity. Yet it's not just their physical form that changes but their emotional makeup as well. One moment they parade their power (Zeus, being the god of the sky, will heave thunderbolts at his enemies), and the next moment they helplessly and pathetically wallow in defeat and agony—you can't help but pity them (Homer's *Iliad* is filled with such stories). Nor can you trust them. One minute they are on your side, but the next they lose their temper, revealing just how whimsical they can be. There is no guarantee, nor any indication, that these gods have control of their emotions. Instead, they look a lot like us. At times, they are even dependent on us, needing us to fulfill their own happiness, satisfy their discontentment, or satiate their own lust.

Every time I looked at one of these paintings in the National Gallery, I was reminded that the God I worship, the God of the Bible, is completely different from these gods and goddesses. Comparing the Christian God to these Greek gods, Michael Horton writes, "If he were determined in his very being by what we do, then we would have no confidence that he, like Zeus, might not as easily destroy us in a fit of rage as weep helplessly over our condition."[5] In theology, there is a term that appropriately describes these gods and goddesses: passible. These gods are passible because they are prone to suffer, having passions that move them and emotions that change them. In other words, they are at the mercy of emotional change.

In contrast to these Greek gods, God has been described throughout church history as *im*passible, or as one who is without passions. Our God is, by nature, incapable of suffering, and he is insusceptible to emotional fluctuation. Rather, we worship a God who is in complete control of who he is and what he does. Never is there any action by God that is out of line with his unchanging character. Instead of being divided by different emotional states or overcome by sudden, unexpected moods, moods that reveal just how vulnerable and dependent he is on what we do, the God of the Bible is a God who never becomes anxious, lonely, or compulsive.[6] He is never at odds with himself, divided over conflicting expressions of his perfections. No, this God is the impassible God.

What Impassibility Is and Is Not

If we are to understand what it means for God to be impassible, it is best to first grasp what it would mean for God to be *passible*. Consider three characteristics from theologian Thomas Weinandy:

1. For God to be "passible" then means that he is capable of being acted upon from without and that such actions bring about emotional changes of state within him.

2. Moreover, for God to be passible means that he is capable of freely changing his inner emotional state in response to and interaction with the changing human condition and world order.

3. Last, passibility implies that God's changing emotional states involve "feelings" that are analogous to human feelings. . . . God experiences inner emotional changes of state, either of comfort or discomfort, whether freely from within or by being acted upon from without.[7]

By contrast, what does it mean for God to be *impassible*? "God is impassible in the sense that he cannot experience emotional changes of state due to his relationship to and interaction with human beings and the created order." Or think of it this way: "God is impassible in that he does not undergo successive and fluctuating emotional states; nor can the created order alter him in such a way so as to cause him to suffer any modification or loss."[8]

That last word—"loss"—deserves highlighting. To say that God is impassible is to shield him from loss. As we saw in our chapter on simplicity (chap. 5), God's essence is without parts, for parts can be gained or lost, added or subtracted. But "there are not parts to God's life, parts which he has lived and which are accessible now only to memory; other parts which he has yet to live, accessible only in anticipation."[9]

Instead, that "which is immutable and impassible is by nature complete."[10] So if God is simple, then he must be not only immutable but impassible. A God whose nature is made up of parts is vulnerable to change, including emotional change. But a God whose nature is without parts is a God who is incapable of fluctuation in any way or form. To clarify, it's not just that God *chooses* to be impassible; he is *incapable* of being passible. It is contrary to his *unchanging nature*.[11]

The fact upon which I stand [handwritten margin note]

Impassibility also means he is not "the victim of negative and sinful passions as are human beings, such as fear, anxiety, and dread, or greed, lust, and unjust anger." To say that God is not passible "is to deny of him all human passions and the effects of such passions which would in any way debilitate or cripple him as God."[12]

Impassibility is the natural, logical, and necessary corollary to immutability, a point we will return to shortly. If God's nature does not change, then neither can he undergo emotional change. Impassibility also stems from God's supremacy, perfection, and infinitude, for any debilitation or crippling of God would inevitably mean that he no longer is that than which nothing greater can be conceived.

What we auto-matically jump to [handwritten margin note]

Does that mean, then, that God is lifeless, stoic, and apathetic? Not at all. God is, as we saw with aseity, the fullness of Being, absolute life in and of himself. He is "supremely blissful," pure *act*.[13] Like immutability, impassibility is a "negative" concept, meaning that its primary purpose is to describe what God is *not*. As we saw in chapter 2, the "way of negation" helps us avoid thinking of God in ways that we should not. If this approach is ignored, one might think impassibility is saying something "positive" about God: he is detached and indifferent, inactive and unconcerned, static and inert. He is apathetic.[14] But that is not what impassibility means; it is an unfortunate misunderstanding, yet a popular caricature.[15] To attribute impassibility to God is not to attribute something positive to him but to deny something detrimental to God—namely, change and with it suffering.

Nor does impassibility mean that God is not loving and compassionate.[16] Rather, it means that such virtues are not true of God as a result of being acted on by someone or something else. Nothing else and no one else caused such virtues to exist in God.[17] Nor does God look to anything or anyone else for such virtues or for the actualization of such virtues. Because God is eternal and immutable, his virtues are affected and impacted by no one. If his virtues were passions, then he no longer would be pure act.[18] Though it may be counterintuitive, impassibility actually protects other attributes like love, because it guarantees that his love will not change or fluctuate. For the church fathers, impassibility was meant to "ensure and to accentuate his perfect goodness and unalterable love."[19]

Impassibility also ensures that his love needs no activation, nor has any potential, as if his perfections need to become something more than they are already. As we have seen, God is pure act, never needing his love, for example, to be actualized. As we will learn later in this chapter, God is *maximally alive*. Impassibility does not mean that God is inert or static, which would preclude him from love. Rather, as the maximal God his impassibility certifies that he could not be any more loving than he already is. He is love in infinite measure.

To affirm impassibility is not to fall prey to a contradiction either, as if God were compassionate, benevolent, merciful, and caring *despite* the fact that he is impassible. Such a view assumes

God's attributes are at odds with one another and incompatible, undermining his oneness and simplicity. Rather, God is compassionate, loving, merciful, and caring because, and only because, he is impassible.[20] Impassibility guarantees that God can act in a way that is personal, involved, and immanent, guarding him from becoming apathetic. In short, *if* God is not impassible, then he cannot be as personal, loving, and compassionate as the Bible says he is. Period.

God Hangs from the Gallows? → God suffers along side of us

Impassibility is, no doubt, the one attribute that strikes against our natural instincts the most, counterintuitive in every way. One of the most famous theologians of the twentieth century was Jürgen Moltmann. Observing the horrors caused by Nazi Germany during World War II, Moltmann put his pen to paper to give hope to suffering people all over the globe. His theology of hope proved timely and is embraced by many still today.

His theology of hope was accompanied by his answer to the problem of evil. As Jews were sent to concentration camps to be tortured, starved, dehumanized, and then slaughtered, these victims, as well as others looking on, asked the probing question: Where is God? Many resonated with Moltmann's answer: God is there suffering with you. He too suffers in the concentration camp, he too suffers in the gas chamber, he too suffers at the gallows. Moltmann believes that the story in the book *Night* by Elie Wiesel says it all: "The SS hanged two Jewish men and a youth in front of the whole camp. The men died quickly, but the death throes of the youth lasted for half an hour. 'Where is God? Where is he?' someone asked behind me. As the youth still hung in torment in the noose after a long time, I heard the man call again, 'Where is God now?' And I heard a voice in myself answer: 'Where is he? He is here. He is hanging there on the gallows.'"[21] In reaction to this gripping, moving, and tragic account, Moltmann echoes that response: God is hanging there on the gallows. "Any other answer would be blasphemy. . . . To speak here of a God who could not suffer would make God a demon."[22] God is and must be a suffering God if the world is to have any hope in all its suffering. "God in Auschwitz and Auschwitz in the crucified God—that is the basis for a real hope."[23]

For Moltmann, God's suffering is so deep that it penetrates not merely to his relations with us but into his very being, his essence, his nature. Moltmann directly confronts the God of the church fathers, patristic and medieval, who would claim God is "absolute" or "pure act," affirming not only impassibility but with it divine immutability, aseity, omnipotence, and infinitude as key to a perfect being.[24] Such a view makes God indifferent, apathetic, and cold. While this classic tradition interprets emotional references to God as anthropomorphic, Moltmann reads them literally. For instance, when the Old Testament talks about God's wrath, this is a "divine *pathos*." Except, such wrath is an "injured love." "As injured love, the wrath of God is not something that is inflicted, but a divine suffering of evil. It is a sorrow which goes through his opened heart."[25] So injured is God's love—like the world's love—that humanity not only "feels sympathy with God" in his suffering but rightly feels sympathy "*for* God."[26]

This sympathy is seen most acutely in the fact that Moltmann's God not only redeems humanity but must redeem himself. God needs saving. So univocal is his suffering with humanity—Israel's exile is his exile—that his people's redemption must also be his redemption, for when they suffer, he suffers. The "Holy One of Israel shares Israel's suffering and Israel's redemption, so that in this respect it is true that 'God has redeemed himself from Egypt together with his people: "The redemption is for me and for you."' . . . Israel is redeemed when God has redeemed himself."[27]

According to Moltmann, the suffering God is most visible at the cross. When Jesus suffered the pain of crucifixion, God himself suffered. Moltmann rejected the response that Jesus was suffering in his humanity only. No, his divinity also suffered at Calvary. And it was not merely the Son who suffered but the entire Triune Godhead, the Father included.[28]

That God suffers at Golgotha means that his being should be "understood as open vulnerability," for "God's being and God's life is open to true man."[29] Moltmann embraces a type of panentheism—God is not identical with the world (pantheism), but there is a mutual dependence between God and the world, so that God is in the world and the world is in God. "Where we suffer because we love, God suffers in us."[30] "The history of the divine pathos is embedded in the history of men."[31] His "self-emptying in the crucified Christ" is what "opens up God's sphere of life to the development of man in him."[32]

One reason so many have resonated with Moltman's suffering God is that this is a God suffering people can relate to. Only a God who truly suffers can authentically understand the suffering we experience in this fallen world. According to many in the culture today, unless God suffers, experiencing human emotions like grief, then he must not be able to sympathize with us in any meaningful sense, let alone love us and care for us.[33] If we are victims, God too must be a victim with us. If we are vulnerable to pain, so must he be. If we are overcome with anguish, God too must be overwhelmed with sorrow. Isn't such empathy, after all, what it means to love? Isn't that what it means to be in a relationship?

Do We Really Want a God Who Suffers? The House Is on Fire

What are we to make of this popular cultural commitment to a suffering God? Is it true that God must suffer to relate to us in a helpful, meaningful way?

As compelling as Moltmann may be at first blush, he makes a faulty assumption, one with dangerous consequences for our doctrine of God. To begin with, this type of reasoning is far more consistent with the monopolytheism (or theistic personalism) we warned against in chapter 3. Dissolving the Creator-creature distinction, we make God in our own image, resembling our attributes, reflecting our human characteristics and limitations.

But we should immediately be concerned about any attempt to humanize the Creator of the universe, reversing the Creator-creature distinction. While there are ways that we, as those made in God's image, reflect who God is, we should not jump to the conclusion that God must be like us to know us, relate to us, or help us.

Not that long ago my home county—Sonoma County, just north of San Francisco—was engulfed in flames due to a natural fire that ignited in nearby hills. What made this fire worse than others was the way it was carried along by the wind with irresistible force. Those driving on the freeway reported that the fire jumped over entire interstates. Not only houses but whole neighborhoods went up in flames in hours. And not merely houses but large businesses, seemingly untouchable, crumbled in ashes.

Imagine if your house were to catch on fire that night. As you barely escape out the front door, you have this sick feeling in your stomach. Your brother and sister are still inside! As the neighborhood gathers to watch, what kind of response would you look for from others? Suppose one woman showed her sympathy by screaming uncontrollably, even ripping out her hair. Or suppose a man so wanted to understand the pain and suffering by those inside that he poured gasoline on himself and lit himself on fire. Understandably, you would look around, not only perplexed, but even outraged at these people.

That is, until a man with a fire suit catches your eye. Calm and focused, the fireman surveys the burning house. So acutely aware is he of the danger, as well as the suffering and turmoil by those within, that he refuses to be moved by emotional outbursts or be overcome by panic. Instead, he runs into the house in order to rescue your brother and sister, while other onlookers uncontrollably weep.[34]

Let's be honest, in that moment we do *not* want someone who changes emotionally or suffers emotional change. We desperately need someone who is impassible; only he or she is able to save others from that burning house. That fireman need not experience all the suffering by others around him to know exactly what needs to be done. We could go further and say that only someone who is not overcome by emotion in that moment is capable of acting heroically.

Many who react against the attribute of impassibility will object that such a belief eliminates compassion. God becomes an uncaring monster of some kind. Ironically, we do not apply that same logic in our human experience. Did that fireman lack compassion? As it turns out, he was the most compassionate of all. While the "compassion" of others led to emotional meltdown, personal panic attacks, and irrational behavior, the compassion of the fireman led him, and him alone, to act in the most heroic way possible. He did not need to suffer at all to be compassionate.[35]

Similarly, we do not *really* want a God who suffers, despite what our first instinct might say. Such a God may be like us, but he cannot help us, let alone redeem us from the evil of this world. If God is to act in a "compassionate" way—rescuing lost sinners—we need him to "remain impassible, unconquered by suffering."[36] We need the type of God Augustine prayed to: "You, Lord God, lover of souls, show a compassion far purer and freer of mixed motives than ours; for no suffering injures you."[37]

Maximally Alive

The danger with the house-on-fire metaphor is that if pressed too far it could convey that impassibility is merely a choice. The fireman could be passible but he chooses not to be for the sake of rescuing those in the house. When we describe God as impassible, however, we do not mean to say that it is optional, as if he simply chose, voluntarily, to be impassible given the circumstances.

Like immutability, impassibility is not merely a choice God makes but is an attribute, a perfection that is true of his essence or nature. It's not enough to say that in this or that situation God acts impassibly. We must say God *is* impassible *by nature*. He simply is not capable of being passible.

In theology, immutability and impassibility are called *modal* terms, meaning that they refer "not merely to what is or is not so, but to what can and cannot be so." To say God is impassible is to say not only that he is not "affected in a certain way" but that he "*cannot* be affected at all."[38] In the last chapter we learned that God cannot choose to change who he is, and we concluded that this is a strength, not a weakness. But if God cannot change, then neither can he be affected. To be affected—emotionally, for example—would mean his perfections alter or change in some way, either for better or worse. Therefore, anytime we say God is immutable, we are also saying in the same breath that he is impassible, and not merely by choice but by nature.[39] Impassible is not something he decides to be on this or that occasion, but it is something he is intrinsically and essentially. He is incapable of change, incapable of being affected.

When we perceive God *as he relates to us*, in his mighty acts and accommodated words, it certainly appears as if he were reacting to us, shifting emotionally. But if impassibility is something not optional but *essential* to God, then we should not think of his will in terms of emotional reactions. If, as we discussed in chapter 5, God's will is tied to his one nature (i.e., there is one will in God), not his three persons (which would tempt tritheism), then we should think of his will, not "as an act, a volition, or a series of volitions, but as an eternal, fully informed disposition." So that when this God is "faced with the knowledge of certain creaturely actions," he "invariably acts in a way that is appropriate to that action (given the divine purpose), and so appears to the creature to *react*."[40] From our finite, human, earthly viewpoint, it is as though God were undergoing emotional change. But as we discovered in the last chapter, in describing God's works, all we have to work with is language that comes out of our mutable, passible, and finite world.

In that vein, we should conclude that impassibility follows if God is "pure act" (*actus purus*). Remember, pure act means nothing in him must be activated, as if something in God must reach its potential. No, God is maximally alive.[41] He is his perfections in infinite measure and is so eternally. God could not be more alive than he already is. Impassibility, then, does not mean that God is inert or static, as if he cannot love, for example. Instead, it means his love is so maximally alive, so fully and completely *in act*, that he cannot become more loving than he already is eternally. Far from undermining love, impassibility actually safeguards God's love, guaranteeing that his love is and remains perfect. Only an impassible love can ensure that our God does not need to be more loving than he already is.

To see such an impassible love in all its perfection, consider the love between Father, Son, and Holy Spirit. Triune love does not change, nor does it need to be improved, or somehow reach its potential, as if the love of the Father for the Son must become more passionate. "It is impossible for the Trinity to be more loving," explains Weinandy, "for the persons of the Trinity possess no self-actualizing potential to become more loving."[42] Their love for one another is maximal, never needing to increase or improve. "The trinity of persons subsists in relation to one another, as the one God, with their love for one another fully and completely actualized."[43] If God is passible, then the love between the three persons not only changes but needs to be improved to reach its full potential. Yet if God is impassible, then his love is maximally alive; the love between the three persons could not be more infinite in its loveliness. Impassibility ensures that the love of our Triune God is perfect.

Impassibility and the Donkey Who Can Talk

At a pivotal point in the book of Numbers, Israel is camping out in the plains of Moab. Moab is terrified of Israel, knowing just how outnumbered they are in battle. Led by Moses, Israel has just come off a winning streak against the Amorites, defeating King Sihon and King Og. God has been giving the enemies into Israel's hands, one by one, fulfilling his promise to give his people the land he promised to Abraham.

When the king of the Moabites, Balak, hears Israel is approaching, his knees begin to rattle. So Balak calls in his ace, Balaam. Balaam is a seer, known to grant success by successfully cursing the enemy in battle. "Come now," says Balak to Balaam, "curse this people [Israel] for me, since they are too mighty for me" (Num. 22:6). But God has other plans. Exhibiting the extent of his sovereignty, God speaks through a pagan like Balaam. Contrary to Balak's wishes, Balaam curses the Moabites.

God, however, becomes angry with Balaam, because Balaam's interest is not in God's message but in the riches he will receive from Balak for prophesying. So the angel of the Lord stands in the path Balaam is traveling, except he is invisible; that is, he is invisible to everyone but Balaam's donkey. When the donkey sees "the angel of the Lord standing in the road, with a drawn sword in his hand," he does what any donkey would do: he refuses to go forward (donkeys do have a knack for stubbornness). After Balaam has beaten the animal repeatedly, the Lord opens the mouth of the donkey, and the donkey talks! "What have I done to you," the donkey says to Balaam, "that you have struck me these three times?" (22:28). Whoever said God has no sense of humor?

Long story short, the Lord opens Balaam's eyes as he did the donkey's so that Balaam, too, sees the angel. "I have come out to oppose you," the angel says, "because your way is perverse before me" (22:32). He tells Balaam that if it were not for the donkey refusing to move forward, the Lord would have killed Balaam and let the donkey live. Convicted, Balaam confesses that he has sinned. He goes with the men of Balak, but he is instructed to prophesy only what God says.

In the story that follows, Balaam does prophesy, as Balak has asked, but Israel, not Moab, receives the blessing. On one occasion, Balak takes Balaam to a field where he can see Israel from a distance and asks him to curse his enemies. Instead, Balaam speaks the word God puts in his mouth:

> Rise, Balak, and hear;
> > give ear to me, O son of Zippor:
> God is not man, that he should lie,
> > or a son of man, that he should change his mind.
> Has he said, and will he not do it?
> > Or has he spoken, and will he not fulfill it? . . .
> The Lord their God is with them,
> > and the shout of a king is among them.
> God brings them out of Egypt
> > and is for them like the horns of the wild ox. . . .
> Behold, a people! As a lioness it rises up . . . ;
> it does not lie down until it has devoured the prey
> > and drunk the blood of the slain. (Num. 23:18–19,
> > > 21b–22, 24)

All in all, Balaam gives four oracles; Balak is persistent, determined to win Balaam over, but with no success. Yet the message should have been loud and clear in the second oracle, quoted above. Balak learns that day that unlike his pagan deities, the God of Israel is not a God who can be manipulated. Unlike Baal, God is not susceptible to emotional change. What God has said, he will do, because by his very nature he is a God who changes not. Notice, God makes this point by specifying that he is *not* a human being. Unlike humans, he does not lie, nor will he change his mind. He is the Creator, not the creature.

This refrain is repeated throughout the Scriptures. In Ezekiel, for example, God says, "I am the LORD. I have spoken; it shall come to pass; I will do it. I will not go back; I will not spare; I will not relent; according to your ways and your deeds you will be judged, declares the Lord GOD" (24:14). The context is different from Balaam's in many ways. Israel is no longer the victor but the victim. Jerusalem is under siege by the king of Babylon, and it's all because Israel has refused to listen and obey the Lord. Therefore, the Lord, through Babylon, will bring disaster on his people, resulting in exile, and Israel can be confident that the Lord will do it and will not relent, since he is a God who changes not.

We saw in chapter 6 that similar language is used in the tragic story of King Saul. God rejects Saul as king due to his direct rebelliousness, and though Saul begs, God makes it clear he will not change his mind: "The Glory of Israel will not lie or have regret, for he is not a man, that he should have regret" (1 Sam. 15:29).

Notice, in each of these stories, especially the last one, God's unchanging will is tied to his unchanging nature, and that nature, unlike a human's, is not one that experiences emotional fluctuation. Unlike humanity, the God without a body, the God without finite limitations, is a God who does not experience emotional vicissitudes like grieving because he is full of regret.

What to Make of Biblical Language

That brings us to a common objection: Doesn't the Bible use emotional language to refer to God? Yes, it certainly does. And for good reason too. God has accommodated himself to us to such a degree that he has chosen to use our human language to make himself known. As John Calvin liked to say, God lisps to us, like a parent or nurse would, using baby talk to speak to a child. "Such forms of speaking do not so much express clearly what God is like as accommodate the knowledge of him to our slight capacity. To do this he must descend far beneath his loftiness."[44]

The Puritan James Ussher makes a similar point when he says, "Almighty God speaks in a broken and imperfect language to us again, for our weakness and understanding's sake." Ussher then uses an illustration: "If the nurse should speak perfectly to the child, as she could to one of greater capacity, the child would not understand her." Now imagine if God did just that: "If God should speak unto us as he could, according to his own nature," then we would never be "able to understand him, nor conceive his meaning."[45]

So the language the biblical authors use of God does communicate something literally true about God, but that does not mean that same language should be interpreted literally.[46] If it did, then passages that say God has hands or feet would have to mean God has a body, and that would result in God being just as restricted by time and space as we are, just as susceptible to change as we are, and just as helpless to implement his plan as we are to implement ours. Yet just as the biblical authors use *anthropomorphic* language (i.e., human form ascribed to a God without form), so too do they use *anthropopathic* language (i.e., human emotions ascribed to a God without passions).

As interpreters, we struggle to accept this point. We want to pick and choose. We want to point to one passage of Scripture and say, "Well, of course, God does not literally have hands and feet" (anthropomorphism). Yet when we come to a passage that says God regrets or grieves (anthropopathism), we hesitate. At the start of the twenty-first century, this inconsistency was exposed in the open theism controversy. Open theists are those who say the future is open to God; he does not know what will happen. Open theists turn to texts that say God "now knows" or "relents" or "regrets" to argue God does not know the future. They insist that these texts must be read in the most literal way possible: God does not know what will happen; God changes his mind; God realizes he has made a mistake. Conveniently, however, when those same interpreters come to texts where God is said to hear, taste, touch, or smell, suddenly they say, "Well, of course this is metaphorical language, not literally true of God." To others, however, the subjective nature of their interpretation is conspicuous.

So why, then, did God choose to employ emotional language to describe himself in Scripture? Is he tricking us into believing something of him that he is not? "It is certain," Calvin answers, "that God is not subject to any human passions, yet He is not able sufficiently to manifest either the goodness or the love that He has toward us, except by transfiguring Himself, as if He were a mortal man, saying that He would take pleasure in doing good to us."[47] In other words, God is well aware of our need for accommodation. Yes, he is impassible, but he is communicating to a world that is not. If that communication is to be meaningful, then he must convey truths through passible mediums, imagery emotional in nature. Otherwise, the door of communication from God to humans remains closed.[48]

As we learned in chapter 2, the beauty of biblical language is that it speaks by way of analogy. Analogical language defines our God-talk because we are not the Creator but the creature, we are not the archetype but the ectype, we are not God but his image. Naturally, then, the biblical authors use a variety of metaphors (light, rock, shepherd, tower, lion, etc.). Yet never do they imply that they have captured God as he is in and of himself, according to his invisible, incomprehensible essence. Instead, they believe they are communicating who God is in relation to the created order by means of his mighty works and words. For example, his "love for his children is *like* that of a father who is afflicted in the affliction of his children, in that he acts so as to deliver them from their affliction as surely *as if* it were his own."[49] Fearfully, we should not conclude that he is literally a father afflicted.

Yet the other side of this coin should be considered as well. Ascribing emotion to God says more about us than God. When we read that God has been merciful, we should think not that God has changed but rather that he has changed us. It's not his status or identity that has undergone a revolution; it's ours. "For when You look upon us in our misery," says Anselm, "it is we who feel the effect of Your mercy, but You do not experience the feeling."[50]

One last point deserves mention. Sometimes the language we force upon God can be misleading. Not only is the word "emotion" foreign to the biblical witness, but the word itself is a very recent invention. In the history of Christian thought, "passions" were contrasted with "affections," the former having negative connotations never to be applied to God lest he be confused with the creature. In the middle of the nineteenth century, however, this language was replaced with the vocabulary of secular psychology: "emotions." Thomas Dixon has pointed to the works of Alexander Bain, William James, and Charles Darwin, to name just a few, and observes how the "new paradigm was physiological, evolutionary and atheological." "It displayed a marked increase in attention to the detailed physiognomy and physiology of emotions while replacing the old moral-theological stories about people as God's *creatures* with natural-historical ones about human beings as evolved *animals*."[51] With this new vocabulary in place, theological discussions took on a new trajectory as people now assumed emotional language in their quest to understand the creature and the Creator. Perhaps this is a lesson to contemporary Christians: talk about God within a framework of human "emotions" is not so much a return to the biblical language as it is an adoption of our modern assumptions about God.

But Didn't Jesus Suffer?

If God is impassible, and Jesus is the Son of God, then how can God remain impassible when Jesus suffers and dies on the cross? Those following the lead of Moltmann will respond that God cannot be impassible, since Jesus suffered on the cross. The assumption is that Jesus must suffer not only in his humanity but in his divinity as well. Whatever occurs in relation to the human nature of Jesus must also be true of the divine nature. The attributes of his humanity must be communicated directly to his divinity. In this view, God *as God* suffers in Christ.[52]

Rather than thinking of Christology from the top down, Moltmann believes we must think from the bottom up, interpreting divinity through the lens of Christ's humanity. "God's being can be seen and known directly only in the cross of Christ."[53] Moltmann blames "traditional Christology" (i.e., the majority of the church throughout history), believing it to have come "very near to docetism" (the belief that Christ only appeared to suffer). The church bought into a "philosophical concept of God," which believed "God's being is incorruptible, unchangeable, indivisible, incapable of suffering and immortal." The result was a "cold heavenly power." By contrast, we need a "human God in the crucified Son of Man."[54]

We cannot explore Christology in all its complexity here, but we can briefly clarify where this logic has gone astray. First, this type of reasoning fails to distinguish carefully how the two natures relate to one another in the person of Christ. Those church fathers who guarded the church from various christological heresies were careful to do just that. For example, consider the creed of Chalcedon (AD 451), perhaps the most important creed to be produced on the subject.

Rather than squishing or smashing together the two natures or, on the other hand, divorcing the two natures from one another, Chalcedon strives for biblical balance, describing the two as related "without confusion, without change, without division, without separation."[55] The denial of those four words (confusion, change, division, separation) is crucial. While we certainly should be fearful of dividing the two natures from one another, thereby severing apart the one person of Christ, Moltmann and company have committed the opposite error. By attributing a human attribute (passibility) to Christ's divinity, one has confused the two natures, subjecting both to change. Such change has resulted in the humanization of the divine.

It also results in a change within the divine nature itself. The divinity no longer is pure divinity. It is unsurprising that when Moltmann discusses councils like Nicaea, a council Chalcedon is expanding on, he approves of their refutation of Arius (who denied the deity of Christ) on the basis that "God is not changeable." But in the very next breath Moltmann is quick to qualify, "But that statement is not absolute." While God may not be "changeable as creatures are changeable," one should not then assume that he is "unchangeable in every respect." The council meant only that God "is under no constraint from that which is not of God."[56] Nevertheless, God is free to will change in himself and to will that he be changed by others. Moltmann denies "absolute and intrinsic unchangeableness" (the view of Aquinas), which would mean God is "incapable of love." Rather, God "voluntarily opens himself up to the possibility of being affected by another." While God does not unwillingly suffer, he does suffer willingly.[57]

In response, I would argue not only has Moltmann misunderstood councils like Nicaea (many fathers did affirm intrinsic unchangeableness), but he has emptied immutability of any authentic meaning. According to Moltmann, immutability can be affirmed only in this sense: God cannot be coerced. So as long as God chooses to be mutable, no harm is done. Notice, Moltmann has used the label "immutability" to advocate for a God who is mutable in every way except one (he cannot be forced). And he has used the unity of the person of Christ (hypostatic union) to justify God's changeability *in his divine nature*.

It is a right instinct to stress the unity present in the incarnate God-man. Nevertheless, Chalcedon also warns that we should be careful to preserve the "distinction of the natures" so that they are "by no means taken away by the union." When we resist the temptation to confuse the attributes of one nature with those of the other, the "property of each nature" is "preserved, concurring

William Lane Craig, #multiple personality disorder

in one Person and one Subsistence"; that Person is simultaneously "not parted or divided into two persons," but there continues to be "one and the same Son, and only begotten, God the Word, the Lord Jesus Christ."[58]

By implication, then, it is illegitimate to think that attributes of the human nature are communicated or transferred over to the attributes of the divine nature during the incarnation. Yes, there is a communication—what has been called the *communicatio idiomatum*, the communication of proper qualities or properties—yet it is not at the level of *nature* but at the level of *person*. Attributes of one nature are not to be predicated of the other nature but instead should be predicated of the person of the Son. When the person of the Son becomes incarnate, he does not undergo a "compositional union of natures"—that creates a Son with parts, contrary to divine simplicity. Rather, by becoming incarnate the person of the Son is "taking on a new manner or mode of existence."[59]

The *Communicatio Idiomatum*

Lutheran View	Attributes of one nature are predicated of the other nature. For Luther, divine attributes (like omnipresence) can be communicated to the human nature. For Moltmann, human attributes (like suffering) can be predicated of the divine nature.
Reformed View	Attributes are not communicated at the level of *nature* but at the level of *person*. The attributes of either nature are predicated of the *person* of the Son. This view is most consistent with Nicaea and Chalcedon.

This can be seen practically when we ask a question such as, Who is it that is suffering at the cross? Answer: the *person* of the Son, who is none other than the divine Son of God. But, as Weinandy points out, if we ask a slightly different question—"What is the manner in which he experiences the whole reality of human suffering?"—our answer changes: the Son suffers "as man!" "It is actually the Son of God who lives a comprehensive human life, and so it is the Son who, as man, experiences all facets of this human life, including suffering and death."[60] This careful nuance allows us to say, on the one hand, that Christ is impassible as he who is true God, and yet he is passible as one who is true man.[61] Or as Gregory of Nazianzus has said, Christ is "passible in His Flesh, Impassible in His Godhead."[62] That explains why Paul can say to the Ephesian elders, "Pay careful attention . . . to care for the church of *God*, which he obtained with *his own blood*" (Acts 20:28), and why he can say to the Corinthians, "None of the rulers of this age understood this, for if they had, they would not have crucified *the Lord of glory* (1 Cor. 2:8)."[63]

There is a tragic irony in the view that says God *as God* must suffer at the cross. For if Christ suffers in his divinity at the cross, then he is not actually suffering *as a man*. But isn't this exactly what the passibilist is after, a Jesus who is *like us* and therefore can *relate to us*? As it turns out, it is the impassibilist who can truly offer humanity a God it can relate to. The person of Christ suffers, but he does so *as a man*. In one of the most moving passages on the subject, Weinandy captures just how thick the irony has become:

> For if the Son of God experienced suffering in his divine nature, he would no longer be experiencing human suffering in an authentic and genuine human manner, but instead he would be experiencing "human suffering" in a divine manner which would then be neither genuinely nor authentically human. If the Son of God experienced suffering in his divine nature, then it would be God suffering as God *in a man*. But the incarnation, which demands that the Son of God actually exists as a man and not just dwells in a man, equally demands that the Son of God suffers *as a man* and not just suffers in a man. Thus to replace the phrase "the Impassible suffers" with "the Passible suffers" immediately purges the suffering of all incarnational significance. . . . This is what humankind is crying out to hear, not that God experiences, in a divine manner, our anguish and suffering in the midst of a sinful and depraved world, but that he actually experienced and knew first hand, as one of us—as a man— human anguish and suffering within a sinful and depraved world.[64]

As counterintuitive as it may seem, if Christ suffers in his deity at the cross—or the Father suffers with him as he looks on—then we have actually excluded the Son from suffering *for us*. "Having locked suffering within God's divine nature," we have "locked God out of human suffering."[65] If the Son of God is going to act on our behalf as our suffering servant, then it is critical that we honor his suffering as truly human. To in effect segregate such suffering to his divinity is to empty suffering in the incarnation from its effectiveness entirely.

A Little Extra

There is a lesson to learn as we conclude: we must always be careful not to restrict or limit the divinity of the Son of God to his human, incarnate experience, nor to let his humanity swallow up his divinity. To circumscribe his divinity to his humanity is to lose his divinity altogether. When the Son becomes incarnate, he does not abandon his divine attributes (impassibility included) nor his divine responsibilities. Even during the incarnation, the person of the Son continues to uphold the universe by the word of his power (Heb. 1:3; Col. 1:15–17).

The Fathers and Reformers called this the "extra." Although the Word becomes incarnate (John 1), nevertheless, the person of the Son cannot be contained by his human nature; due to his divinity, he continues to exist and operate outside, or beyond, his flesh as well. As Thomas Aquinas said, "Not even in the hypostatic union is the Word of God or the divine nature comprehended by the human nature. Although the divine nature was wholly united to the human nature in the one Person of the Son, nevertheless the whole power of the divinity was not, as it were, circumscribed."[66] For that reason, then, the person of the Son remains impassible in his divinity while at the same time truly suffering in his humanity. Although it is mysterious, the person of the Son is actively and concurrently engaged in and through both natures.

The *Extra Calvinisticum*	The "extra" is not original to John Calvin but is found in the theology of Athanasius, Augustine, Cyril of Alexandria, Thomas Aquinas, and many others. Nevertheless, Calvin's name is associated with it because he famously appealed to the "extra" in his debates with Lutherans over the presence of Christ in the Lord's Supper. Calvin writes, "Here is something marvelous: the Son of God descended from heaven in such a way that, without leaving heaven, he willed to be borne in the virgin's womb, to go about the earth, and to hang upon the cross; yet he continuously filled the world even as he had done from the beginning!"[a]

[a] Calvin, *Institutes* 2.13.4.

Impassibility, the Gospel, and the Christian Life

If God were passible, would that change the gospel and its promises for the Christian life? Absolutely. If God undergoes emotional change and if his perfections, his essence, or his actions fluctuate in response to the creature, then it is reasonable to wonder whether God's promises, Christ's saving work to fulfill those promises, and the application of those promises both now and in the future are entirely certain. If God's perfections change, if he fluctuates from one emotional state to the next, then his promises might change as well.

A passible God would leave us in a state of anxiety, unsure whether he will remain constant in who he is and what he says. His wrath would not be just, because his retribution is potentially uncontrollable. His love would not be steadfast, as the Psalms repeatedly say it is, for a possible love guarantees no certainty of devotion. Impassibility, it must be granted, is the basis on which God's steadfast love and justice are built.[67]

If God is passible, we might also conclude that God is pathetic. At first, it might feel comforting to hear someone say, "You are suffering? God suffers with you." But any immediate comfort gained quickly dissipates when we realize that such a God needs just as much help as we do. A suffering God is a God we start to feel sorry for, not a God we seek help from or take refuge in. What we need is a God who does not suffer, a God who is our rock and fortress (see chap. 6). Only that kind of God is then able to help those who do suffer; only that kind of God is free to relieve the suffering of others. "The absence of suffering allows God's love to be completely altruistic and beneficent."[68] Not only God's power to rescue but his ability to do so out of love significantly depends on his impassibility.

The cross is a case in point. It is precisely because God does not suffer that he is able to send his Son to suffer for us as a man. As we learned, that does not mean that Christ's *divine nature* suffers; we must be careful not to confuse the human nature with the divine nature, humanizing his divine attributes. But it does mean that the *person* of the Son suffers on the cross in the fullness of his humanity. Yet he is able to do so only because suffering does not victimize him in the first place. If God is just as much a victim of suffering as we are, then he is helpless, powerless, and hopeless to embark on a rescue mission. That is not the picture we see in the Gospels. The Gospels portray the Son of God fully in control of his mission. Again and again, as he sets his face toward Calvary, he announces, even predicts, his redemptive suffering, putting on full display his total sovereignty (Matt. 16:21–23).

Not only does impassibility guarantee that Christ can save sinners, but impassibility guarantees that God's love and grace are free. If God is passible, then his love is contingent on the creature. According to Moltmann, God's love depends on the creature for its fulfillment. A real give-and-take relationship requires passionate love, a love that is mutually dependent and changed by the one it loves. However, such passionate love is entirely conditioned on humans. Grace is no longer free, mercy no longer a gift, and love no longer gratuitous. God must look to those outside himself for love.[69] The Bible teaches throughout that God's love is unconditional, free, and purely altruistic (Rom. 9:16; Eph. 2:4–5; 1 John 4:10). Why? Because this love is impassible. It does not look to the creature for its effectiveness. It is rooted in God's immutable nature.

In the end, only a God who does not suffer can accomplish redemption for a suffering humanity. Only one who is impassible can become incarnate as the suffering servant. And only one whose love depends on no one can offer grace that is free of charge.

Idolatry-Free Zone

More than any other attribute, impassibility may be the most counterintuitive to Christians today. The way the culture has influenced our thinking about God, coupled with the way we have been taught to read the Bible in the most literal way possible, means that a perfection like impassibility is foreign to us, even strange. But as we've seen in this chapter, impassibility is essential. Without it we risk confusing Zeus with the God of Abraham, Isaac, and Jacob, the God who is "I AM." We risk, in short, making God a lot like us, which is the essence of idolatry. Ultimately, impassibility is so important because it creates an idolatry-free zone.

8

Is God in Time?

Timeless Eternity

> Of old you laid the foundation of the earth. . . .
> They will perish, but you will remain;
>   they will all wear out like a garment.
> You will change them like a robe, and they will pass away,
>   but you are the same, and your years have no end.
> The children of your servants shall dwell secure.
>
> PSALM 102:25–28

> Before Abraham was, I am.
>
> JESUS, IN JOHN 8:58

> [God's eternity is] the whole, simultaneous and perfect posses-
> sion of boundless life.
>
> BOETHIUS, *The Consolation of Philosophy*

Preparing Hell for Idiots? Augustine's Answers to Tough Questions

Saint Augustine was asked, "What was God doing before he made
heaven and earth?"[1] Many today think Augustine humorously

responded that God was preparing hell for idiots that ask questions like that.[2] Today, we laugh at such a response, as many did in Augustine's day. Actually, Augustine never found it funny; in fact, Augustine never gave such a response. In *Confessions* he explains how some have responded with such a joke, but in his opinion the joke is "to evade the force of the question." "It is one thing to laugh, another to see the point at issue, and this reply I reject." How, then, did Augustine respond? "I would have preferred him to answer, 'I am ignorant of what I do not know,' rather than reply so as to ridicule someone who has asked a deep question and to win approval for an answer which is a mistake."[3] That comment is pure Augustine: humble, never to dismiss a serious theological question.

The question was, in context, more of an objection. Some who posed it did so as an argument against God's eternity and immutability. If God was "unoccupied" and "doing nothing," they asked, "why does he not always remain the same for ever, just as before creation he abstained from work?" "For if in God any new development took place and any new intention, so as to make a creation which he had never made before, how then can there be a true eternity in which a will, not there previously, comes into existence?" The will, they objected, is tied to God's substance. So it follows that if there is a new act or change of will, there must be a change of substance, and any change would preclude God from being an eternal being. Or if God is everlasting, then based on such logic, so must his creation be.[4]

For Augustine, theological questions, or in this case objections, were never to be separated from matters of the heart. "They attempt to taste eternity when their heart is still flitting about in the realm where things change and have a past and future; it is still 'vain' (Ps. 5:10)."[5] Augustine counters such objections with such sternness only to then embark on a discussion of time itself, defending a God who is not limited by time but transcends time, is external to time, and is timelessly eternal. He is not a God of change, as if he had a past and a future; this God is timelessly eternal, insusceptible to the change that comes with being in time. As we will discover, that means we must conceive of God's will and that which he creates not in creaturely ways but in ways appropriate to a God whose actions do not defy but complement his eternal nature.

The eternality of God is just one implication of his infinite nature and ultimately the outcome of a God who is the most supreme, perfect being. Time is fraught with limitations; a being in time is a being bound by all the characteristics of time: change, composition, dependency, and impotence. But a perfect being can have no such limitations because he is, by definition of being perfect, infinite in nature. He is his attributes in all their fullness, to the absolute degree.[6] Timeless eternity is but the child, the heir, of two proud parents: divine perfection and infinitude, who themselves are married to one another and cannot be divorced.

From Everlasting to Everlasting

Scripture constantly refers to God's eternal nature. He has no beginning; he has no end. He always *is*. Here is a concept our finite minds are barely able to handle: someone who exists but never came into existence.

Consider the ways—the many ways—Scripture testifies to God's eternity.[7] Moses prays in Psalm 90:

> Lord, you have been our dwelling place
> in all generations.
> Before the mountains were brought forth,
> or ever you had formed the earth and the world,
> from everlasting to everlasting you are God. (90:1–2)

Moses then contrasts God's everlasting existence with the fate of the people.

> You return man to dust
> and say, "Return, O children of man!"
> For a thousand years in your sight
> are but as yesterday when it is past,
> or as a watch in the night.
>
> You sweep them away as with a flood; they are like a dream,
> like grass that is renewed in the morning:
> in the morning it flourishes and is renewed;
> in the evening it fades and withers. (90:3–6)

A dream? Like grass? Moses is making the point that our life span is but a moment. In an instant the floodwaters gush, and we become dust once more. Like grass, we sprout up in the morning, only to wither by sunset. Not God; he is everlasting. As the prophet Isaiah says, "The LORD is the everlasting God, the Creator of the ends of the earth" (40:28). Not only is his name "Holy," but as the Holy "One who is high and lifted up," he also "inhabits eternity" (57:15).[8]

Many of the prologues and benedictions in the New Testament highlight the eternal nature of this holy God as well. Paul calls him the "immortal God" (Rom. 1:23), the "eternal God" (Rom. 16:26), and the "only Sovereign, the King of kings and Lord of lords, who alone has immortality" (1 Tim. 6:15–16). John addresses the seven churches in Asia and says, "Grace to you and peace from him who is and who was and who is to come" (Rev. 1:4). He then concludes his greeting with the words of God himself, "I am the Alpha and the Omega, . . . who is and who was and who is to come, the Almighty" (1:8).

Since God is everlasting, his perception of time is not like ours. For us, we see one moment followed by the next because that is how we experience time. To transcend time is impossible for us. We are in it, bound to it, and formed by it. But with God, time is perceived differently. As one who is not bound by time or limited by its count, he sees all time at once. While it may seem as if the Lord will never return, Peter reminds his readers not to count slowness as some do. With "the Lord one day is as a thousand years, and a thousand years as one day" (2 Pet. 3:8).

Without Succession, without Measure

As in many theological debates, simply citing a biblical word does not necessarily settle controversy. In the past, theologians have debated the meaning of "everlasting." Does it mean God is *in time* yet never had a beginning or an end? If so, then God is not strictly eternal but more appropriately everlasting. Or does it mean that God is outside of time altogether, unrestricted by the boundaries of time? If so, then for God to be called an everlasting God means he is timelessly eternal. Today, many are attracted to the first view. Yet to say that God is in time is to bind him to time with all its limitations. What are such limitations?

First, to be in time is to be restricted by a succession of moments. For example, when you woke up this morning you may have had breakfast at 7:00, dressed for work at 7:30, and sat in traffic until 8:00 (angry, too, since you were late!). You took each minute as it came. Every person sitting in traffic, late for work, wishes he or she could transcend time. But that's impossible, and we all know it. Time will not speed up or slow down, despite our wishes. Nor can you skip over time, bypassing its grip. No, each minute comes and goes. You experience each second, each minute, each hour one by one, successively.

That word "successively" is key. Augustine says the reason we struggle to understand God's eternal nature is that we can think only in this category. We try to "compare eternity with temporal successiveness which never has any constancy," a terrible mistake, especially since "no comparison" is "possible." The reason we sit in traffic and it feels like forever is that time is "constituted of many successive movements which cannot be simultaneously extended."[9]

143

Is this the way we should speak of God and time? If it is, it certainly limits the one who is supposed to be limitless (infinite). How so? For starters, it means God now has *potential*.[10] Having potential, in our human vocabulary, is a good thing. If your son is in Little League and hits a home run, you would say as a proud parent that your son has great potential. What does potential assume? It assumes we go from bad to better, from good to great. That is a perfectly acceptable concept when we're speaking about human, finite, mutable creatures.

But the moment we apply this concept to God we have a massive problem. If God were to reach his potential, that would assume he was not perfect before. He would be a God who is becoming something he was not before. He would change, says Thomas Aquinas, because "in any change there is successiveness, one part coming after another."[11] Naturally we would wonder whether this is a God we can trust. After all, this God changes, either for better or for worse.

Second, if God experiences a succession of moments, it is hard to see how he is not one who can be measured. As humans, we have a past, present, and future. We are inherently assessable, computable, calculable beings. "Granny is eighty-five years old." "My sister just turned sweet sixteen." "You look so much older than the last time I saw you." Statements like these reveal that we are always *becoming* and *in process*. And as such we are measurable. It's even built into our conversations: "He didn't really measure up to my standards."

Would we dare say the same of God? Is he a being that can be measured? Not if he is infinite. By definition, an infinite, eternal God cannot be measured. And if he cannot be measured, then he must not be a temporal being, for a temporal being can always be measured in some way. Why? Because experiencing one moment and then another successively means one is in the process of *becoming*. But "God is not a process of becoming," says Herman Bavinck, "but an eternal being."[12] "In the eternal," observes Augustine, "nothing is transient, but the whole is present."[13]

Third, experiencing one moment before the next also would mean God is made up of parts and therefore changes. "If God does first one thing and then another He cannot be simple because His essence must stay the same over time, and thus be something other than the part that does the changing." Time always involves and includes "motion and change."[14] Motion poses a problem because God does not have parts that can be moved into motion; he is simple. Motion also assumes one shifts, even changes, from one minute, or motion, to the next; God, however, is immutable.

It is far better to understand God's everlasting and eternal nature as precluding not only a beginning and an end but also any succession of moments. We could call these—no beginning, no end, and no succession of moments—the three marks of eternity.[15] These three are captured best by Anselm, who says no part of God's eternity will "leak away with the past into non-existence, or fly past, like the scarcely existing momentary present, or, with the future, wait, pending, in not-yet existence."[16] Instead, the great "I AM" just is: time-free, and forever so. It is true of eternity, and it is true of God: he exists, says Aquinas, as an "*instantaneous whole* lacking successiveness."[17]

We must conclude, then, that eternity and time are entirely different, antithetical to one another. "Eternity measures permanent existence and time measures change." Here lies the essential difference. Even if time were unending, it would not be an "instantaneous whole."[18] That category applies only to eternity and with it to an eternal God. Only if God is an instantaneous whole can he avoid the change that comes with time.

Eternal Present?

So far we've described what God is not—he is not in time or a temporal being. He has, as Anselm labels it, no "temporal present."[19]

Can God's eternity be described positively, though, in a way beyond merely confessing God to be eternal? Honestly, it is hard, very hard, which explains Augustine's famous comment: "What then is time? Provided that no one asks me, I know. If I want to explain it to an inquirer, I do not know."[20]

As difficult as it is for time-bound creatures to describe a time-free God, some have said that all time is like an eternal present to God.[21] "God possesses being perfectly," explains Katherin Rogers, "because all of His own life is present to Him, and He knows and causes all things at all times because all of time is immediately present to Him."[22] Tertullian may have had a similar idea in mind when he said, "Eternity has no time. It is itself all time."[23] Yet describing God's eternity as time immediately present to him still has its weaknesses. We are still using time-bound categories (eternal *present*) to describe a being who is time*less*, which runs the risk of misunderstanding.

For example, one might assume eternity for God is merely time "stretched out."[24] But if God experiences no duration, then an unending line is a misleading illustration. All we've done is taken time and pulled it, stretched it, and extended it until we see no beginning or end. An eternal duration is still a *duration*, a succession of moments. It is crucial to clarify, then, that "God does not have to be temporally extended to encompass all of time."[25] Rather, as the one who is timeless, "God sees all things together, and not successively," says Aquinas.[26]

The "Gloss and Lustre" of All Perfections

Perhaps a better way to understand what it means for God to be timeless and time-free is to appreciate the many ways eternity is tied to all the other attributes.[27]

"Eternity is the choice perfection of God" and the "gloss and lustre" of all other attributes, says Stephen Charnock. The reason is that every "perfection would be imperfect, if it were not *always* a perfection."[28]

These words should arrest our attention. In each chapter we've explored how any one attribute is tied to other attributes; remember, the attributes are like a spider web in which each silk strand is connected to the rest of the web. Eternity, however, is one silk strand that is especially noteworthy—apart from it all the other perfections cease to be. Without eternity, perfections such as omniscience, immutability, love, and countless others lose their steadfast radiance. They fade out because they are not forever true of the being of God. God's love is extinguished like a flame in the wind, for it cannot forever keep the ones he loves. His justice fails to charge forward, making right every wrong, but instead allows his nemesis to have the last word. And his nature itself is susceptible to change, for his immutability is no longer attached to eternity.

To see the "gloss and lustre" of eternity sparkle, consider a few more ways eternity is wedded to other perfections.

A River or an Ocean? Immutably Eternal, Eternally Simple

Previously we concluded that God is not susceptible to a *succession of moments*. Succession in time would introduce change in God, but he is *immutable*. Charnock uses the illustration of the sea in contrast to a river. A river changes, moving from place to place, sometimes even shifting its location or destination, depending on its environment (e.g., heavy rain and flooding). It is highly susceptible to being affected by something external to itself.

Not so the ocean. It's as if it never changed. Always in the same place; always the same body of water from year to year. It's fixed and stable. If a river ever came into contest with an ocean, there would be no contest. The ocean would swallow up the river.[29] The sea is such a vast body of water that it remains constant.

God is more like an ocean than a river. As the Infinite One, he is an "unbounded sea of being."[30] But he's not only infinite, he is eternally and immutably infinite. While the river of time is always changing and developing, the ocean of the divine remains constant, consistent, and invariable. He is changed by no succession of moments, for he has none. He has no beginning; he has no end. He just is. And because he just is, he does not fluctuate. God's "immutable eternity means," says Anselm, that he "exists without qualification: you cannot talk of change, that it 'was' or 'will be.' It does not exist in a changeable way. It is not now something that it has not been, or will not be. It is not now not something that it has been, or will be. But it is what is, once, simultaneously and unendingly."[31] For that reason, God's eternity serves to protect, a "shield against all kinds of mutability."[32] If he is not eternal, time-free, then his essence is vulnerable to all types of change.

In part, God is immutably eternal because he, well, has no parts. A creature, like you or me, changes with time because we have parts that change with time. To be bound by time implies we are beings that are made up of parts, parts that vary from one state to the next. Such perpetual variation means "something is acquired" or something is "lost every day."[33] We are the victims of addition and subtraction.

A being who is outside of time, however, cannot have parts. Imagine, for a second, how God's essence would be affected if he were bound by time. The "supreme essence," says Anselm, "would be cut up into parts along the divisions of time. For if its life span is drawn out along the course of time, it must have, as time does, a present, past and future." God would be one thing one minute and another thing the next. He would have "parts scattered about throughout time."[34]

Such a conception may be consistent with a composite being, but not with a God who is "supremely simple and supremely unchangeable."[35] That which is in time has a "beginning" and grows "up by degrees," because there it is characterized by a "succession of parts."

Not so for that which is eternal. "Eternity is contrary to time, and is therefore a permanent and immutable state; a perfect possession of life without any variation."[36] Charnock concludes, "As the nature of time consists in the succession of parts, so the nature of eternity is an infinite immutable duration."[37] No parts, no change, no time. All three are inseparably tied together. God cannot be added to or subtracted from, for he has no parts. He does not become either greater or lesser. He does not change for the better or the worse. But that is only because he is eternal, always existing, always remaining the perfect God that he is, immutably eternal and eternally simple.[38]

As a result, God's attributes or perfections can never be added to or subtracted from his essence; they are his essence. Nor do they grow greater or smaller with time; they remain forever the same. Unbound by time, our God is who he has always been and always will be. "He is not in his essence this day what he was not before, or will be the next day and year what he is not now. All his perfections are most perfect in him every moment; before all ages, after all ages."[39] As long as God remains unlimited, infinite in being, he cannot be said to be constrained by time and space. He necessarily "exists everywhere and always."[40]

Caused by None, Deprived by None: Self-Existent, Eternal, Omnipotent, Infinite Life

One reason divine eternity is so important is that apart from it God would be at the mercy of another. Think about it. If God were created, coming to exist at a particular point in time, then he would be caused by another. Whoever created him must be more powerful. That creator gave life and surely could take God's life too. In short, God would no longer be God, for his existence would depend on another.

That God is eternal is really good news. Being immortal means he is also self-existent and self-sufficient. It is precisely because

God has no beginning that he is dependent on no one and no thing. Instead, he is "immovably fixed in his own being," for "none gave him his life," and so "none can deprive him of his life."[41] To be God, at least a God who is independent, he must necessarily be eternal. The attributes of aseity and eternity go hand in hand, which explains why Boethius cannot define the latter without including the former: God's eternity is "the whole, simultaneous and perfect possession of boundless life."[42]

If no one else gives God life, then our God has life in and of himself. He is independently eternal. He does not gain life as we do, nor is he granted life as we are, but he *is* life. Surely his name "I AM" (Exod. 3:14) implies this much, which is why many in ages past have titled him "pure act." "All life is seated in God, as in its proper throne, in its most perfect purity. God is life; it is in him originally, radically, therefore eternally. He is a pure act, nothing but vigor and act; he hath by his nature that life which others have by his grant."[43] Deservedly, then, it is to "the King of the ages, immortal, invisible, the only God," that we should ascribe "honor and glory forever and ever" (1 Tim. 1:17). Our worship of God will never cease, for the God we worship never ceases, being life in and of himself always and forever.

One last point. If God has life in and of himself (indeed, he *is* life), then it must also follow that he, unlike the creature, experiences his life not moment by moment but all at once. Contrast God with the creature: God "'possesses' His unlimited life 'at once,'" but the creature leads "a dreadfully 'disconnected' life in that at each present instant we have little access to or power over all the other instants of our lives."[44] God is not only the self-existent, eternal God, but he is omnipotent life itself, for he has power over all of his life at once, whereas we are restricted to experience life one instant at a time. We cannot forget, either, that the life he has power over all at once is an infinite life; it is unlimited and unbounded. What can we conclude but that our God is *self-existent, eternal, omnipotent, infinite life*?

Just as God's power is not to be severed from his immutability, his immutability is not to be disconnected from his eternity. As Paul Helm says, "Only a God who is immutable in a particularly strong sense can (logically) perform all that Scripture claims that God performs, and a God can only be immutable in this strong sense if he exists timelessly."[45]

Eternal Decrees and Creation

Understandably, one could lob an objection at this point, the same sort of objection lobbed at Augustine when he was asked what God was doing before he created heaven and earth. If God is timelessly eternal, then how can he act? How can he create the world, for example? To act or will anything seems to suggest temporal succession, especially if there are a series of acts that stem from the will of God. Creation, so the argument goes, proves that God cannot be eternal. This objection is parasitic, latching onto the historic idea that there is an *order* to God's decrees, which seems to imply that one decree occurs after another.

To answer this inquiry, we need theological precision on our side. When we speak of the decrees of God, we are referring to an *eternal* reality. Such an order cannot be a *temporal* order; instead, it is a *logical* order. While such a distinction sounds pedantic, it's common to our everyday experience. When you walk into a room and turn on the light switch, what happens first, the turning on of the light switch or light brightening the room? In time, they appear to happen simultaneously. But logically? Logically it's obvious: the light switch. It's not the light in the room that causes the light switch to turn on but the light switch that causes light to brighten the room, thanks to the discovery of electricity. Logically, one comes before the other even though they appear to happen in time simultaneously.

Similarly, when we refer to the divine decrees, seeking to understand which one comes *before* the other, we need to remember that a logical, not temporal, ordering is in view. Such decrees are eternal, for they are issued by the timelessly eternal God. God wills immutably and eternally because the God who wills *is* immutable and eternal. As argued in chapter 5, God's will is identical with his essence.[46] Therefore, it does no good trying to sneak change (and with it, time) into an act of God's will, since his will and essence cannot be divorced from one another. Even in willing creation, God remains unchanging, timelessly eternal. If he did not, then creation would somehow meet some unfulfilled potential in God. He would no longer be pure act. But as pure act, God "needs to 'do' nothing further than *be* in order to cause the world."[47]

That's not to deny that in the execution of God's decrees in salvation history there is a temporal order and succession as experienced by the creature. But that succession does not describe change *in God* as it does describe change in humans as we move, for example, from a state of ungodliness to reconciliation. The sinner who has been called and regenerated by grace does experience a temporal sequence. Such a person is, for example, justified first and then glorified. A lifetime of perseverance comes in between. Nevertheless, justification, perseverance, and glorification, though experienced by temporal creatures temporally, are ordained by God eternally, cemented in the mind of God in timeless eternity.[48]

All that to say, we can describe God as one who brings the created order into existence, but we should not assume that he, then, is a God bound by time as is that which he creates. Rather, the work of creation is one that stems from the eternal decree of the eternal God. This means, as Augustine says, that the God who is "everlasting without time" can change the created order "without any change in himself."[49] He creates, nurtures, and changes all things all the while remaining the same, timelessly eternal.[50]

It is good news to us feeble and fickle Christians that God's decrees take on an eternal nature, much like the God who decrees them. It means that God does not decree one thing only to change his decree and to will another thing later. Rather, what he has decreed in eternity remains firm, and it will play itself out in its proper time. When God makes a promise, he comes through on that promise. That said, we are now ready to see the practical implications of an eternal God.

Eternal Judge, Eternal Judgment

God's eternal nature is both the worst news in the world and the best news in the world. While an eternal God is a comfort to believers, reassuring them of eternal life to come, an eternal God is a torment to unbelievers, perpetually reminding them of the judgment to come. Let's begin with the bad news.

For the unbeliever, God's eternal nature is the source of enormous discomfort. Christians love to quote John 3:16, which rightly turns to an eternal God as the fountain of eternal life for those who believe. Equally true, though far less popular, is John 3:18: "Whoever believes in him [the Son] is not condemned, but whoever does not believe is condemned already, because he has not believed in the name of the only Son of God." It has been commonly said that Jesus spoke of hell's eternity more often than any other biblical author. A simple survey of the Gospel accounts reveals that claim to be true. Unembarrassed and unashamed, Jesus never hesitates to warn his listeners of the eternal wrath to come (Matt. 18:8; 25:41).

The biblical notion of eternal condemnation is despised by many (most?) in the twenty-first century, deemed politically incorrect and abrasively pessimistic. However, in past generations contemplating eternal punishment proved indispensable to authentic renewal and revival, moving entire churches and cities to repentance and faith in Christ. You might resonate with that all-too-common experience of sitting in a university classroom as your English teacher sneers at the primitive rhetoric found in that threatening sermon by Jonathan Edwards (1703–58), "Sinners in the Hands of an Angry God." Few professors pay attention to the context in which Edwards ministered. Edwards saw the miraculous and sudden conversion of many in Northampton only because he followed in the footsteps of Jesus, warning his listeners of the wrath to come unless they ran to the gracious arms of God; there only would they find eternal life.

Yet Edwards was, in many ways, the last of a long line of Puritans. A century before him, Stephen Charnock also preached sermons full of such trepidation: "How dreadful is it to lie under the stroke of an eternal God! His eternity is as great a terror to him that hates him, as it is a comfort to him that loves him; because he is the 'living God, an everlasting king, the nations shall not be able to abide his indignation' (Jer. [10:10])." Charnock goes on to say that though "God be least in their thoughts, and is made light of in the world, yet the thoughts of God's eternity, when he comes to judge the world, shall make the slighters of him tremble." God is a judge who punishes the wicked. Yet this judge lives forever, which is "the greatest grievance to a soul in misery, and adds an inconceivable weight to it."[51]

God's eternal nature is the source of much greater fear in the unbeliever than his power. Why exactly? Apart from eternity, God's power does not last, and the wicked will escape eventually. When power is coupled with eternity, however, there can be no end to the punishment God inflicts. "His eternity makes the punishment more dreadful than his power," because though "his power makes it sharp," it is his eternity that "renders it perpetual." Since it endures forever, it "is the sting at the end of every lash."[52]

So sharp is the sting that one might wonder, especially if we are honest with our own sinfulness, whether there is any hope. In one sense, there is no hope, as long as we are looking to escape divine, eternal judgment by our own works and on our own terms. Should we give up and look outside ourselves to the eternal God himself, we discover that the same God who is just to condemn us for all eternity has taken the initiative to grant us *eternal* life. How can this be?

Eternal Covenant, Eternal Priest

The answer to that question is found in the person of Melchizedek, who appears in the book of Genesis and is a figure full of mystique. First off, he is a king-priest. In Genesis 14 we witness an encounter between Melchizedek and Abraham. Keep the context in mind: Abraham has just rescued his nephew Lot, his family, and his possessions from several kings, one of whom was the king of Sodom. When Abraham returns from battle victorious, he encounters Melchizedek, who is not only king of Salem but "priest of God Most High" (Gen. 14:18). As a priest, Melchizedek pronounces a blessing on Abraham, attributing Abraham's victory over his enemies to the hand of God, and Abraham in return pays tithes to Melchizedek, accepting Melchizedek's blessing.[53]

Melchizedek's name is significant, for it means "King of Righteousness," in contrast to the wicked king of Sodom who opposed Abraham. As the "King of Righteousness," Melchizedek would foreshadow the king-priest yet to come—that is, the Messiah. As hinted at in Psalm 110, as a priest in the order of Melchizedek, the Messiah hails from an eternal priesthood, a priesthood grounded on a righteousness that can atone for sins definitively.[54]

That is a point the author of Hebrews is not shy to make: "He [Melchizedek] is without father or mother or genealogy, having neither beginning of days nor end of life, but resembling the Son of God he continues a priest forever" (7:3). It is doubtful the author means Melchizedek never died or had physical parents. Rather, the author is making the simple observation that in the Genesis narrative Melchizedek just appears suddenly without any explanation and then disappears from the story without any warning. No genealogy is given; Scripture never records when he was born or when he died. It's as if his priesthood had no end.

Continuing as a priest forever (Heb. 7:3), Melchizedek is a type of the Messiah to come. "The former priests were many in number, because they were prevented by death from continuing in office, but he [Jesus] holds his priesthood permanently, because he continues forever. Consequently, he is able to save to the uttermost those who draw near to God through him, since he always lives to make intercession for them" (7:23–25).

As a better priest, a priest by divine appointment (7:20–21), Christ could bring about a better covenant. Remember, Christ is a priest in the order of Melchizedek, whose name means "King of Righteousness." Unlike the priests of old, who were sinful and had to offer sacrifices not only for the people's sin but for their own sin, Christ is a priest "holy, innocent, unstained," and as the perfect priest he could offer up himself as the perfect, sinless offering for the forgiveness of sins (Heb. 7:26–27; cf. 10:11–14).

Apart from the eternal priesthood of our sinless mediator, we have no sacrifice that can deal with the eternal punishment our sins deserve. Only the eternal Son of God himself can fit the bill (Heb. 7:3; cf. John 17:5; Col. 1:16–17). "Could our sins be perfectly expiated," asks Charnock, "had he not an eternal divinity to answer for the offences committed against an eternal God? Temporary sufferings had been of little validity, without an infiniteness and eternity in his person to add weight to his passion."[55] Those previously doomed by the eternal consequences of their sins can now rejoice and say with great confidence, "We have such a high priest, one who is seated at the right hand of the throne of the Majesty in heaven" (Heb. 8:1).

Mud Pies in a Slum or a Holiday at Sea?

The marvel of an infinite, eternal God is that he, and he alone, can offer life eternal. In the apostle Paul's letter to Titus, he says he is writing "for the sake of the faith of God's elect and their knowledge of the truth, which accords with godliness, in hope of eternal life, which God, who never lies, promised before the ages began and at the proper time manifested in his word through the preaching with which I have been entrusted by the command of God our Savior" (1:1–3). The Christian has every assurance of life eternal because God, who is himself eternal, is a God who does not, indeed cannot, lie (Heb. 6:18). Just as God's decrees do not change because God himself does not change, so too does the sinner who trusts in Christ have every assurance of eternal life because the giver is life, and eternally so.[56]

What kind of joy does eternal life bring to the believer? A joy that never ends, a joy that never ceases to satisfy. As David rejoiced,

> You make known to me the path of life;
> in your presence there is fullness of joy;
> at your right hand are pleasures forevermore.
> (Ps. 16:11)

Is this not the type of joy the world tries to find in everything but God? Those outside of Christ look everywhere—politics, money, fame, sex, possessions, relationships, and so on—for a happiness that will last. With each quest for ultimate happiness, one is left dissatisfied, frustrated, and jaded. The Christian is not destined for such short-lived, inferior happiness. Why? Because the believer has been made to know and enjoy God forever, the true source, and only source, of joy unending. The reason God can offer us joy that cannot rust or fade away is that *he himself* is the one we enjoy. Christianity is not about coming to God so that he can direct us to something or someone better than himself, some other thing that will make us ultimately happy. No, *God himself* is the one in whom all our joy, pleasure, and happiness are found. If we are made for infinite happiness—and that is what every person in the world is groping after—then the only place one will find it is in the one, and only one, who is infinite. As Augustine prays, "You stir man to take pleasure in praising you, because you have made us for yourself, and our heart is restless until it rests in you."[57]

John Piper has spent a lifetime proclaiming this truth. "God is most glorified in us when we are most satisfied in him."[58] His point is not new, as seen in Augustine's prayer above. The Westminster Shorter Catechism—a product of the Puritan era—says something similar in its opening question: "What is the chief and highest end of man? Man's chief and highest end is to glorify God, and fully to enjoy him for ever." Piper has commented that he would only slightly tweak that sentence, changing "and" to "by": "Man's chief end is to glorify God *by* enjoying him forever."[59] I doubt the authors of the catechism would have disagreed; that is their point. We were made to glorify God, for he is the most glorious, infinite being (see chap. 3), and the way we most glorify God is by enjoying who he is, because he is the most infinite, glorious being that exists.

This side of heaven, we struggle to live this way. We are spiritually nearsighted. Seduced by the pleasures of this world, we fail to see past immediate gratification to the *eternal* pleasure found in the Infinite One himself. In view of the "unblushing promises of reward and the staggering nature of the rewards promised in the Gospels," laments C. S. Lewis, our "Lord finds our desires not too strong, but too weak." How so? "We are half-hearted creatures fooling about with drink and sex and ambition when infinite joy is offered us, like an ignorant child who wants to go on making mud pies in a slum because he cannot imagine what is meant by the offer of a holiday at the sea. We are far too easily pleased."[60]

Everything we enjoy in this world is dissatisfying for two reasons: (1) it doesn't last but is short-lived, and (2) the object itself does not prove ultimately satisfying but falls short in some way. God defies both. Since he is an eternal being, enjoyment of God will never cease. Since he is an infinitely beautiful, majestic, and glorious being, enjoyment of God will prove more than we could ever take in. If we think about God's being only in comparison with objects in this world, we struggle to understand how both of these truths can be true. "How can I spend eternity enjoying God? Won't that get old?" No, it never will. Why? Because each attribute of God is infinite. His love is an infinite love, his grace an infinite grace, his holiness an infinite holiness, his power an infinite power. It will take an eternity to enjoy God, because he is an infinitely grandiose being. "Happiness cannot perish as long as God lives," says Charnock. "He is the first and the last; the first of all delights, nothing before him; the last of all pleasures, nothing beyond him." But will our delight in this God grow stale? "The enjoyment of God will be as fresh and glorious after many ages, as it was at first. God is eternal, and eternity knows no change; there will then be the fullest possession without any decay in the object enjoyed."[61]

God's immutability should inform how we perceive eternity. If God is unchanging, then the joy, the happiness, the satisfaction that we experience in eternity will never be in jeopardy. Our happiness will be forever precisely because the object of our eternal happiness does not, indeed cannot, change. How incredibly different this experience will be from how our desires operate in this world.[62]

As much as we enjoy turning through an old photo album, as we do so our heart longs once again for an experience that is now no more. On the other hand, glancing at the calendar on your refrigerator brings to mind a future meeting with someone special, or perhaps a much-needed vacation. Naturally, the joy of what lies ahead cannot come soon enough, and we pray nothing gets in the way of that future joy.

Our enjoyment of God for eternity will be altogether different. We will enjoy him without the threat of such joy passing by and being no more. We will desire him but without the fear that it may never come. The happiness of eternity will be as if it is always present, because the eternal God we enjoy does not change, and the dispensing of his glory never wanes. "Time is fluid, but eternity is stable; and after many ages the joys will be as savory and satisfying as if they had been but that moment first tasted by our hungry appetites."[63] God possesses the "variety to increase" our "delights" as well as "eternity to perpetuate them." God is more like a fountain than a cistern. Cisterns only contain so much water, but the water never stops gushing over from a fountain.[64] He is a fountain of eternal delight.

How foolish it is to place our delight in that which is transient, momentarily satisfying, when the greatest pleasure, the supreme delight our souls were made to enjoy, is not only offered to us through Christ but lasts for eternity. The eternity of God should rebuke us for thinking that something impermanent, and only temporarily sufficient, could be better than a God who is eternally fulfilling.[65] Not only is he everlasting in comparison to earthly pleasures that fade away, but our God is incomparably better, someone than whom none greater can be conceived. For David, this resulted in one passion:

> One thing have I asked of the Lord,
>   that I will seek after:
> that I may dwell in the house of the Lord
>   all the days of my life,
> to gaze upon the beauty of the Lord. (Ps. 27:4)

9

Is God Bound by Space?

Omnipresence

I will fear no evil,
for you are with me.

PSALM 23:4

"Behold, the virgin shall conceive and bear a son,
and they shall call his name Immanuel"
(which means, God with us).

MATTHEW 1:23

O whole and blessed truth, how far You are from me who am so
close to You! How distant You are from my sight while I am so
present to Your sight! You are wholly present everywhere and I
do not see You. In You I move and in You I have my being and
I cannot come near to You. You are within me and around me
and I do not have any experience of You.

ANSELM, *Proslogion*

The Highest Heaven Cannot Contain You

Solomon had every reason to be proud of himself. Building the temple was one of the greatest achievements in the history of Israel. This temple was to be the very dwelling place of God with his people. Meticulous detail went into every piece of furniture, each being embedded with symbolism. At its inception, the ark of the covenant itself was placed in the temple, though within the Most Holy Place "underneath the wings of the cherubim" (1 Kings 8:6). When the "priests came out of the Holy Place, a cloud filled the house of the LORD, so that the priests could not stand to minister because of the cloud, for the glory of the LORD filled the house of the LORD" (8:10–11).

But why did Solomon build this temple to begin with? Solomon explains: "The LORD has said that he would dwell in thick darkness. I have indeed built you an exalted house, a place for you to dwell in forever" (8:12–13). Solomon then stands before the altar with Israel present, lifts up his hands to heaven, and exclaims that there is no God like his God, neither "in heaven above or on earth beneath, keeping covenant and showing steadfast love to your servants who walk before you with all their heart" (8:23). Solomon goes on to praise the Lord for keeping his covenant with his father David and asks that this steadfast commitment to the covenant continue with him.

Just imagine: Solomon has built a house for God! Here is the home where God will dwell amid his people. If there were ever a point at which Solomon would be tempted to think much of himself, it would be now. Yet building the Lord a temple has the exact opposite effect. Solomon is sobered by the fact that his God is *not* a God who can be contained. He asks, "But will God indeed dwell on the earth?" Then comes Solomon's theologically packed answer: "Behold, heaven and the highest heaven cannot contain you; how much less this house that I have built!" (8:27). Notice Solomon's logic: not even heaven itself can contain God, so how much less this house built by human hands?

We feel the weight of Solomon's own inadequacy when we read a parallel response in 2 Chronicles 2:6: "But who is able to build him a house, since heaven, even highest heaven, cannot contain him? Who am I to build a house for him, except as a place to make offerings before him?" God may choose to make his presence known in a special way to his covenant people (more on this in a minute), but it is never safe to assume that the manifestation of his presence at any one place to any one person is the containment of his being to that place. This God defies the limitations of space entirely. Unlike his finite creatures, the Creator is not limited to a "somewhere."[1] "God, because infinite, fills all," says Stephen Charnock, "yet so as not to be contained in them. He is from the height of the heavens to the bottom of the deeps, in every point of the world, and in the whole circle of it, yet not limited by it, but beyond it."[2] The reason why is simple: God does not have a body.

God without a Body: Nonspatial Ubiquity

"Incorporeal." It's an old-fashioned word few use today. Applied to God, it means God is without a body. Not only is it true that he is a God without parts (simplicity), but he is a God without physical parts (incorporeal). His being cannot be identified with matter.

Having no material composition sets the God of Christianity apart from the gods of many other religions. At the beginning of Israel's journey, Moses continually warns the people against idolatry. His rationale has everything to do with God's incorporeal nature: "Watch yourselves very carefully. Since you saw no form on the day that the LORD spoke to you at Horeb out of the midst of the fire, beware lest you act corruptly by making a carved image for yourselves, in the form of any figure" (Deut. 4:15–16). Here is the fundamental difference between the one true God and the gods of the surrounding nations, nations tempting Israel with gods they can see.

What Israel continually fails to realize, however, is that the gods with bodies are gods limited in every way. You can see them, but they cannot talk, they cannot listen, and they certainly cannot defy the limits of whatever space the hands that made them have placed them in. Material gods are materially bound.

But not the God of Israel. He has no body. He has no parts.

If God is not composed of physical parts, then he is *not* a spatial being. Just as he is *atemporal* (timeless) so is he *aspatial* (spaceless). That one letter *a* placed in front of the word "spatial" indicates he is *not* a being located in space, nor does he have spatial dimensions.

We, as creatures, are physical beings, severely limited by space. Our presence fills one location and only one location at a time. But these spatial limitations do not apply to the Creator. Space cannot restrict, confine, or bind one who is without material form. God is spirit, invisible to our sight, incapable of being touched (Exod. 33:20, 23; John 1:18; 6:46; Rom. 1:20; Col. 1:15; 1 Tim. 1:17; 6:16; 1 John 4:12, 20).

That does not mean, however, that God is uninvolved with those in time and space. Being nonspatial enables him simultaneously to be everywhere with his whole being. As we will see, he is a God who is everywhere and cannot be limited by anywhere.[3] We might label this "nonspatial ubiquity," ubiquity meaning he is everywhere present.[4]

No Single "Somewhere": Infinite Essence, Infinite Presence

Like many of the other attributes, God's defiance of spatial categories stems from his infinite nature. We finite human beings always exist *somewhere*; anybody with a body exists somewhere. That intrinsically defines who we are and what we can (and cannot) do. Not only can our life span be measured by time, but our location can be measured by space. I am six feet two, weigh around 190 pounds (pure muscle, of course), and can usually be found occupying one of a few different spaces: my writing desk, my leather recliner to cheer on the Los Angeles Lakers, or the dinner table to enjoy my family. As much as I love all three of those spaces, I can occupy only one of them at a time—unless, of course, my family decides dinner needs to be eaten while we watch a Laker's game. But even then, I still exist in only one "somewhere," and that somewhere is very predictable as a result.

Herman Bavinck makes this point more scientifically: "Whatever is finite exists in space. Its limited character carries with it the concept of a 'somewhere.' It is always somewhere and not at the same time somewhere else. Regardless of all measurable distance from other points (extrinsic location), an intrinsic location is characteristic of all creatures, not excepting even spiritual being." Bavinck admits that "steam and electricity" may expand our understanding of space—and in 2019 perhaps we could say "internet and smartphones"—and yet, "a limited and local existence will nevertheless always be characteristic for all creatures."[5]

God, as the Creator, escapes this creaturely limitation, nor is it even possible for him, as one who is infinite, to be limited in this way. As one who has an "infinite essence," so must he also have an "infinite presence." The latter follows from the former, for if God is infinite in his essence, then it is impossible for him to be demarcated by or contained within a finite space. While finite creatures, like you and me, are bounded by space, the same cannot be said of an infinite being.[6]

Does this mean, then, that God is absent from this world, as is the case in some forms of deism? No, not at all. God transcends space, but it's only because he is by nature not a spatial, physical being that he is able to be wholly present everywhere (omnipresence). That adverb "wholly" is essential. It is possible for light and air to be spread out in different spaces all at once, an image we will return to shortly.[7] But that is not a limitation for a God without a body.

No Diffusion, Division, or Mixture: Simple Omnipresence

There are several errors to avoid when speaking about divine omnipresence.

First, by omnipresence we do not mean that God simply stretches himself out. That would imply some type of finitude, as if God could be measured, increasing or decreasing. With air and light there is a type of diffusion that takes place.[8] But there is no diffusion of essence with God. Instead, he is present with his *whole* being everywhere simultaneously.[9] No one place has part of God. Remember, God is simple and has no parts. So he is not spatially divisible.[10] Nor does one place contain all of God. He is not spatially contained. We must be on guard from thinking that God is stretched out, *diffused* across numerous spaces, or that God's being is *divided*, divvied up into a variety of spaces. Let's consider the dangers of each.

If God were omnipresent by diffusion, then God would "fill" a place like any bodily object would. "Bodies fill places by excluding other bodies from where they are," Thomas Aquinas explains. Not so with God. "God's presence in a place does not exclude the presence there of other things. Rather, God fills all places by giving existence to everything occupying them."[11]

If God were omnipresent by means of his essence being divided up, God would be multiplied.[12] Omnipresence wrongly defined and applied destroys God's simplicity. If part of God "is in every time and place and part is not," then God "has parts, which is false." He does not "partly exist in every time and place."[13]

By contrast, God remains one, undivided, and simple, present everywhere and always with his *whole* being. We should not think, Charnock warns, that "God is here or there, but only a part of God here, and a part of God there." Rather, this God "is as much a god in the beneath as in heaven above (Deut. [4:39]); entirely in all places, not by scraps and fragments of his essence."[14] Simplicity and a correct understanding of God's omnipresence go hand in hand.

[margin handwritten note: A part of God filling form place]

Older generations of Christians made this point by ascribing *immensity* to God quickly on the heels of their affirmation of his infinitude. It is because God is infinite, without limitations, that he must be immense, unrestricted by space, transcending all space, able to be present in all places at once with his whole being.[15] "As no place can be without God, so no place can compass and contain him."[16]

Time and Space in Relation to an Infinite God

Eternity	Immensity
No duration of God's essence: endless, infinite	No diffusion of God's essence: boundless
God not measured by time but timelessly eternal	God not bound or contained by place/space but nonspatial
God is always and always is (eternal)	God is everywhere (omnipresence, ubiquity)

Note: Some of the phrases in this chart come from Charnock, *Existence and Attributes of God*, 1:281.

Second, by omnipresence we do *not* mean there is any *mixture* between God and his creation. Pantheism is the view that God is the universe and the universe is God. They are one and the same. Advocates believe only such synonymy can make God truly present. Actually, by mixing God with the creation, they lose God altogether, for he is no different than the creation. Ironically, divine presence is lost whenever the Creator has been swallowed by his creation. The root of the problem is a neglect of divine simplicity. Mixing him assumes he has parts to mix.

God, however, is "most simple"; his essence is "not mixed with anything." Yes, he is *everywhere* present, but we should not go so far as to think that he becomes *everything* in the process. Such a process would spell disaster, dividing God's being as if he were to be meshed with the creation, absorbed by the creature, dissolving the Creator-creature distinction. God may be present with the world, but he does not become one with the world.[17] The "finite and infinite cannot be joined."[18] Consider the way the sun produces light. The light illumines a room, but that does not mean the light becomes the air.[19] The two remain distinct. Likewise with the Creator and his creation.

To conclude that God's omnipresence stems from his *infinite* nature is also to conclude that it is the necessary outcome of a *perfect* being. As Charnock reminds us, "No perfection is wanting to God; but an unbounded essence is a perfection; a limited one is an imperfection." God's ability to be everywhere present with his whole being makes him a superior being to one who is confined to one place. "What is everywhere, is more perfect than that which is bounded in some narrow confines. . . . Where anything hath limitation, it hath some defect in being; and therefore, if God were confined or concluded, he would be as good as nothing in regard of infiniteness."[20] If God is to be someone than whom none greater can be conceived, then he cannot be spatially confined.

King Always, King Everywhere: Omnipresent Power, Omnipotent Presence

Divine omnipresence is not only a natural entailment of God's infinite nature, but it is also inseparably connected to his omnipotent nature. *If our infinite God is omnipresent, then his power is extensive, his kingdom rule pervasive, and his sovereignty comprehensive.*

Consider what would happen if God were not omnipresent. If his presence were bounded to one place, restricted and confined, so too would his power become impotent, handicapped to one place at one time. "If God did not fill the whole world, he would be determined to some place, and excluded from others; and so his substance would have bounds and limits, and then something might be conceived greater than God."[21] So again, God's *perfect* being is at stake. To delimit his presence is to handcuff his power, which makes him less than perfect. No longer is he the greatest being; now he has weaknesses, unable to be everywhere by his power.

Yet Scripture teaches us, says Charnock, that "where God works by his power, he is present in his essence; because his power and his essence cannot be separated. . . . His essence cannot be severed from his power, nor his power from his essence." As the "power of God is everywhere, so is his essence." Should we "confine him to a place" we ultimately "measure his essence" and "confine his actions," constraining his power.[22]

God's power is "no less infinite" than his essence, and his essence no less infinite than his power, for the two are one and the same (simplicity).[23] Where he is, there his power is present. *His power is an omnipresent power, and his presence, an omnipotent presence. The two cannot, and must not, be divorced from one another.* "Where the power of God is, his essence is, because they are inseparable; and so this omnipresence ariseth from the simplicity of the nature of God; the more vast anything is, the less confined."[24]

Our King of kings is wherever he has power to act, and we know from Scripture that there is nowhere off-limits to God's rule and reign. If God's "eternity renders him King alway[s], so his immensity renders him King everywhere."[25]

The Island with a Motor Boat: Immutable Omnipresence

God's power is not the only attribute interconnected with omnipresence; so is his immutability (God does not change). And it's a good thing it is, because an omnipotent omnipresence would mean little (and could be scary) if it were susceptible to change.

Follow this logic: If God were confined to one place at a time, then he would have to move from one place to another, as opposed to his whole essence being present everywhere at once. But if God moved—something we do as physical, finite beings—then he would be a God who changes, one who is mutable. He would move to a new place where he was not present previously. "He would not fill heaven and earth at once, but successively."[26] He would be little better than us finite beings who change as we move and move as we change. Fixed to one place, we must change in order to occupy another place. Applied to God, this principle would mean he would have to change whenever he became mobile.

But doesn't Scripture describe God as one who does move from one place to another? Was not Solomon's hope that God would descend on the temple? And is it not a basic Christian truth that God is in heaven? Yes, yes, and yes. However, in none of these biblical descriptions do we ever see the biblical author or the divine author say that God's presence is confined to one place. Heaven "is the court of his majestical presence, but not the prison of his essence."[27] As we will see shortly, while God may be omnipresent, his presence with certain people and in certain places may take on a meaning that is special and unique. While he is present with all people, he is present with *his* people covenantally, to save and redeem, to justify and sanctify.[28] While his presence in heaven is bliss, hell cannot lock him out simply because he is not there to bless. God is present everywhere equally, even if he is present somewhere uniquely. He can be in both places equally though differently due to the immensity of his essence.[29]

To clarify, while God's essence is everywhere present, the effects of his actions in relation to humankind are felt differently. He operates in a diversity of ways but always as the same essence.[30] So yes, he may be described as "near" or "far," but that is only to describe the manner and effect of his presence, not his essence itself. When God is described as "far," could it be that the biblical author is trying to communicate that God is exercising his wrath, punishing the wicked, acting as judge, dispensing his justice? "When he comes to punish, it notes not the approach of his essence, but the stroke of his justice." When God is described as "near," could the biblical author be communicating that God's blessing has been given? "When he comes to benefit, it is not by a new access of his essence, but an efflux of his grace." Charnock's summary is right on target: "He departs from us when he leaves us to the frowns of his justice; he comes to us when he encircles us in the arms of his mercy; but he was equally present with us in both dispensations, in regard of his essence."[31]

Consider the way you approach land in a boat.[32] Suppose you were in a motor boat, and it broke down one hundred yards from an island. The people on the island are good people, so they attach a rope to your boat, head back to the island, and pull you in. Forgive me asking an obvious question, but what is it that is moving? From the vantage point of the boat, it appears to be the shore. It is coming closer and closer with each passing minute. However, in reality the shore remains fixed; it is the boat that is moving as it floats to the shore. So it is with God. He remains that island, an immutable rock. Yet such a rock anchors the boat, so that it might be drawn into the safety of the rock in the midst of a storm. "God's drawing near to us is not so much his coming to us, but his drawing us to him."[33] *Relates to our language of God.*

Two Types of Divine Presence

As hinted at already, omnipresence has much to do with divine providence. God is everywhere present as the Creator, sustainer, and governor of the universe. Charnock helps us see the many ways God's presence is manifested providentially through the other attributes:

Authority: "He is present with all things by his authority, because all things are subject to him."

Power: He is present "by his power, because all things are sustained by him."

Knowledge: He is present "by his knowledge, because all things are naked before him."[34]

Authority, power, knowledge—each is critical. God "is present in the world, as a king is in all parts of his kingdom regally present: providentially present with all, since his care extends to the meanest of his creatures. His power reacheth all, and his knowledge pierceth all."[35] As king, in other words, God is present over all, for his kingdom rule and reign is over all (authority). This king is clearly powerful, for that which he reigns he also sustains. Nor can we forget his knowledge; this king is not only present to sustain and govern, but he does so as one who knows all things. None of his subjects are strangers, for he knows them by name. Everything is "naked before him."

Omnipresence, when tied to providence, sets the Christian God apart from the deistic God. Deism was popular during the Enlightenment period (seventeenth–eighteenth centuries), and it continues to be influential among the masses to this day.[36] Deism teaches that God created the world but then took a step back, intentionally having little to no providential involvement with the world thereafter. In short, the deistic God is absent; providence is an unnecessary doctrine. Or if providence is affirmed in a limited way, supernatural intervention is out of the question.[37]

But the Christian God, the God of the Bible, is actively involved, not only creating his world but preserving and governing the world according to his divine purpose and plan. Such providential involvement requires his presence. As Paul says to the philosophers at the Areopagus, quoting one of their own poets, God "is actually not far from each one of us, for 'In him we live and move and have our being'" (Acts 17:27–28).[38]

Is God's presence merely providential? Or is this king also present with his people in a way that is unique, special, gracious, and intimately supernatural? And if so, is he present in different ways with different people? Is he with the righteous in a way he is not with the wicked? Is there a special sense in which he is present with his covenant people that cannot be said of those who are not his covenant people?

The answer to these questions is yes. As one church father said, "God is in everything in a general way by his presence, power and substance, but we say that he is in some things in a more intimate way by grace."[39] It is appropriate to distinguish between God's *essential* presence and his *gracious* presence. His "essential presence maintains our beings," observes Charnock, "but his gracious presence confers and continues a happiness."[40] His essential presence sustains, preserves, and governs his creation, but his gracious presence regenerates, justifies, and sanctifies his chosen people.

What does God's gracious presence with his people look like?

Covenantal Presence

God's gracious, covenantal presence is immediately present at creation. The first couple is said to walk with the Lord in the garden in the cool of the day (Gen. 3:8). The garden is a temple for God's presence, and Adam is entrusted as its keeper, a priest exercising dominion as God's representative. Sadly, Adam fails to guard God's temple from a deceptive intruder, the serpent, who questions the credibility and authority of Adam's Creator. The result of Adam's sin is not only death but separation from God. Adam and Eve are cast out of the garden, and cherubim with a flaming sword deny access to the tree of life. Nevertheless, God is gracious, promising an offspring from Eve that will one day crush the serpent (3:15).

The fruit of that promise matures when God cuts a covenant with Abraham, the man through whom the promised offspring will come. To ensure the promise, animals are cut in half and God—symbolized by a smoking fire pot—walks between the bloody carcasses (Gen. 15). By passing between the carcasses, God is declaring to Abraham that if he (God, that is) breaks this covenant, he will become like these dismembered animals.

The covenant presence Abraham experiences is known by Joseph as well. Just when it seems as though the future of Abraham's offspring is in jeopardy, threatened by famine, God raises up Joseph to save the lineage of Abraham. Countless times in Joseph's life it seems as though all is lost; he is sold into slavery only to spend years in prison. But repeatedly we read that the Lord is with Joseph, and ultimately God's presence will redeem not only Joseph and his family but all Egypt. In everything Joseph does, all can see that God is with him to bless him (Gen. 39:2–3).

God's redeeming presence is most memorably felt in the exodus of Israel. Fleeing for his life after murdering an Egyptian, Moses encounters the holiness of God's presence in the burning bush as God reveals his name and plan for the children of Abraham. Moses is afraid and overwhelmed by the task, but God promises to go with Moses to liberate Israel from slavery and to bring God's people into the land he promised Abraham (Exod. 3). Never has Israel seen God's presence so powerfully as when God thunders plague after plague, only to lead his people out of Egypt by day in a pillar of cloud and by night in a pillar of fire (13:21).

Yet this pillar of cloud can also be an object of great wrath. Moses speaks with God face-to-face to receive the law of the covenant at Sinai, but the mountain is "wrapped in smoke because the LORD ha[s] descended on it in fire" (19:18). So heavy is the smoke, so loud the thunder, and so bright the lightning that the mountain trembles greatly (19:18). The Lord "come[s] down on Mount Sinai in the sight of all the people" (19:11), but Israel is not to go up the mountain lest she be put to death. One would think that such an experience would strike fear into the hearts of the people. Not so. As Moses talks with God, Israel commits idolatry, inviting God's wrath, which would have destroyed the people if Moses had not interceded (Exod. 33). While Israel barely avoids total annihilation thanks to God's mercy, God announces he will not go with Israel into the land of promise. But Moses knows that unless God is present with his people, the nations will not know that God has had favor on this people (33:16). "My presence," says the Lord in response, "will go with you, and I will give you rest" (33:14).

Unfortunately, Sinai is not the last time Israel presumes upon God's holy presence. Aaron, Moses's right-hand man, is consecrated by the Lord, along with his two sons, Nadab and Abihu, in front of all Israel at the entrance to the tent of meeting (the tabernacle). Through a bloody sacrifice of a bull, Aaron and his sons are atoned for (Lev. 8:34), qualifying them to then discharge the duty of a priest, a duty that involves mediating atonement on behalf of a sinful people so that they can remain in covenant with a holy God (9:7). When atonement is made, God's acceptance is communicated whenever the glory of the Lord appears to the people and fire comes out from before the Lord to consume the burnt offering (9:23–24).

Everything goes terribly wrong when Nadab and Abihu offer "unauthorized fire before the LORD, which he had not commanded them" (Lev. 10:1). Instantly fire from the Lord consumes them. There is reason to believe that Aaron's sons may have been drunk and, worse yet, have dared to enter into the Most Holy Place (see 16:1–2). A curtain separates the Holy Place from the Most Holy Place, where the presence of God dwells. Who knows whether Nadab and Abihu made it in; they may have been struck dead the moment they touched the curtain! But God's message is loud and clear: "Among those who are near me I will be sanctified, and before all the people I will be glorified" (10:3).

Just on the heels of this death sentence, Leviticus 16 opens with a somber tone, introducing the Day of Atonement. On this day, the Lord will appear in a cloud just over the mercy seat. Aaron is to come into the Most Holy Place and perform several offerings, one of which includes sprinkling the blood of a bull on the mercy seat. The blood of this sacrifice and other sacrifices are the means by which Aaron will make atonement for the people. They are an unclean people, and due to their transgressions they cannot enter into the presence of God, or their fate would be the same as that of Aaron's sons. But if the high priest enters the presence of God on the Day of Atonement and makes a sacrifice on their behalf, God's wrath against their sin will be appeased and satisfied. In turn, they will be at peace with their covenant Lord. Holy is the Lord, and holy must his people be to dwell with him. And yet, these sacrifices, as necessary as they may be, are but a temporary fix, a shadow, a type of the final sacrifice to come. What is needed is a sacrifice that will once and forever deal with sin so that humanity's communion with God can be forever healed. Only then will Eden be restored.

Generally speaking, God's presence in the Old Testament is not only limited (to the tabernacle, as seen above), but it is sporadic; the Spirit of God is said to come upon certain leaders for special occasions, not necessarily upon all Israel at all times. In Numbers 11 the elders of Israel are gathered before the Lord in the tent when the Lord comes down in the cloud and takes "some of the Spirit" that is on Moses and places it on the elders (11:17). Receiving the Spirit, these elders prophesy. Unexpectedly, two other men have the "Spirit rest on them," though they have "not gone out to the tent." They too prophesy, though they are "in the camp" (11:26). Worried observers report the news to Moses, expecting him to be angry. But Moses responds, "Would that all the Lord's people were prophets, that the Lord would put his Spirit on them!" (11:29). Moses longs for a day, a day he does not see, when the Spirit of the Lord will rest upon every covenant member permanently.

Prophets like Ezekiel and Joel likewise long for this day. The Lord promises through the prophet Ezekiel that one day he will give his people a new heart. A "new spirit I will put within you" (36:26). "I will put my Spirit within you, and cause you to walk in my statutes and be careful to obey my rules" (36:27). The Lord also promises through the prophet Joel, "I will pour out my Spirit on all flesh," and "your sons and your daughters shall prophesy" (2:28).

Immanuel, God with Us

The New Testament begins with this great prophetic hope. What is astounding about the start of the New Testament is that God

176

will come through on his prophetic promises not by manifesting his presence through the temple or only with a select, chosen leader like Moses. No, God himself will step down from the heavens. How is this possible, when we know God has no body and is not in time or space? The answer is remarkable: the Father sends his Son to become incarnate.

At the start of his Gospel, John calls Jesus the Word and says this Word is eternal, not only eternally with the Father but the one we can rightly label God himself (see 1:1–2). Here is the essence of the incarnation in all its mystery: the eternal, divine Word "became flesh and *dwelt among us*, and we have seen his glory, glory as of the only Son from the Father, full of grace and truth" (1:14). Previously we saw that not even Moses could see the glory of God; yet John says he has seen it.

Given the story line so far, your jaw should hit the floor at this point. Deity dwelling with humanity? Unbelievable. Surely God must have an incredibly significant reason why he would stoop so low as to become incarnate, even dwell among a sinful people. And he does. The reason is in verse 14: this Son from the Father is "full of grace and truth." "For from his fullness we have all received, grace upon grace" (1:16). Moses gave us law, but Jesus, the Christ, the Messiah, "became flesh and dwelt among us" in order to give us "grace and truth" (1:14). Here, in the person of Christ, is the redemption Adam, Abraham, Moses, and David longed desperately to see and never saw. Yet now that the Word has come, says John, we have seen him, and through him we have received grace to be saved. "No one has ever seen God," yet "the only God, who is at the Father's side, he has made him known" (1:18). Could there be a greater or more intimate manifestation of divine presence than the Son himself dwelling with us?

Matthew makes a similar point at the start of his Gospel. Describing the birth of Jesus, Matthew highlights the angel's appearance to Joseph. Joseph need not fear to take Mary as his wife, "for that which is conceived in her is from the Holy Spirit" (1:20).

The child's name, the angel says, will be Jesus, "for he will save his people from their sins" (1:21). Matthew then quotes the Old Testament, Isaiah 7:14 to be exact:

> Behold, the virgin shall conceive and bear a son,
>   and they shall call his name Immanuel. (Matt. 1:23a)

What does this name mean? It means "God with us" (1:23b).

Here is the essence of the gospel; here is the nucleus of Christianity. And it has everything to do with the presence of God. Our sins will be taken away once and forever only if the Son of God himself becomes incarnate, dwells among us, and—as Matthew's narrative will reveal—is put to death by us. The Day of Atonement has finally found its fulfillment.

Temples of the Holy Spirit

"Hold on," you might object. "I know my Bible well enough to remember that Jesus not only rose from the dead but also ascended into heaven. And Jesus did not stay with his people; he left them. So how can God's presence remain with us still?"

Now that's a great question, and one that worried the disciples too. Scared to death at the thought that Jesus would leave them, the disciples are comforted by Jesus in John 14 as he tells them not to let their hearts be troubled. Yes, he will go, but he will go to prepare a place for them in his Father's house. In the meantime, he will "ask the Father," and the Father will give them "another Helper, to be with [them] forever, even the Spirit of truth" (14:16–17). The world cannot receive the Spirit "because it neither sees him nor knows him." Not so for believers. "You know him, for he dwells with you and will be in you" (14:17). Jesus has not left believers as orphans; the Spirit comes not only to make us alive (regeneration / new birth) but to cause us to walk in newness of life (Rom. 6:4).

Jesus's promises are fulfilled at Pentecost in Acts 2. Before he ascended into the heavens, Jesus told his disciples to wait for the Spirit. With unprecedented force, the Spirit now descends on them as tongues of fire, and they start speaking in the tongues of the nations, bearing witness to the crucified and risen Messiah. When onlookers wonder what is happening, it's no surprise that Peter explains everything by quoting Joel 2. With redemption accomplished, the Spirit has now come to apply what Christ has purchased to those who believe.

The ramifications for those who believe today are many. Considering the Spirit's mission, Paul can say that Christians are temples of the Holy Spirit (1 Cor. 6:19). To those Christians taking this honor with less seriousness than they should, Paul issues a warning: "If anyone destroys God's temple, God will destroy him. For God's temple is holy, and you are that temple" (3:17; cf. 6:19). In the Old Testament, the Israelite cannot enter into the Most Holy Place, that inner sanctuary of the tabernacle and temple. A massive curtain separates Israel from that inner sanctuary. But when Jesus, the true temple of God (John 2:19–22), is crucified, the curtain of the temple is torn in two, from top to bottom (Matt. 27:50–51). There is but one person who can pass through this curtain in the Old Testament, the high priest, and even he can do so only on the Day of Atonement (Lev. 16). Yet now that our great high priest, Jesus Christ, has mediated for us, sacrificing himself in our place (Heb. 9), the curtain is torn by God himself, and a great multitude enters into the Most Holy Place; indeed, they become temples of the Most Holy One.

As those who are indwelt by the Holy Spirit (Rom. 8:9), we are being transformed by the Spirit into the image of Christ. Paul tells those in Rome that Christians were predestined by God for this very purpose (Rom. 8:26–29). Writing to the Corinthians, he similarly describes believers as those who are "being transformed into the same image from one degree of glory to another." Who does this transforming work? "This comes from the Lord who is the Spirit" (2 Cor. 3:18).

The Indwelling Spirit and the Christian Life

Not only does the Spirit indwell us, but he is renewing us more and more into the image of our Savior, who is the true image of God (2 Cor. 4:4). Genesis 3 has resulted in an image very much damaged by sin. In the Spirit's work of regeneration (i.e., being born again; John 3), that image has been awakened to its true intention. Yet, this side of heaven, the restoration of that image is a process. One day the Spirit's work of renewal will be complete, and "we shall be like him, because we shall see him as he is" (1 John 3:2). The indwelling of the Spirit, comments J. I. Packer, results not only in a "personal fellowship with Jesus," as well as "personal transformation of character into Jesus's likeness," but it also results in the "Spirit-given certainty of being loved, redeemed, and adopted through Christ into the Father's family" (cf. Rom. 8:17).[41] Not only does the Spirit's presence mark us off as a child of the Father, bought with the precious blood of Christ, but his presence also assures us that we are his child, adopted into his family, and safe in his hands until we one day see our Savior face-to-face.

Until that day, we are commanded to *be filled* with the Spirit. Do not "get drunk with wine," Paul commands the Ephesians, but instead "be filled with the Spirit" (Eph. 5:18). As those filled with the Spirit, we walk not according to sinful flesh but according to the Spirit (Rom. 8:4). We are those who keep in step with the Spirit (Gal. 5:16, 25). Step-by-step, with the Spirit's help and by the Spirit's sanctifying grace, we put sin to death (mortification) and put on the fruit of the Spirit (vivification; cf. Col. 3:5–17; Eph. 4:17–32), knowing that one day we will experience the presence of the Holy One uncorrupted, untainted by sin. John speaks of this forthcoming day, a day that will last for an eternity: "Behold, the dwelling place of God is with man. He will dwell with them, and they will be his people, and God himself will be with them as their God" (Rev. 21:3). On that day David's desire will take on new dimensions: "One thing I have asked of the LORD, that will I

Complete, not just emotional experience

seek after: that I may dwell in the house of the LORD all the days of my life, to gaze upon the beauty of the LORD and to inquire in his temple" (Ps. 27:4; cf. 23:6).

While we may long for that day with great expectation, we do not look for it as those who have not tasted of it here and now. While the banquet may be yet to come, already we have tasted its firstfruits. We may await the new heavens and earth, but on this earth, this side of glory, the Spirit is with us and within us. Every guarantee of that future day is assured in the ongoing, persistent, and unrelenting presence of the Spirit in our daily Christian lives. Every little victory over indwelling sin and every little desire to love others as Christ has loved us is a sign that the Spirit is at work in us, preparing us for that final day. The Spirit truly is a gift through whom we, as his little temples, enjoy fellowship with our Triune God (Matt. 12:28; 28:19–20; Mark 13:11; Luke 11:13; 12:12; 24:49; John 3:5–8; 14:26; 20:22).[42]

Drawing Near to God in All the Wrong Places

Regrettably, many today do not understand this. As Martin Luther experienced in the sixteenth century, some people take pilgrimages to Rome to somehow find God and make peace. But, says Bavinck, "going to God and seeking his face does not consist in making a pilgrimage but in self-abasement and repentance." The sinner's distance from God is due to sin, yet this distance is not "*locally* but *spiritually* (Isa. 59:2)." "To abandon God, to flee from him, as Cain did, is not a matter of local separation but of spiritual incompatibility."[43] As Augustine said, "It is not by location but by incongruity that a person is far from God."[44]

On the other hand, sinners "who seek him, find him—not far away, but in their immediate presence. For in him we live and move and have our being."[45] In Augustine's words, "To draw near to him is to become like him; to move away from him is to become unlike him."[46] The great doctor of grace, as Augustine was called, says in his *Expositions on the Psalms*: "No matter where you flee, he is there. You would flee from yourself, would you? Will you not follow yourself wherever you flee? But since there is One even more deeply inward than yourself, there is no place where you may flee from an angered God except to a God who is pacified. There is absolutely no place for you to flee to. Do you want to flee from him? Rather flee to him."[47] Augustine is right. Do not "flee from him. . . . Flee to him." Only then will God's omnipresent omniscience be a great comfort, for he will be present, no longer to judge and condemn, but to justify and sanctify, to bless and bring us into union with his Son. Only in Christ will his immensity be a gift of saving grace and his omnipresence a covenant blessing.[48]

10

Is God All-Powerful, All-Knowing, and All-Wise?

Omnipotence, Omniscience, and Omnisapience

The LORD is the everlasting God. . . .
He does not faint or grow weary. . . .
He gives power to the faint,
    and to him who has no might he increases strength.

ISAIAH 40:28–29

Ah, Lord GOD! It is you who have made the heavens and the earth by your great power and by your outstretched arm! Nothing is too hard for you.

JEREMIAH 32:17

God, being power, is not made up of things that are weak.

HILARY OF POITIERS, On the Trinity

Your thoughts of God are too human.

MARTIN LUTHER TO DESIDERIUS ERASMUS

The King Who Ate Grass

The history of the world is the story of the rise and fall of kings and nations, from Egypt's pharaohs, to Rome's caesars, to France's Napoleon. They were the most powerful rulers of their day, reigning over the most powerful territories of their day.

In the days of Daniel, that great man of God thrown into the den of lions, the most powerful man on earth was Nebuchadnezzar, king of Babylon. Nebuchadnezzar and his Babylonian army had besieged Jerusalem and taken Hebrews, like Daniel, into captivity.

Nebuchadnezzar was a ruler without competition, commanding his people as he pleased. At the snap of his fingers, heads literally rolled. He simply gave the order, and his armies would claim any kingdom on earth he desired. To those in his kingdom, Nebuchadnezzar was like one of the gods. Until one day, something happened that would change Nebuchadnezzar forever.

As Nebuchadnezzar is walking on the rooftop of his palace in Babylon, admiring the power, beauty, and extensiveness of his kingdom, he looks over his kingdom and says with unequivocal confidence, "Is not this great Babylon, which I have built by my mighty power as a royal residence and for the glory of my majesty?" (Dan. 4:30). At that moment, before the words even finish leaving his mouth, a voice from heaven says, "O King Nebuchadnezzar, to you it is spoken: The kingdom has departed from you, and you shall be driven from among men, and your dwelling shall be with the beasts of the field. And you shall be made to eat grass like an ox, and seven periods of time shall pass over you, until you know that the Most High rules the kingdom of men and gives it to whom he will" (4:31–32).

The next scene is a ghastly one. Instantly, this king, whose power is incomparable to that of anyone on earth, is no longer eating at the banqueting table in his palace but is on all fours eating grass like any other animal of the field. No longer is he clothed with royal robes, but now he is wet from the morning dew, having slept outside all night. Previously he was groomed, but now his hair is so long it could be mistaken for the feathers of an eagle. Before this moment, we may suppose Nebuchadnezzar has received the best manicures and pedicures the Babylonian fashion industry had to offer, but now his finger- and toenails are so grossly overgrown that they look like the claws of a bird. You get the picture: one minute Nebuchadnezzar is sipping wine from a gold chalice; the next he could be hunted as a wild beast of the forest. By anyone's assessment, Nebuchadnezzar has gone insane. What's happened?

What's happened is Nebuchadnezzar lost perspective and forgot who is Lord. He looked at his power and affluence through human eyes only. Through human eyes it looked as though he were the one who had built the most powerful nation on earth. If he had only looked at his kingdom from a God's-eye point of view, he never would have dreamed of boasting. By claiming he had built Babylon, Nebuchadnezzar was essentially removing God from his throne and taking his seat there instead. We often think that only happens deliberately, but Nebuchadnezzar's downfall is proof that it can happen simply by neglecting to acknowledge who is really King in this world.

Nebuchadnezzar learns the hard way that our King *is all-powerful (omnipotent), all-knowing (omniscient), and all-wise (omnisapient)*. These three attributes will be our focus as we not only define what each means but how each relates to the others, as well as many other attributes in God.

God Laughs

Psalm 33 gives us this God's-eye point of view. Calling all the "inhabitants of the world" to "stand in awe of him," the psalmist says God simply "spoke" and the universe "came to be" (33:8–9). At his word, the "heavens were made," and oceans were put in their place (33:6–7). What, then, is a nation in God's hand? Even the most powerful nation on earth is like a pebble in the hand of the Almighty. When the nations rage against him, "He who sits in the heavens laughs" (Ps. 2:4). He laughs! He is the Lord, the one who "brings the counsel of the nations to nothing" and "frustrates the plans of the peoples" (33:10). The prophet Isaiah puts everything into perspective:

> Behold, the nations are like a drop from a bucket,
>   and are accounted as the dust on the scales;
>   behold, he takes up the coastlands like fine dust.
>   (Isa. 40:15)

> All the nations are as nothing before him,
>   they are accounted by him as less than nothing and
>   emptiness. (40:17)

Nebuchadnezzar is but a drop of water in God's bucket, a speck of dust on the scales of eternity. Nebuchadnezzar thinks he has created his kingdom, but it has been God's doing all along, which is why his boasting is so offensive in the ears of the reigning King. To clarify who really possesses ultimate power, God simply speaks the word and Nebuchadnezzar goes from his palace rooftop to eating weeds in manure.

God, however, has mercy on Nebuchadnezzar. "At the end of the days"—a phrase that communicates that God is the one in charge, determining Nebuchadnezzar's destiny—this Babylonian king lifts his eyes to heaven, and his reason returns. God gives him back his sanity. Now Nebuchadnezzar recognizes who is the true King: "I blessed the Most High, and praised and honored him who lives forever,

> for his dominion is an everlasting dominion,
>   and his kingdom endures from generation to generation;
> all the inhabitants of the earth are accounted as nothing,
>   and he does according to his will among the host of
>   heaven
>   and among the inhabitants of the earth;

and none can stay his hand
or say to him, "What have you done?" (Dan. 4:34–35)

Those last lines are sobering. God's will cannot be thwarted. So invincible is his power that no one, not even the greatest king or nation on earth, can "stay his hand." No one, absolutely no one, has the right to question him, asking "What have you done?" He alone is Lord of heaven and earth; he does as he pleases; he answers to no one but himself. The story of Nebuchadnezzer can be summarized by Solomon, who says, the "king's heart is a stream of water in the hand of the LORD; he turns it wherever he will" (Prov. 21:1).

In my own theological journey, the story of Nebuchadnezzar was a game changer. It became obvious that whatever conclusions I came to, none of them could violate this one biblical fact: God is absolutely sovereign. The title "Lord" now took on a whole new meaning. His lordship is universal in its scope and exhaustively meticulous in its control, extending to events as colossal as the crucifixion of Jesus (Acts 2:23; 4:27–28) and as small as apparently "random" or "chance" occurrences, like the casting of lots in the story of Jonah (Jon. 1:7). The lot may be "cast into the lap, but its every decision is from the LORD" (Prov. 16:33). Such sovereignty had to mean that the God I worshiped is not merely powerful; he is all-powerful. He is omnipotent.

What's So Special about Power, Anyway? The Simplicity of Independent Power

It may seem odd to ask what is so special about God's power. Isn't power . . . well . . . power, plain and simple? Not really, actually. The type of power that characterizes the Creator is very different from the type of power that characterizes his creatures.

To understand why, we must first remember our doctrine of divine simplicity. God does not merely possess power or have power, he *is* all-powerful. His power and his essence are one and the same. It follows, then, that "simple power" is true of God, but it cannot be true of us, the creature.

Some of the greatest military leaders in American history are from the time of the Civil War. Ulysses S. Grant was a lion in the North, leading the Union to victory eventually, but it had to overcome a nearly impenetrable stance from Confederate generals like Robert E. Lee and Stonewall Jackson in the South. Regardless of which side each of these generals was on, they all had one thing in common: their strength in battle depended on the men they led. These generals might concoct the most brilliant plan of attack, they might procure the latest weaponry for their soldiers, but apart from the unique power each battalion brought to the battlefield, these generals were powerless. They were, in other words, reliant on others for their own power in warfare.

God's power, on the other hand, is dependent on no one. Here is where omnipotence and aseity meet up. Since God is self-sufficient, his power must be self-sufficient. Yet in light of simplicity, it's not just that God's power is independent, but it is independent because he *is* his power. It's not as if he must draw his power from elsewhere. He *is* all-powerful in and of himself. To put the point more technically, power "is originally and essentially in the nature of God, and not distinct from his essence."[1]

"Not so fast," you say. "Doesn't God act through others when he exercises his power?" He does. But he doesn't have to; he chooses to. So yes, God does use means to accomplish his will. He chooses to spread the good news of salvation through human proclamation; he chooses to sanctify his saints by means of the ordinances and the preached word; and he works providentially in the minute details of life through individuals who sometimes deny his very existence. And yet, if he wanted to, he could have chosen to dispense with means altogether. His power may work through others, but it is *intrinsic* to God himself, depending on no one. He is that powerful. Indeed, his essence is his power.[2]

A Distinction Too Powerful to Miss: Absolute and Ordinate Power

You've heard the saying "The devil is in the details." It's true. But it's also true that "God is in the details." I know, it's not quite as catchy as the first saying, but it's just as important. In theology, it's the details that matter, determining whether one is a heretic or a Bible-believing Christian. That is why theology is all about making distinctions.

One distinction too important and too powerful to miss is the distinction between God's absolute and ordinate power. *Absolute* power refers to God's ability to do all things, including those things that are possible for God but that God, for any variety of reasons, chooses not to do. In the medieval era, theologians like Duns Scotus abused God's absolute power. So high did Scotus elevate God's *will* that God's ability to do anything meant he could even sin! God's power had become arbitrary; his will turned into "absolute indifference."[3] But others saw this abuse for what it was, arguing instead that God's will cannot be divorced from his moral nature (a point I stressed in chap. 5).[4] Since God is simple, his will and nature are one, and since his nature is identical with all his perfections (holiness included), in no way can his will be set over against any attribute.[5]

God's *ordinate* power, on the other hand, refers to those things that God has ordained, decreed, and willed to do. God's ordinate power is not another power in God but is part of his absolute power.[6] It is only because he has the power to do anything and everything that he has the power to do those specific things he has ordained and willed to do.

Do you remember that nail-biting story about Peter cutting the ear off the servant of the high priest who tried to arrest Jesus? Jesus has been betrayed by Judas, and he is about to be seized, when Peter, seemingly out of nowhere, does what only seems right: he draws his sword to defend Jesus. What is fascinating for our purposes is not the bloody ear Peter chopped off but Jesus's response: "Put your sword back into its place. . . . Do you think that I cannot appeal to my Father, and he will at once send me more than twelve legions of angels? But how then should the Scriptures be fulfilled, that it must be so?" (Matt. 26:52–54). There you have it, God's absolute and ordinate power in two sentences.

As the Son of God, Jesus is all-powerful; if he said the word, he could have an army of angels at his side, sending his opponents running away terrified. But God has a greater purpose in mind, one he promised through his prophets in the Old Testament: the atoning death of his Son on the cross for the forgiveness of sins. So yes, Jesus could exercise such power, but it would then be at the expense of the Father's plan to redeem his people. Calling down the armies of heaven certainly would exhibit absolute power, but at this moment it is God's ordinate power that is necessary, and ironically, such omnipotence is powerfully displayed in the crucifixion and death of King Jesus.

Can God Create a Rock So Big He Cannot Lift It? Infinite Omnipotence

It would have been something to have been there, witnessing Peter cut off that ear, only to see Jesus pick it up and put it back on the man's head, as if it never happened. Remarkable. Jesus's response to Peter—that he could call down legions of angels—is an *aidemémoire*, an aid to our memory, that just beneath the surface of the events surrounding Jesus's ministry is the full force of divine omnipotence.

The full force of divine omnipotence resides in the infinite and eternal nature of God. Think about it: God's power is *infinite*; he is power in infinite measure. Plus, God's infinite power is *eternal* as well, meaning it will never wane. He can never stop being as omnipotent as he always has been and will be. To put it simply, what we mean when we say God is omnipotent is that there are no limitations to his being. Omnipotence, notice, is another way of saying our God is *infinite*.

"Hold on; no limitations, you say? Surely there are things God *cannot* do, right?" Can God create a rock so big he cannot lift it? Can an omnipotent God tell a lie? Can God create another being who is equally unlimited in power? Can an all-powerful God make an unmade person?[7] Can an eternal, infinite God die? These questions are meant to throw into doubt the infinite nature of God's power, exposing the fact that there are some things God *cannot* do, and therefore he cannot be *all*-powerful.

Unfortunately, we are looking at the picture upside down. We should be asking just the opposite: If God could do these things, would it be a display of impotence rather than omnipotence? Anselm corrects our misconception: "For he who can do these things can do what is not good for himself and what he ought not to do. And the more he can do these things, the more power adversity and perversity have over him and the less he has against them. He, therefore, who can do these things can do them not by power but by impotence."[8] By asking such questions we are so amused and impressed by our own cleverness that we fail to see just how contradictory our words have become. For God to do anything that would violate his other attributes does not complement his power but destroys it.

In a world in which *doing* things (doing everything) has become a sign of authority, we struggle to understand that there are situations in which *not doing something* is a far greater signifier of power. Joseph does not commit adultery with Potiphar's wife; Jesus does not command stones to turn into bread—these non-acts display the greatest degree of power. To have done any one of these would have been not powerful but weak, even sinful. Self-control is not a weakness but a sign that one is more powerful than those who cannot control themselves or their actions.

So it is with God. His power is just as powerfully manifested in what he cannot do as what he can do.

Can God Whisper a Secret He Cannot Know? Omnipotent Omniscience

There is, however, another puzzling conundrum that is a bit trickier to answer: Is it possible for God to create someone who can keep a secret even God himself cannot know?[9] If the answer is no, then how can God remain all-powerful? If the answer is yes, then how can God remain all-knowing?

Yet doesn't our doctrine of simplicity come to the rescue once again? Far from bifurcating attributes from one another, simplicity demands their unity. God's knowledge is an omnipotent knowledge, and his power is an omniscient power. Applied to the conundrum above, these truths mean that there is no choice to be made between knowledge and power.

The relation between power and knowledge is key. God's thought life is not like our thought life. Last time I checked, I cannot make objects levitate or buildings shift places merely with my mind. Yet God's knowledge is directly tied to his omnipotence. More precisely, his knowledge is his power, and his power is his knowledge (simplicity). He is omnisciently omnipotent and omnipotently omniscient, so that when he "thinks," things happen. His knowledge is causal, not merely contemplative, like ours. He is no spectator. He is the Creator, the one who determines all things. His knowledge is not *a posteriori*, like the creature's, as if he knew by observing, but his knowledge is *a priori*, meaning he observes what he already knows and has decreed eternally.[10]

Creator's Knowledge	Creature's Knowledge
a priori	*a posteriori*
Knowledge that is eternal and independent (*a se*) of others	Knowledge gained by observation; knowledge that is dependent on others.

The implications for God's creation and providential care are significant. First, the Creator's knowledge is *a priori* in the act of creation, which means one can never say God was somehow ignorant until he created. "It is true of all his creatures," says

[margin note: Arg on PJ 199, L 201]

Augustine, "both spiritual and corporeal, that he does not know them because they are, but that they are because he knows them. He was not ignorant of what he was going to create. So he created because he knew, he did not know because he had created."[11] God's omnipotent knowledge brought creation into existence out of nothing (*ex nihilo*). "By thinking He creates," says John of Damascus, "and, with the Word fulfilling and the Spirit perfecting, the object of His thought subsists."[12] John of Damascus also highlights the trinitarian nature of creation. It is the Triune God who, by thinking, creates, the Word fulfilling his Father's command and the Spirit perfecting what the Father has spoken through the Word, his Son.

Second, God's omnipotent knowledge not only brings about creation but also sustains creation. "God's omnipotence entails," observes Katherin Rogers, "that everything that has any sort of being at all, besides God, is kept in existence from moment to moment by God's causal power. Since God's power is His knowledge, whatever is *is* because it is being thought right now by God." Rogers warns, "To hypothesize something which exists on its own not immediately caused by God's thought is to deny God's omnipotence."[13] Notice the logic:

1. God is omnipotent, so everything exists by his causal power.
2. God is simple: his power is his knowledge; his knowledge is his power.
3. Therefore, all that exists only exists because God knows it to exist.

The conundrum—Can God create a secret he cannot know?—is flawed from the start because it assumes that God's thought life is irrelevant to his power. Not so. God's knowledge is not passive, merely receptive in what it knows. It is, rather, entirely proactive. As Augustine remarks, "God does not know all creatures . . . because they exist; they exist because he knows them."[14]

For that reason, your theological antennae should stand up whenever you hear someone attempt to limit or condition what God knows upon what human creatures do or think.[15] Not only is it the case that God knows *all* things past, present, and future, as Scripture confirms (e.g., Ps. 139:17–18; Isa. 41–48), but God's knowledge is *not dependent* on our knowledge, nor is it reliant on our actions, let alone our existence.[16] He knows all things, including all future things, because he has determined all things.[17] It is not the "world but the decrees" that "are the medium from which God knows all things."[18] His knowledge is unconditional, depending on no one. He is self-knowing, his omnipotent omniscience being rooted in his aseity. "He knows all things in and of and by himself."[19]

Neither does God learn as he goes, as if he grew or increased in knowledge. His knowledge is not becoming or evolving, which would undermine its infinite and eternal nature. To be eternal, as we've noted in chapter 8, means God experiences no succession of moments. But that also means God experiences no succession of *knowledge*. God's "vision of occurrences in time is not temporally conditioned," says Augustine.[20] What God knows now he has always known, and he has known it perfectly. His knowledge does not develop over time. Can you imagine if it did? How could we ever trust his decisions? Perhaps his decision today is based on knowledge that will improve tomorrow. Thankfully, such is not the case with an eternally omniscient God. He knows everything by one eternal act.[21] Everything is as if it were present to God, even things that have yet to occur in our experience, because he does not grow in his knowledge, knowing something that he did not know before. To be exact, there is no "before" or "future" with God. He knows everything timelessly, eternally.

His knowledge, in other words, is primary, always preceding who we are and what we know. If anything exists or acts, it exists and acts ultimately because of him (Acts 17:28). His knowledge is, in short, *creative* and *causal*. If some thing or person escaped the mind of God, then it would not exist in the first place.[22] Nothing exists independently of God's knowledge, lest his knowledge be robbed of its power.

In summary, we are yet again reminded of simplicity's importance: we may distinguish between God's power and knowledge, but never are they to be separated from one another.

God's Power Is Always and Everywhere

If simplicity means God's power and knowledge are inseparable, then so too does it mean that God's power is inseparable from his timeless eternity and omnipresence.

First, God is not merely powerful in the sense that he is powerful at one moment and then, later on, at another moment. As the timelessly eternal God, he is eternally powerful. His power cannot come and go, rise and fall. He is as powerful today as he was yesterday. He will be no more powerful tomorrow than he is today. His power is as long-standing as he is, for he *is* power. His power is as everlasting as his nature.

Second, his power is everywhere. It is omnipresent. His enemies cannot escape it no matter where they hide, and his friends rejoice that it is their shield in the darkest of valleys (Ps. 23). Omnipotently omnipresent, his power is wholly present in all places simultaneously.

If God's power is both eternal and omnipresent, it cannot be accidental (nonessential) to who he is and what he does. It is, rather, substantial and essential. Anselm explains the difference: God's "power is indeed not accidental," since he cannot "exist without power." God's power must be "substantial," for "it is either part of his essence or the very thing that is his whole essence." Yet it cannot be "part of his essence," Anselm qualifies, since God's essence is not "divided into parts." Power must be "the very thing that is his whole essence." And if it is his whole essence, then it is "always and everywhere, so whatever is God is everywhere and always."[23]

How Powerful Is God's Power?

If God's power is infinite, everywhere, and always, then there is no event in the history of humankind that escapes his say-so. Some in the history of the church have argued that though God is all-powerful, he chose to relinquish that power, voluntarily abstaining from acting in the world as he who is in control of all things. However, Scripture paints a completely different picture of God. As seen with Nebuchadnezzar, the God of the Bible is actively omnipotent not only in the overall, sweeping plan of history but even in the smallest details. There is no sphere, no matter how big or small, that is off-limits to God.

Consider salvation. At the opening of his letter to the Ephesians, Paul explains that "before the foundation of the world" God "chose us in him [Christ]" (1:4). In love "he predestined us for adoption . . . according to the purpose of his will, to the praise of his glorious grace" (1:5–6). Chosen, predestined—it could not be clearer who is the master architect behind our salvation.

One might object, "What guarantee can I have that I will receive this great inheritance?" The answer is found in verse 11: "In him we have obtained an inheritance, having been predestined according to the purpose of him who works all things according to the counsel of his will, so that we who were the first to hope in Christ might be to the praise of his glory." Did you miss it? Two words cannot be overlooked: "all things." Not some things, but all things. God works "all things according to the counsel of his will." If you are a child of God, then Paul has this to say to you: there is nothing, absolutely nothing that happens in your life that has not been planned by God before the foundation of the world. In every single aspect of your life God is at work to accomplish his eternal, unchanging, omnipotent, and gracious will. As Paul says elsewhere, "And we know that for those who love God *all things* work together for good, for those who are called according to his purpose" (Rom. 8:28).[24]

"Sure, God is in control of salvation, but what about all the evil in the world? Surely that falls outside his jurisdiction?" When Scripture says God is *Lord*, it means he is Lord especially over evil, which is, no doubt, the greatest threat to his kingdom. Evil cannot win if God is all-powerful. But don't take my word for it; listen to what God himself says.

As Moses looks back on his life—especially the way God has delivered Israel from the hands of Pharaoh, the most powerful ruler on earth at that time, commanding the Red Sea to consume his army—he recounts God's words:

> See now that I, even I, am he,
> and there is no god beside me;
> I kill and I make alive;
> I wound and I heal;
> and there is none that can deliver out of my hand.
> (Deut. 32:39)

Everyone agrees that God is the one who makes alive and heals, but kills and wounds? Yes, even kills and wounds, as the exodus of Israel demonstrates.

Moses is not alone. After devoting her son, Samuel, to the Lord's service after he answered her prayer and gave her—a barren woman—a child, Hannah says something similar:

> The Lord kills and brings to life;
> he brings down to Sheol and raises up.
> The Lord makes poor and makes rich;
> he brings low and he exalts. (1 Sam. 2:6–7)

Sure, the Lord brings to life, raises up, makes rich, and exalts, but kills, makes poor, and brings low? Yes, he even kills, makes poor, and brings low. And no one knows this so well as Hannah, who experienced some real lows from the hand of God. Her inability to have children was no accident. The "Lord had closed her womb"

(1:6), which is why Hannah went directly to the Lord himself to ask that he open her womb. She knows that the same Lord who takes away is also a Lord who gives, for he is in control of both.

Job, too, knows the pain of God's secret providence. While we are let in on the backstory to Job's suffering, Job is left in the dark by God. He is being tested, and what a test it is. In one day Job loses his family and his wealth. Next, Job loses his health, brought to the very brink of death itself. But what does Job say when this dark, evil hour hits? "The Lord gave, the Lord has taken away; blessed be the name of the Lord" (1:21).

As the reader, we are given VIP access behind the curtain of divine providence. After roaming the earth, looking to unleash havoc, Satan appears before God. Shockingly, it is not Satan but God himself who asks Satan if he has considered his servant Job, a man who truly fears God (1:8). Claiming Job only fears God because God has blessed him, Satan challenges God to remove his blessing. God then gives Satan permission to kill and destroy Job's family, animals, and possessions, which Satan does. Notice, however, that Satan cannot touch anything unless God says so.

When Satan sees Job still won't curse God, he appears again before God, and once more it is God who asks Satan if he has considered Job (2:3). Satan claims Job will curse God if his own health is taken and he is made to suffer. But again, Satan cannot touch Job unless God gives him permission (1:12). Job is right; although Satan has destroyed everything Job was and had, it is the Lord who first gave to Job, and it is the Lord who has now taken everything away (1:21). Few stories convey God's absolute control over evil, including Satan himself, like the story of Job does. Satan cannot lift a finger without God's permission.

Yet no text is as shocking as Isaiah 45. You may recall King Cyrus, that Persian king God raised up to deliver Israel from exile. What is astonishing about Isaiah 45 is that it was written long before Cyrus was even born. Yet God calls Cyrus by name (45:4–5), declaring beforehand that he will raise Cyrus up as his instrument for deliverance. When he does so, everyone will know that "there is none besides" him (45:6). And then comes a stunning statement by God himself:

> I form light and create darkness;
>> I make well-being and create calamity;
>> I am the LORD, who does all these things. (Isa. 45:7)

Do you see just how exhaustive and meticulous, extensive and comprehensive God's sovereignty is here? There is no limit! He is God; he is in control of all things, including evil. Not only does God say he creates light, but he says he creates darkness as well, not only well-being but calamity.

In the Hebrew, the word here for "create" is *bārā'*, an Old Testament word that has God as its subject.[25] For example, in Genesis 1:1 we read: "In the beginning God *bārā'* the heavens and the earth." Do you now see why it is so startling that this same word is used in Isaiah 45 to say God creates darkness (evil)? Similarly, consider the word for "calamity" (*ra'*). Other Old Testament passages actually translate this word as "evil," "bad," "harmful," or "wicked." There are not too many words in the Hebrew language that so strongly convey that which is horrendous, wicked, and despicable.[26] Now you can see why it is so unexpected that the same word would be used in Isaiah 45 to refer to God's control over evil.

God's point is to make it crystal clear that he is the one who is in control of *all things*. Not even the most threatening acts against his kingdom, the evil actions of his enemies, are beyond his control. In the context of Isaiah 45, God makes this shocking statement because he wants his people to know, without a shadow of a doubt, that he, and he alone, is God. "I am the Lord, who does all these things."[27]

Is An All-Powerful God Still Good?

These passages, and countless others, demonstrate that God is all-powerful, even over that which might threaten his power most—namely, evil itself. But if God's control is that extensive, is God still a good God? If he controls evil, is he then evil himself?

It is telling that when God permits Satan to harm Job, Job not only says it is the Lord himself who has taken away (1:21), but the narrator then concludes this opening scene by saying, "In all this Job did not sin or charge God with wrong" (1:22). Even Job, who is completely in the dark as to God's dealings with Satan, understands that the same God who is in total control of the horrific evil done to him and his family is and remains good. As mysterious as it may be, God's holiness, his ethical purity and impeccability, is in no way compromised by his exhaustive, meticulous control over the evil he ordains. How do we make sense of this apparent paradox?

First, God is equally in control of evil and of good, but we should not assume that he relates to both in the same way. While he dispenses the good from his hand directly and proximately, he ordains evil and sees to it that it occurs indirectly, mediated through someone else from whom that evil originates. God's control of good and evil is asymmetrical. "Though evil is ever so much under God's control," says Herman Bavinck, "it cannot in the same sense and in the same way be the object of his will as the good."[28]

Consider Job once more. When harm comes to Job, it is God who has ultimately "taken away," but God's intentions in the decision are good (as the ending of Job reveals). Satan's are not. Satan intends to destroy Job, and so he uses the wicked Sabeans and Chaldeans to put Job's family and animals to death (1:15, 17). So yes, God has ordained this evil, but the evil itself originates in Satan and stems from the motives of the Sabeans and Chaldeans.

Just as remarkable is the story of Israel's exile under the Assyrians. Keep in mind, the Assyrians were a wicked, pagan people.

They were as godless as a nation can be. Their intent against Israel was perverse all along. And yet, it is God who sends Assyria to punish his people for their idolatry, though Assyria knows it not and has nothing but wicked motives.

> Woe to Assyria, the rod of my anger;
> the staff in their hands is my fury!
> Against a godless nation I send him,
> and against the people of my wrath I command
> him. . . .
> But he does not so intend,
> and his heart does not so think;
> but it is in his heart to destroy,
> and to cut off nations not a few. (Isa. 10:5–7)

Assyria does not think he is serving God. His motives are entirely degenerate. He even boasts in his villainous accomplishments: "By the strength of my hand I have done it, and by my wisdom, for I have understanding" (10:13). Nevertheless, as God himself says, Assyria is merely the "rod of my anger," the weapon God wields to afflict his own people (10:5).

> Shall the axe boast over him who hews with it,
> or the saw magnify itself against him who wields it?
> (10:15)

God goes on to say he will punish Assyria for his wickedness (10:16–19). But wait, isn't Assyria the instrument God has used to punish his people? Indeed. And yet, it is not God who is evil but Assyria; so Assyria will be held responsible. As in Job's story, here we see God's asymmetrical control. He may permit evil, though it is no bare permission; he is in complete control of Satan and Assyria.[29] Nevertheless, God's control is indirect. He uses means. And while those means have only ill motives, God's intentions are for good (e.g., to turn Israel from idolatry and to repentance).

- God sustains the rapist, and the rapist commits sin.
- God sustains satan.

201

No event in history so models this asymmetrical control like the cross. At the cross, wicked, evil people put Christ to death. The intentions of Herod, the Jews, and the Romans were strictly malicious and malevolent. And yet we read twice in the book of Acts, once from the lips of Peter and once from the church as a whole, that the crucifixion was the predestined plan of God (2:23; 4:28). On the one hand, God's *moral, preceptive, revealed will* condemns the evil at the cross. On the other hand, the cross is the fulfillment of God's *sovereign, decretive, and secret will*, issued in eternity, progressively revealed in history, but only explicitly announced at the time of Christ.[30] His sovereign, decretive will is as "eternal, immutable, independent, and efficacious" as he is.[31]

Two Aspects of the One Will of God

God's Moral, Preceptive, Revealed Will	God's Sovereign, Decretive, Secret Will
God's moral commands revealed to humankind concerning right and wrong, good and evil	God's immutable, independent, and efficacious decree in eternity concerning all things; secret to the council of God

God is not duplicitous in ordaining that which he condemns. Consider an illustration: "Just as a father forbids a child to use a sharp knife, though he himself uses it without any ill results, so God forbids us rational creatures to commit the sin that he himself can and does use as a means of glorifying his name."[32]

Second, although we are not always told the reasons why God ordains evil (Job never was), we are told in Scripture that God has done so for our good and his glory (Rom. 8:28).[33] The cross is the ultimate proof. If we had stood there at the foot of the cross on that dark day, it would have seemed as though evil had triumphed once and for all. That is how God's providence looks in the moment, on the ground, in the heart of the storm. But if we had been there when the disciples ran to the tomb and discovered it empty, we would have realized that God had our good in mind all along.

As William Cowper (1731–1800) says in his hymn "God Moves in a Mysterious Way,"

> Ye fearful saints, fresh courage take,
>   The clouds ye so much dread,
> Are big with mercy, and shall break
>   In blessings on your head.
> Judge not the Lord by feeble sense,
>   But trust Him for his grace;
> Behind a frowning providence,
>   He hides a smiling face.

The predestined plan of God, a plan that often is accomplished through the evil actions of humans, demonstrates that the power and sovereignty of God are always accompanied by his unfailing goodness and infinite wisdom, which brings us to our next point.

The King Who Is Father: The Wisdom of Omnipotence

One of the scariest threats the world will ever know is a ruler who has all the power in the world but not the wisdom to know what to do with it. Adolf Hitler, Josef Stalin, Saddam Hussein—each of these men had power at his fingertips but used power for great evil. Cold-blooded, power hungry, and brutally negligent of human life, these rulers are just a few examples of what power looks like when wisdom is absent. As John Dalberg-Acton so famously has said, "Power tends to corrupt, and absolute power corrupts absolutely. Great men are almost always bad men."[34]

How true that is . . . with everyone but God. The reason has to do with *who* God is: he is no man. He is God. And because he is God, his absolute power does not corrupt but is instead guided by the wisdom and righteousness that define his essence. "His sovereignty is one of unlimited power, but also of wisdom and grace. He is both king and father at one and the same time."[35]

God's wisdom pervades our world in every way. Throughout the Old Testament the biblical authors praise God for his wisdom in redemption, but in doing so they cannot help but be drawn to his wisdom in creation (Deut. 4:6–8; Job 9:4; 12:13, 17; 37:24; Pss. 19:7; 104:24; Isa. 40:28; Jer. 10:12). They understand that the same wisdom that created the cosmos is at work in the salvation of those created in the image of God. When that wisdom is displayed in all its finality in and through Christ, New Testament authors like Paul cannot help but conclude their letters with doxologies like this one: "To the only wise God be glory forevermore through Jesus Christ! Amen" (Rom. 16:27; cf. 1 Tim. 1:17; Jude 25; Rev. 5:12).[36]

Of course, the wisdom of God's omnipotent plan is very different from ours. As mentioned, few of us would have stood at the foot of the cross and concluded that God's power and wisdom were present, let alone prevailed. The king was crucified; evil had the last word.

Or did it?

The apostle Paul tells the Corinthian church that the "foolishness of God is wiser than men, and the weakness of God is stronger than men" (1 Cor. 1:25). Paul does not actually mean God is foolish or weak. Rather, the apparent foolishness and weakness of God are seen at the cross, because in the eyes of unbelievers nothing appears to be a greater indication of impotence than the shame of crucifixion and the death it brings. How can Jesus be "King of the Jews," as the caption above his cross read, when he is dead? While "Jews demand signs and Greeks seek wisdom," says Paul, "we preach Christ crucified, a stumbling block to Jews and folly to Gentiles, but to those who are called, both Jews and Greeks, Christ the power of God and the wisdom of God" (1:22–24).

The greatest symbol of weakness up to that point in history— the cross—would now be the greatest sign of God's power over sin and death. Through his Son's death on a cross, the wrath of God was satisfied on behalf of sinners like you and me (Rom. 3:25–26). When Jesus cried out, "It is finished" (John 19:30), our debt was paid, our forgiveness was won, for on that cross Jesus bore the penalty for every one of our trespasses. That the Father was satisfied with his Son's payment for our sin was publicly declared by raising Jesus from the dead (Rom. 4:25). The cross and empty tomb are the greatest picture we will ever have of the wisdom of our all-powerful, all-knowing God.

Is God Too Big to Care?

The temptation with a chapter on omnipotence is that you walk away thinking, "Yes, God is big, but is his bigness so big that he cannot possibly care about little me?"

Francis Schaeffer famously has said, with a very big God in mind, that there "are no little people."[37] He was right. It may feel awkward to think this way, but it is precisely because God is so big that there are no small people. It is because he is all-powerful, all-knowing, and all-wise that he can care so much about you. But why? To think that he is too big to care is to impose a limit on a God who has no limits. If he truly is infinite, limitless in his power, knowledge, and wisdom, then restricting him to an aloof existence will not work. "To believe that God is too transcendent, too infinite, to know or care about us here on planet Earth is to limit God. An omniscient God *must* have numbered the hairs on our heads!"[38]

If you struggle to believe in the wisdom of God's omnipotent care, you are not alone. We all remember the remarkable faith of Abraham. However, Abraham's wife, Sarah, struggles too. That's not to say faith is absent, but her faith has a limp to it, as does Abraham's at times. So much time has gone by since God has promised an heir; the couple has clearly aged past the time of childbearing years. Pregnancy is simply impossible. Can you hear Sarah's tears? Her doubts? Seemingly out of nowhere, the Lord appears to Abraham by the oaks of Mamre, this time by means of three men (Gen. 18). Quickly, Sarah runs to prepare a meal. As she whips up her delicious cakes, she overhears the conversation. In just one year Sarah will give birth to a son. Sarah laughs to herself, "saying, 'After I am worn out, and my lord is old, shall I have pleasure?'" (18:12). Here is the laugh of a woman who knows her own body, but it is also the laugh of a woman who doesn't know the care of the one who is omnipotent. One year later, just as God has promised, Sarah gives birth to a baby boy. His name is Isaac, and he is the seed out of which a nation will bloom.

Hundreds of years later, another barren woman will have the same struggle as Sarah. Her name is Hannah. So painful is her barrenness that when she pours out her soul before the Lord in prayer, Eli, the priest of Israel at the time, rebukes her for being drunk. Explaining that she is not drunk but distressed, Hannah expresses her "great anxiety and vexation" (1 Sam. 1:16). Hannah is a godly woman; she has promised the Lord that if he will give her a child, she will devote this child to the Lord's service for life. Here is a woman who believes in the power of God, so much so that she thinks God Almighty cares enough to listen to her petition. And she is right. God does listen, God does care, and God does honor her promise by doing what is impossible by human strength: blessing Hannah with a son.

Who is this son? His name is Samuel, and he will be Israel's next priest and prophet, the very one who will anoint King David. Just as God cared for Sarah, God cares for Hannah, and he shows his care by exercising his omnipotent hand. His omnipotent hand is also tied to his big plan, a plan to redeem his people. Though women like Sarah and Hannah were embarrassing to society—barren and cursed—they were God's instruments of salvation, through which the seed of Genesis 3:15 would come to crush the serpent's head. The point is, the wisdom of God's power is displayed in our weakness. His wise omnipotence shines bright in our darkest hour.

Though Sarah was slow to see that omnipotence and care go together, Hannah sees it and bursts with praise:

There is none holy like the LORD:
    for there is none besides you;
    there is no rock like our God. . . .
For the LORD is a God of knowledge,
    and by him actions are weighed.
The bows of the mighty are broken,
    but the feeble bind on strength. . . .
The LORD kills and brings to life;
    he brings down to Sheol and raises up.
The LORD makes poor and makes rich;
    he brings low and he exalts. . . .
For the pillars of the earth are the LORD's,
    and on them he has set the world.
            (1 Sam. 2:2, 3b, 4, 6–7, 8c)

Many centuries later, the same omnipotent care will be experienced by a young girl named Mary. She too will have a son, a son in the lineage of Sarah's son, Isaac. Yet this Son is unlike any son before, for he is conceived of the Holy Spirit. Mary, when first told the news, can hardly believe it. "How will this be, since I am a virgin?" (Luke 1:34). Sarah and Hannah would have nodded at the angel Gabriel's response to Mary: "Nothing will be impossible with God" (1:37).

When there is no room in the inn, the King is born in a manger. The power of God could not be more real; a virgin has given birth, and this impossible conception is the advent of the eternal Son of God, the King of kings and the Lord of lords. Yet such omnipotence is wrapped in swaddling cloths and placed in the feeding trough of animals. No palace, no throne, no scepter. Omnipotence himself is laid upon straw. Why? Because God cares. He cares so much he sends his Son to be born as a man, suffer, and die, so that sinners like you and me might be forgiven and reconciled with God.

Only an omnipotent God can do that. And he has done it for you and for me.

11

Can God Be Both Holy and Loving?

Righteousness, Goodness, and Love

The LORD works righteousness
and justice for all who are oppressed. . . .
The LORD is merciful and gracious,
slow to anger and abounding in steadfast
love. . . .
He does not deal with us according to our sins,
nor repay us according to our iniquities.

PSALM 103:6, 8, 10

Truly, then, you are merciful because You are just.

ANSELM, *Proslogion*

And heaven's peace and perfect justice
Kissed a guilty world in love.

WILLIAM REES, "HERE IS LOVE,
VAST AS THE OCEAN"

The Murderer Who Talked with God

He's a murderer. A cold-blooded murderer. Sure he grew up in a palace, the palace of Pharaoh to be exact, enjoying all the comforts Egypt could offer, but now that he has killed a man, those comforts are a thing of the past.

It all happens one day when Moses sees an Egyptian abusing a Hebrew slave. Moses may have grown up in Pharaoh's palace, but he is a Hebrew by birth. Seeing his own people brutally beaten by the Egyptians has been agonizing. Day after day he has watched as his Hebrew brothers and sisters toil under the slavery of the Egyptians.

Moses can take it no longer. Watching this Egyptian master beat this Hebrew slave is the straw that breaks the camel's back. Moses looks to the right and then to the left—the coast is clear. Full of anger, Moses strikes down the Egyptian and hides him in the sand. Not exactly the perfect cover-up story. Clearly Moses is no Jason Bourne; his assassination of this Egyptian is spotted by other Hebrews. The next day Moses tries to stop a fight between two Hebrews, but one of them calls Moses out: "Who made you a prince and a judge over us? Do you mean to kill me as you killed the Egyptian?" (2:14). Like I said, Moses is no trained assassin; his little secret is out, which means Pharaoh will have his head for this capital offense.

Moses does the only thing he can do: he flees into the wilderness, where no one can find him or hunt him down.

Or so he thinks.

"I AM WHO I AM"

One day Moses approaches Horeb, the "mountain of God" (Exod. 3:1–15), the mountain that will become known as Mount Sinai. Without notice, Moses is caught off guard by a very strange sight. In front of him is a bush, and it is on fire. Oddly enough, the burning bush is not burning up. Curious, Moses steps closer to get a better look, when out of nowhere he hears a voice:

"Moses, Moses!" God himself is speaking to Moses.

No doubt terrified, Moses answers, "Here I am."

"Do not come near; take your sandals off your feet, for the place on which you are standing is holy ground."

Moses is petrified. Will he be consumed by this fire? Has God found him out, murderer and all? How can he, a mere mortal, stand in the presence of the holy? And why in the world would God want to speak with him? No time to ask questions; his sandals have to come off.

God then says to Moses, "I am the God of your father, the God of Abraham, the God of Isaac, and the God of Jacob."

If Moses was petrified before, now he is absolutely terrified. This is God himself, the same God who led his forefathers. How could a lowly Hebrew outlaw on the run, hiding in the wilderness, be of any interest to the God who has established *the* covenant with Abraham? Moses knows his theology; mortals, sinful mortals especially, cannot look at God. So Moses hides his face, for he is afraid to look at God.

As Moses hides, God explains to Moses that he has heard the outcry and groaning of his chosen people in bondage. Moses will be the one to deliver God's people out of Egypt, further fulfilling God's covenant promises to Abraham.

Moses is, as you might expect, completely shocked. He did not see this coming at all. "If I come to the people of Israel and say to them, 'The God of your fathers has sent me to you,' and they ask me, 'What is his name?' what shall I say to them?"

What God says next may be the greatest five words in the Old Testament: "I AM WHO I AM."

If the people ask, Moses is to say to them, "I AM has sent me to you."

But who is this "I AM"?

"Say this to the people of Israel, 'The LORD, the God of your fathers, the God of Abraham, the God of Isaac, and the God of Jacob, has sent me to you.' This is my name forever, and thus I am to be remembered throughout all generations.'"

"I AM WHO I AM." What does God's name mean?

Covenant Lord: Aseity and Covenant Presence

There is a sense of mystery to this name, "I AM," but it does reveal at least two crucial aspects of God's nature. First, it means *God is set apart*. Unlike the Egyptian gods, gods that were identified with certain objects or places (the sun, the moon, the river, etc.), God is above his creation. For example, "He is not like Amun or Ptah," two Egyptian gods; "he cannot be assigned a place and identity in the cosmos as one of the gods."[1] He is not just another god in the long list of gods, but he is unique, distinct from the created order. He is not a "contingent being"; his "identity is not tied to any shrine, cult, city, people, or title." Rather, he is the one who "exists independently of all things, and is the only being for whom existence is part of his essence." In short, "everything else is contingent on him. . . . He is the one, eternal, all-powerful, creator God. . . . 'I AM' implies absolute existence without limitation either in time or contingency. He is not contingent upon anything, and everything is contingent upon him."[2] The title "I AM" conveys God's absolute independence. He alone is the self-existent, self-sufficient Creator. He alone is life in and of himself.

Second, the divine name also communicates God's *covenant presence*. Context is key; not only is Moses to say to Israel, "I AM has sent me to you" (Exod. 3:14), but this "I AM" is "the LORD, the God of your fathers" (3:15). Earlier in the narrative, just before God reveals his name to Moses, when Moses is afraid to look at God, the Lord says, "I have surely seen the affliction of my people . . . and have heard their cry" (3:7). Instructing Moses to go to Pharaoh, the Lord promises, "But I will be with you" (3:12). "More than ontology is at stake."[3] And yet, to be accurate, it is God's ontology (his absolute aseity) that is the basis on which he can then freely stoop down, enter into the covenant with his people, and promise to be with them no matter what. "I AM" means not only "I am the one who is" but "I am the one who is . . . with you." And that is a message Moses desperately needs to hear as he prepares to face off with Pharaoh. Yes, "I AM" is God transcendent, but "I AM" is *with* his chosen, covenant people, and his presence is the guarantee of their deliverance.

Moses knows this firsthand. At the start of this book, we pictured Moses hidden in the cleft of the rock (Exod. 33). Remember, Moses has asked the unimaginable: "Please show me your glory" (33:18). Not possible. "You cannot see my face . . . and live," says God (33:20). He is incomprehensibly transcendent in his glory. Nevertheless, God hides Moses in the cleft of the rock, covering him with his hand, allowing Moses to see his back. As he does so, God reveals his name, "The LORD," and makes his goodness pass by, declaring his grace and mercy. This God may be high and lifted up, but he has chosen to stoop down and be immanent for the sake of his people. He reveals himself not only as covenant *Lord* but as his people's *covenant* Lord.[4] And for that reason, the gods of Egypt are no match.

Someone Than Whom None *Holier* Can Be Conceived: Self-Excellency

Moses's encounter with God on Mount Sinai confirms that God's holiness first and foremost means God is set apart. His aseity is what distinguishes him from all other gods. Countless times when Scripture refers to God as the Holy One, it is this fundamental meaning that it has in mind. Nonetheless, that does not exhaust the meaning of divine holiness. Such aseity has implications for God's moral character. As the self-sufficient, self-existent God, he must also be the *self-excellent* God. His aseity applies not only to his existence but to his moral purity, a point we stressed in chapter 4.

Let's return to the story of Moses. After God reveals his name to Moses, God comes through on his word, liberating his people from Pharaoh. As Israel then begins her journey out of Egypt to the land God has promised Abraham, the first stop is Mount Sinai, just as God has promised Moses (Exod. 3:12). At the mountain God makes a conditional promise: "Now therefore, if you will indeed obey my voice and keep my covenant, you shall be my treasured possession among all peoples, for all the earth is mine; and you shall be to me a kingdom of priests and a holy nation" (19:5–6). Descending on the mountain in a thick cloud, with smoke and fire, causing the mountain to tremble, God writes down his law on tablets of stone. Here is the constitution of the nation, God's law to live by so that Israel might keep the covenant and be set apart as his holy nation.

Since these ten commandments reflect God's moral perfection, his people are to be an image of his moral excellency, not only set apart but *consecrated* to him in every way. Whether it be through worship ("You shall not make for yourself a carved image"; 20:4), the family ("Honor your father and your mother"; 20:12), or possessions ("You shall not covet your neighbor's house . . . wife . . ."; 20:17), God's chosen people are to display to the nations around them what their God is like.

Not only is Israel's God unlimited by the created order, contingent on no one, Lord over all, but his moral excellence radiates brighter than the sun. Israel's God not only is perfection itself but is the very standard of morality, the very source of sanctification and holiness. Right and wrong are determined by looking to him, who is himself the Truth. We might call him the *summum bonum*, the supreme, highest, greatest good that can be imagined.[5] All good is measured against him, for he is the greatest good. If Anselm is right that God is someone than whom none greater can be conceived, then it must also be true that God is someone than whom none *holier* can be conceived.

Unlike Israel, who is dependent on God for her holiness—even her genesis as a holy nation is his doing—God is dependent on no one for his moral excellency. Putting into practice our doctrine of simplicity once more, if God is independently holy (self-excellent), then it is fitting to say this God *is* holy. Holiness is not something someone gives to him, nor is it a quality he acquires over time (which would undermine his immutability). He is holy in and of himself. His essence is, by definition, holy. It always has been, it always will be. Our God is *eternally*, *immutably* holy.

To understand the magnitude of divine holiness further, we need to travel in time from Moses, a criminal on the run, to a sixteen-year-old king who makes a mistake he will never forget.

Incense, a King, and One Leprous Forehead

You've heard it said that pride goes before a fall. Never has that been truer than with Uzziah. Who is Uzziah, you ask? Uzziah is king of Judah. I don't know what you were doing at sixteen years old, but I was in high school and spent most of my time playing basketball. Not Uzziah. At sixteen he is king, ruling a nation.

Unexpectedly, at just sixteen Uzziah is actually a good king. As inexperienced as he may be, he fears God. Uzziah shouldn't get all the credit; starting off on the right foot is also due to having the right prophet, and the right prophet is Zechariah. Uzziah sets himself "to seek God in the days of Zechariah, who instructed him in the fear of God, and as long as he sought the LORD, God made him prosper" (2 Chron. 26:5). Every Jedi needs a master, and Zechariah is that master to Uzziah.

Notice, however, that 2 Chronicles says God makes Uzziah prosper as long as he seeks the Lord. That phrase "as long as" makes you nervous, doesn't it? It should. If you are a parent, you might use that phrase too. "As long as you do your homework, you can go to the dance." "As long as you eat your dinner, you can go play football." The phrase introduces a condition. And such a condition is placed on Uzziah, as it is on every other king and judge of Israel. If only the story ended there, then Uzziah would remain a king who seeks God and listens to the advice of God's prophet.

Unfortunately, that is not the end of the story of Uzziah. "But when he was strong, he grew proud, to his destruction. For he was unfaithful to the Lord his God and entered the temple of the Lord to burn incense on the altar of incense" (2 Chron. 26:16). Didn't we say that pride goes before a fall? The Bible says Uzziah is "unfaithful." The word "unfaithful" (*mā'al*) "carries the sense of affronting God's holiness" and "failing to accord him his due worship."[6]

What is so affronting about walking into the temple and burning incense on the altar? You may remember from chapter 9, how Nadab and Abihu offer "unauthorized fire before the Lord, which he had not commanded them" (Lev. 10:1) and instantly they are consumed by fire from heaven. To approach the presence of the living God in his own dwelling place without following his own instructions is to invite his wrath. Not even the king is exempt.

The success of Uzziah, the strength and power he has acquired, have gone to his head. He assumes, even presumes, that he is the exception to the rule. After all, he is the king; no one is greater than he. Uzziah's head is so large he has forgotten not only who has given him his kingdom but who he is. Yes, he is a king, but he remains a sinner, in need of a priestly mediator to atone for him. As king he should especially know better, for God has prescribed that he is to be approached and worshiped according to his regulations. Uzziah thinks he can bypass those regulations and worship God however he sees fit. He has no more need for the priests but wants to bypass them altogether and claim ultimate spiritual authority in God's house.[7]

Azariah the priest tries to stop the king. With eighty priests by his side, he marches after Uzziah and confronts him. "It is not for you, Uzziah, to burn incense to the Lord, but for the priests, the sons of Aaron, who are consecrated to burn incense. Go out of the sanctuary, for you have done wrong, and it will bring you no honor from the Lord God" (2 Chron. 26:18). The king will not listen but instead becomes angry, infuriated that Azariah would deny him, the king, a priestly role.

At that moment, Uzziah could repent, but instead he becomes livid. So God instantaneously afflicts Uzziah with leprosy. There they are, in a standoff, when instantly leprosy covers Uzziah's forehead! Leprosy was a death sentence in those days. And for a king, like Uzziah, it also would mean his reign was virtually over. The rest of the story is tragic. Uzziah "was a leper to the day of his death, and being a leper lived in a separate house, for he was excluded from the house of the Lord" (2 Chron. 26:21). His son Jothan has to govern the people instead.

The Trisagion

King Uzziah dies a leper. His death must leave the people worried. Despite his tragic end, Uzziah has brought security and peace. Now where will Israel look for a king? Where will hope be found with the king now dead?[8]

That same year, the prophet Isaiah has a vision of a king (Isa. 6). "In the year that King Uzziah died I saw the Lord sitting upon a throne, high and lifted up; and the train of his robe filled the temple. Above him stood the seraphim. Each had six wings: with two he covered his face, and with two he covered his feet, and with two he flew" (6:1–2). Previously we saw that Moses covered his face when he encountered the voice of God at the burning bush. That was but a bush, but here Isaiah actually approaches the heavenly throne and sees God sitting on it in all his sovereignty and supremacy, in all his infinite beauty and excellence. Isaiah feels "the raw edge of terror at being where humanity dare not go."[9]

The scene is one of royalty. As the Lord sits on his throne, "high and lifted up"—a phrase that stresses divine sovereignty—his robe is said to fill the temple. The robe's seemingly unending length is a symbol: this is the King, supreme in his omnipotence, immense in his omnipresence, and unsurpassed in his glory. His rule and reign, as well as the glory of his name, extend as far as his robe.

Flying above him are seraphim. What kind of creatures are seraphim? We are not given a total visual, but some speculate, based on how the word is used elsewhere in Scripture, that they may look like either a serpent or a dragon. Others believe the word itself conveys they are fiery creatures.[10] Either way, we do know they have six wings. As they hover over the divine throne, their wings serve a key purpose. Two wings cover their *eyes*, lest they look upon the Holy One himself. They may be heavenly beings, but they too are created, finite creatures, unworthy to glance at him who is infinite and eternal. The sheer brightness of his glory would blind them immediately. Two wings cover their *feet*. Now that's strange. Or is it? Feet, in the ancient world, were that part of the body associated with either filthiness or immodesty. Exposed feet before a king, let alone the King of kings, would be a sign of disrespect and defilement, inviting impurity into the presence of the Holy One.

The last set of wings is used to fly, and as these six seraphim fly they call out to one another, "Holy, holy, holy is the LORD of hosts; the whole earth is full of his glory!" (6:3). Why say "holy" three times? This phrase is often referred to as the Trisagion. Hebrew scholar John Oswalt says it is "the strongest form of the superlative in Hebrew," indicating that "Israel's God is the most 'godly' of all the gods."[11] It is to stress, as emphatically as possible, that no one is holy like the Lord. His holiness places him in a realm all by himself.[12]

[margin handwritten note:] Contrast with the story of Moses

Notice, there is no limitation to the extent of God's glory. His glory fills the whole earth, a phrase that attests not only to the omnipresence of his glory and its infinitude but to the scope of his sovereignty. There is no land, no place, untouched by his power, rule, and authority. All the earth knows the presence of his power, and with it his grandeur.

But then something terrifying happens. As Isaiah listens to these seraphim, the room fills with smoke, and the "foundations of the thresholds" start to shake violently. Growing up in the Bay Area of California, I am not unfamiliar with earthquakes. Every school year our class would undergo earthquake drills, preparing for "the big one." Ducking under desks or doorways always felt ridiculous. Was this really necessary? Then, one day in October of 1989, an average day by any estimation, an earthquake hit, 6.9 on the Richter scale. I will never forget it. I was in my living room, where we had a very large fish tank. It was as if a giant had reached down and scooped the water out with one swipe of his hand.

After we huddled together as a family under a doorpost, the earthquake finally stopped. If you've ever been in an earthquake, it's like being in a slow-motion scene from the movies; it seems like an eternity until it's over. Afterward, we turned on the news, only to see people crushed to death under collapsed structures. The 880 freeway looked like a series of waves in the ocean. Most will remember a top portion of the Bay Bridge collapsing onto cars on the bottom level. Cars were literally falling off the bridge. That day, San Francisco was brought to its knees.

As Isaiah stands in the presence of God—seraphim flying over the throne, smoke filling the air—the ground under him and the walls around him violently shake from the cries of the seraphim, and Isaiah is brought to his knees. Can you imagine just how petrified he must be? Isaiah surely thinks he is about to be swallowed whole. In that moment, no doubt Isaiah sees his life flash before his eyes. Never before have both the *finitude* of his existence and the *sinfulness* of his soul been so exposed. Such is the effect of standing in the presence of the Holy One.

"Woe Is Me!"

Isaiah then does the only thing he can do; he cries out in despair, "Woe is me! For I am lost; for I am a man of unclean lips, and I dwell in the midst of a people of unclean lips; for my eyes have seen the King, the LORD of hosts!" (Isa. 6:5). Isaiah's response is telling. Standing in the presence of the one who is "holy, holy, holy" brings one face-to-face not only with the *total, utter otherness* of the Lord but with his *absolute purity* as well. And that is a massive problem for Isaiah. He is a sinner, standing before the one who *is* holy. There is no escape for Isaiah, only confrontation with his own guilt and pollution. Isaiah stands condemned, and he knows it; he feels it.

Isaiah sees not only his own plight—"Woe is me! For I am lost"—but his people's as well: "I dwell in the midst of a people of unclean lips." Lips give expression to the heart. They express what truly lies within us, even our deepest, darkest thoughts. James says the tongue is a "fire, a world of unrighteousness." It stains the "whole body, setting on fire the entire course of life, and set on fire by hell" (3:6). It is, James laments and warns, a "restless evil, full of deadly poison" (3:8). "With it we bless our Lord and Father, and with it we curse people who are made in the likeness of God" (3:9). Isaiah, long before James, knows this to be true of himself and of his people. How can he stand in the presence of the Holy One with such lips and survive? He can't.

Your Guilt Is Taken Away: Holy Love

In the twenty-first century, "love" is a word that means virtually nothing anymore. We use it of everything, so that it refers to nothing. On a Sunday it is likely you "love" church, pizza with a football game, and a long nap . . . and in that order. The point is, we use the word so frequently and with such equality that the word itself has lost its meaning. It used to be the case that we "liked" things (cars, movies, BBQ), and saved "love" for those things we cherish most (family, God). Not anymore. We love everything and anything.

God's love, however, is not so superficial. When he expresses his love or declares that he will set his love upon someone or something, that means something special. In the Bible, divine love is so rich that it has a variety of shades to it, each color contributing to a magnificent mosaic in the end. D. A. Carson outlines five different shades of God's love in Scripture:

1. "The peculiar love of the Father for the Son, and the Son for the Father" (John 3:35; 5:20; 14:31)
2. "God's providential love over all that he has made" (Matt. 6)
3. "God's salvific stance toward his fallen world" (John 3:16; 15:19; 1 John 2:2)
4. "God's particular, effective, selecting love toward his elect" (Deut. 4:27; 7:7–8; 10:14–15; Mal. 1:2–3; Eph. 5:25)
5. "God's love . . . directed toward his own people in a provisional or conditional way—conditioned, that is, on obedience" (Exod. 20:6; Ps. 103:8; John 15:9–10; Jude 21)[13]

Many of these have been encountered already in previous chapters. Yet what is so striking about Isaiah 6 is the way it ushers God's effective love to the center. In the most personal way possible, God sets his redemptive love on Isaiah, and in a way Isaiah will never forget.

Does something move God to love Isaiah in a saving way? No, at least nothing external to God himself. That answer may be shocking; after all, we think highly of ourselves. "Surely I am a lovable person!" we protest. But that gut reaction merely reveals our blindness to the pervasiveness, offensiveness, and hideousness of our own depravity. When we stand before the heavenly courtroom—sinners before the throne of a holy God—our guilty stains show themselves. Even our best works are but filthy rags before the one who is perfect in holiness, a point Isaiah himself is not shy to make (Isa. 64:6).

Our utter unworthiness, however, makes God's love all the more lovely. His electing, saving love for us as sinners is not conditioned upon our inherent worth or the worthiness of our good works. If it were, we would have no hope. Our cry is the same as Isaiah's: "Woe is me!" Truth be told, God loves us when we are unlovely (1 John 4:10; Rom. 5:8). While Isaiah still has that "woe" on the tip of his tongue, one of the seraphim flies over to him with a burning coal from the altar. This coal is so hot that not even the seraph, a fiery creature, dares to touch it. The seraph has to use tongs to pick up this burning coal. With that coal the seraph touches Isaiah's mouth and declares, "Behold, this has touched your lips; your guilt is taken away, and your sin atoned for" (6:7).

Heat is powerful. A flame can become so hot that it actually purifies an object. In Psalm 12:6 we read, "The words of the LORD are pure words, like silver refined in a furnace on the ground, purified seven times." The purity of God's word is proved by a hot furnace. A furnace is so scorching it removes any impurity, and that which is pure is showed for what it is. God's word is so pure that it can be compared to silver that has been put into the flame seven times, seven being the number of perfection. Similarly, the coal from the altar purifies, most fundamentally because it originates from God, who is himself a "consuming fire" (Deut. 4:24; Isa. 33:14; Heb. 12:29; cf. 2 Thess. 1:8).

Isaiah stands condemned in his guilt, but God removes that guilt completely, making atonement for Isaiah's sin. Such atonement, such forgiveness, is pictured by the burning hot coal touching Isaiah's lips, the focal point of Isaiah's guilt. Isaiah is a new man with clean lips and a pure heart. Forgiven, atoned for, Isaiah will never forget God's holy love.

The Just and the Justifier: Fatherly Love and Retributive Justice

The atonement for guilt that Isaiah receives points to a much greater atonement to be found in the sacrifice of Jesus Christ. It's critical to clarify that Isaiah experiences God's love not apart from God's holiness but through it and because of it. It is God's love—a love that provides the atonement needed for forgiveness—that not only upholds but fulfills the conditions of divine holiness.

Many today are of the opposite conviction. They think that a holiness that would execute justice by means of wrath can have nothing to do with a God who is love and bestows love. The cross, in this view, is all about God's love but not at all about the holiness, justice, and judgment of God. In such a scheme, the cross becomes merely an example as to how one might love others, but it is not an atonement for sin. Sin would imply wrongdoing, and wrongdoing the breaking of a divine law, and with the breaking of a divine law the necessity for divine wrath and judgment. Love cannot have anything to do with judgment.

Or can it?

I really enjoy watching detective movies. My infatuation started with Agatha Christie's fictional detective Hercule Poirot, that Belgian genius (played by David Suchet in the PBS series) who seems to notice all those critical details necessary to solving the most enigmatic cases. Other friends of mine are drawn more to Sherlock Holmes and his sidekick Dr. Watson. Whether you are a Poirot or Holmes fan, detective mysteries typically end the same: the evil villain, who stalks the street murdering the innocent, is caught, tried, and found guilty. But imagine, for a moment, if the villain were caught, placed on trial, and found guilty, but then the judge let the villain go.

Two Key Components of God's Distributive Justice

Remunerative Justice	Retributive Justice
God distributes rewards (remunerates) for obedience to his holy law	God distributes punishment (retributes, penalizes) for breaking his holy law
Stems from God's covenantal love and grace	Stems from God's holiness, righteousness, and justice in the form of divine wrath
Deut. 7:9–13; 2 Chron. 6:15; Ps. 58:11; Mic. 7:20; Matt. 25:21, 34; Luke 17:10; Rom. 2:7; 1 Cor. 4:7; Heb. 11:26	Job 41:11; Matt. 5:22, 28–30; 10:28; Luke 17:10; Rom. 1:32; 2:9; 12:19; 1 Cor. 4:7; 2 Thess. 1:8

Note: For more on these distinctions, see Berkhof, *Systematic Theology*, 75.

It is one thing to talk about the movies, but imagine if this happened in real life. The child molester, the rapist, the serial killer, the terrorist—all let go, all set free. What would be the response of the victims and their families? Outrage. And rightly so. Why? Because justice was not served. A society characterized only by *remunerative justice* (a justice that rewards those who do good) and not *retributive justice* (a justice that repays the wicked with the penalty they deserve) is a society that allows the wicked to rise up and crush the innocent. As much as our culture protests a God of retributive justice, we dare not imagine a society without it.

Yet for some reason we think that our sin, before a perfectly holy God, is the exception, as if God could turn a blind eye without his own righteousness being polluted by his acceptance of injustice. Have we forgotten that we stand trial before a *holy* judge, one whose eyes are so pure that he cannot even look upon evil (Hab. 1:13)? "Vengeance is mine, I will repay, says the Lord" (Rom. 12:19). Justice is not merely a consequence of God's decisions or his will; it is an essential property of God himself (Ps. 5:4). If he is righteous by nature and hates sin as the one who *is* intrinsically and absolutely holy, then he must punish iniquity.[14]

Coming to grips with our own guilt before the throne of a holy God—much as Isaiah does—gives us a radical appreciation for what happened at Calvary. Isaiah himself speaks of that dark day:

He was despised and rejected by men,
    a man of sorrows and acquainted with grief. . . .

Surely he has borne our griefs
    and carried our sorrows;
yet we esteemed him stricken,
    smitten by God, and afflicted.
But he was pierced for our transgressions;
    he was crushed for our iniquities. . . .
All we like sheep have gone astray;
    we have turned—every one—to his own way;
and the LORD has laid on him
    the iniquity of us all. . . .

Yet it was the will of the LORD to crush him;
    he has put him to grief;
when his soul makes an offering for guilt,
    he shall see his offspring; he shall prolong his days.
      (Isa. 53:3a, 4–5a, 6, 10)

Here is the gospel according to Isaiah. We, sinners, have turned our own way, the way of iniquity. Before a holy God, we stand guilty, deserving his eternal condemnation. But God sent his suffering servant to bear that condemnation in our place. The iniquity that was ours was laid on him instead. Substituted for us, this servant was wounded for our transgressions, crushed for our iniquities. The penalty for our sin, the wrath that should have been ours, was placed on him instead, and he bore it in our stead. His soul made an offering for our guilt that day. Notice that holiness, and the justice it brings, is not bypassed by God; rather, the law's penalty is satisfied. Justice is served.

The New Testament authors have a word for this: "propitiation." Christ was put forward as a propitiation, meaning he satisfied the penalty for our sin by bearing on the cross the wrath of God that we deserve. No one captures our sin and Christ as our propitiation as beautifully as Paul: "For all have sinned and fall short of the glory of God, and are justified by his grace as a gift, through the redemption that is in Christ Jesus, whom God put forward as a propitiation by his blood, to be received by faith. This was to show God's righteousness, because in his divine forbearance he had passed over former sins. It was to show his righteousness at the present time, so that he might be just and the justifier of the one who has faith in Jesus" (Rom. 3:23–26; cf. Heb. 2:17; 1 John 2:2; 4:10). According to Paul, there appeared to be a problem for God. God had "passed over former sins." How can a holy, just, righteous God do that? Is he not like that judge who looks at the guilty criminal and lets the criminal go free? Equally problematic is how a holy, just, righteous God can then justify sinners when the due penalty for their sin has not been met. If God is to remain holy and just and righteous, this is an impossibility.

Then why is Paul so ecstatic? It is because the just God has not compromised his holy character by passing over sins but has put forward *his own Son* as a propitiation. He has not given grace at the expense of his righteousness, but his righteousness itself has produced grace.[15] Christ is the perfect sacrifice, the holy substitute, whose spilled blood satisfies divine justice itself. The cross is the way—the only way—God can remain righteous and just yet legitimately justify guilty sinners, like you and me. At the cross, justice and mercy kiss. For God is both "just and the justifier of the one who has faith in Jesus." "Wrath, judgment, punishment—that doesn't sound very loving," some say. I beg to differ: it is the most loving act there ever has been.

Baseball is America's pastime. There is a reason high schoolers think American history class is so boring; it is because most teachers fail to tell the history of America from the bleachers. From the Great Depression, to World War II, to the Civil Rights movement, it was baseball that got America through. And it still does. After a long week at work, there is nothing like taking the kids to grab a hot dog, a cold soda, and a seat in the bleachers in hopes of catching a home run from your favorite big league hitter. The smell of peanuts, the crunch of Cracker Jack . . . well, this is starting to sound like the seventh inning! But no matter what game you attend, it seems like there is always that guy or gal holding up that sign for the camera: "JOHN 3:16." If you are lucky, you might even see them running across the infield waving the sign before they are tackled by security.

Everyone knows John 3:16, but few ever consider how it begins. "For God *so loved* the world, that he *gave his only Son* . . ." There it is: the love of God. Apparently, John did not think Christ's sacrifice, which he too calls a propitiation (1 John 2:2), was opposed to divine love. Quite the contrary, it is the love of God that motivated the cross in the first place. If God did not love, he would not have sent his Son to endure the cross for our sake. As John so powerfully says, "In this is *love*, not that we have loved God but that *he loved us* and sent *his Son* to be the *propitiation* for our sins" (1 John 4:10).[16] Calvary is the greatest display of God's holy love we will ever see.

The Judge of All the Earth Will Do What Is Right

"Yes, John 3:16 is great, but listen, Professor, I still see a lot of evil in the world. Does the holy love of God exist this side of the cross?" Now, that's a good question.

We live in a world where everyone, it seems, likes to take a shot at God. When something catastrophic happens, God becomes the universal punching bag. Christians too succumb to this temptation. The wicked appear to prevail in this life, and we lose all hope. "Oh, God, where are you?" Or perhaps we cry out in anger: "If you really are God, why don't you stop this evil?"

If there ever was a people who dripped with wickedness, it was Sodom and Gomorrah. After God has appeared to Abraham and Sarah, promising them an heir through whom God will make a great nation, setting his electing love on Abraham and his children as a people who will "keep the way of the LORD by doing righteousness and justice," God declares that he cannot ignore the "outcry against Sodom and Gomorrah," for their "sin is very grave" (Gen. 18:19–20). The last time wickedness was this great, God sent a flood and wiped humanity nearly off the face of the earth (Gen. 6–9). Sodom and Gomorrah deserve the same fate. Here is a people who rape and murder the innocent, women and children included, for mere fun. Pure evil.

Knowing God's wrath is imminent, Abraham worries that justice will be forgotten: "Will you indeed sweep away the righteous with the wicked? . . . Shall not the Judge of all the earth do what is just?" (18:23, 25). Abraham then begins one long negotiation with God—that's right, *with God*. What if only fifty . . . or forty-five . . . or forty . . . or thirty . . . or twenty righteous are found? The Lord responds that he will not destroy the city if only twenty righteous are present. Abraham, knowing he is crossing the line of what any creature has the right to ask of God, then asks, What if only a mere ten righteous persons are found? "For the sake of ten I will not destroy it," says the Lord (18:32). How incredibly gracious our God is. He is willing to spare all if but a handful of God-fearing people are found. Sadly, not even ten are found; at the end of the story God destroys Sodom and Gomorrah with sulfur and fire from heaven.

"Shall not the Judge of all the earth do what is just?" Abraham learns that day that the answer is always yes. Even in the midst of horrendous wickedness on earth, God is not like those passible Greek gods who fly off the handle in capricious anger. Far from whimsical, this God puts on his black robe, enters into his courtroom, and evaluates every thought and action—indeed, every person—before he swings his gavel and declares his verdict: "Guilty."

The Judge of all the earth always does what is right. In the midst of a world that is wicked and evil and overlooks crimes against the innocent, we can take great comfort knowing that our God is just, and one day he will make all things right.

Until that day of final judgment, we point the unjustified to the cross, for there and there only will they find peace with a holy God of love.

12

Should God Be Jealous for His Own Glory?

Jealousy and Glory

You shall worship no other god, for the LORD, whose name is Jealous, is a jealous God.

EXODUS 34:14

For we ought to think of God even more often than we draw our breath.

GREGORY OF NAZIANZUS, *Theological Orations*

Once upon a Time in the Land of Shittim

If the story were made into a movie, it would be rated R. People being hanged and left to bake in the hot sun, a plague that wipes out twenty-four thousand Israelites, and an adulterous couple slaughtered in the bedroom—this is a story too gory for the family theater. I am referring to the story in Numbers 25.

It all begins in the land of Shittim. God's people, the Israelites, begin "to whore with the daughters of Moab" (25:1).[1] These women woo Israelite men to then sacrifice to their gods. "Israel yoked himself to Baal of Peor" (25:3). Much later in Israel's history, Manasseh, king of Judah, leads God's people to worship Baal in Jerusalem and then burns his own son as an offering (2 Kings 21:6). So when God warns his people against marrying women in other nations, you can see why.

In Numbers 25, Israel has indulged in idolatry, whoring after Moabite daughters and worshiping their gods. Israel has committed not only physical adultery but spiritual adultery as well, for sleeping with these women was part of the worship of Baal, the Canaanite god of fertility. The covenant God has so graciously established with his people has been violated. Israel has been an unfaithful spouse.

It's little surprise that "the anger of the LORD was kindled against Israel" (Num. 25:3). The consequences of her actions are deadly. The Lord commands Moses to gather "all the chiefs of the people and hang them in the sun before the LORD." Until Moses does so, the "fierce anger of the LORD" will not "turn away from Israel" (25:4). The scene is graphic: to "hang" these men means thrusting them through, impaling them, and then digging the pole into the ground so that their corpses can be seen by everyone. This is a shameful death; rather than being buried with one's ancestors, one's body is left to bake in the sun and be eaten by birds, impaled for all to see.[2]

Then, the unthinkable happens. "One of the people of Israel came and brought a Midianite woman to his family, in the sight of Moses and in the sight of the whole congregation of the people of Israel, while they were weeping in the entrance of the tent of meeting" (25:6). The scene is shocking. In front of all the people, in front of his own family, and in front of the tabernacle itself, the very dwelling place of God (!), this man is committing adultery with this Midianite woman. It is a wicked thing to commit adultery in secret, but to do it for all to see and right in front of God's house, that is the height of perversity, the pinnacle of idolatry.

Someone has to put a stop to this madness.

And that someone is Phinehas, son of Eleazar, son of Aaron the priest. Consumed with righteous anger (think Jesus throwing over tables in the temple), Phinehas takes a spear, hunts down this man and woman in their chamber, and thrusts both of them through so that they are impaled on one spear, right through the belly. God had sent a plague on Israel; but now, instantly, the plague stops. Twenty-four thousand lay dead.

The scene is one that could be in a movie like *Gladiator*, except Phinehas is filled with a godly zeal for the glory of the Lord. Notice God's response to Moses: Phinehas "has turned back my wrath from the people of Israel, in that he was jealous with my jealousy among them, so that I did not consume the people of Israel in my jealousy" (25:11). The heroic boldness of Phinehas comes out of a jealousy for God and a jealousy that stems from God's own jealousy for his name.

"Jealousy," a Very Bad Word

Society today does not like the word "jealousy." It's a bad word. It typically conjures up the image of someone who is insecure, obsessive, and full of envy. Modern psychology usually sees jealousy as an unpredictable emotion based on whimsical impulses like uncontrollable rage. It's no wonder that Christians today are embarrassed, even repulsed, by the many biblical passages that attribute jealousy to God.[3] However, they have projected a human, and very distorted, conception of jealousy back on God, which explains their disgust.

First things first: we need to remember that the Creator is not the creature. Whenever we describe God, we do so in human language using symbols and objects found in our human world, in our human experience, and so our language is analogical by definition (as opposed to univocal; see chap. 2). For we are describing a being who is not only greater than us but a totally different *type* of being altogether. Moreover, even when our human experience is used to describe the one who is not human, finite, and physical, we should never ascribe to God a human attribute in an *amoral* sense. Unfortunately, since our culture associates jealousy with reproachful behavior, we have to correct misconceptions of what jealousy means (and doesn't mean) for God.

The place to begin is to clarify that the way Scripture speaks of jealousy is not the way our culture understands jealousy. God is not insecure, overcome by envy, and unpredictably full of irrepressible, immoral rage. Jealousy, for God, means something else entirely. For starters, jealousy is not the same thing as *envy*. In Scripture, envy is always considered a sin. Envy is tied to coveting, lusting after something that does not belong to you, resenting someone for having something you do not have or for being someone you are not.[4] Envy is characterized by a malicious, bitter, and irrational spirit.

Jealousy, on the other hand, is an "ardent desire to maintain exclusive devotion within a relationship in the face of a challenge to that exclusive devotion."[5] Jealousy, as the Bible defines it, does not describe the raging mad, jealous husband, the lunatic who is unjustifiably suspicious and beats his wife as a result. No, jealousy describes something more like the husband who so loves and cares for his wife and is so devoted to the commitment reflected in the promises they made on their wedding day that he seeks to earnestly draw his wife back to himself should she be flirting with adultery. No one would look at that second husband and think he is crazy for lovingly insisting on marital fidelity, the type that should always be present whenever two individuals have entered into a binding covenant with one another.

In our age of *in*clusivism, *ex*clusivism is considered intolerant, but if we really think about it, intolerant is sometimes the most loving thing we could be. No woman wants to marry a man who is so tolerant that he could not care less if she has affairs with other men. At the end of the day, we justifiably don't want the irrational, abusive spouse, but we most definitely want a spouse who will give his or her life to keep and save the exclusive devotion promised in those wedding vows. Intolerant love is the type of jealousy we cannot do without.[6] Apart from it, we have no reassurance that our spouse loves us enough to pursue us.

His Name Is Jealous

When we describe God as jealous, his jealousy is not first and foremost about us. Yes, he is jealous for his people, but he is most importantly jealous for his own name and his own glory. Whenever he is described as jealous for his people, it is because he is jealous for the glory of his own name.

First, let's explore the ways God is jealous for his own glory. Since he is the one, true, and living God, all glory belongs to him. He will not give his glory to another (Isa. 42:8). He alone is God; therefore, he alone is to be worshiped, not the gods of the surrounding nations. Idolatry is the ultimate affront to his exclusive claim to divinity. Jealousy means God "always responds to the abrogation of his exclusive right to be acknowledged as the only true God."[7]

As soon as Israel is liberated from Egypt, the first item God addresses is idolatry. Idolatry is a lethal cut to the jugular of divine glory. It is the act of giving glory to the created rather than the Creator. And so, God says unambiguously, "I am the LORD your God, who brought you out of the land of Egypt. . . . You shall have no other gods before me. . . . For I the LORD your God am *a jealous God*" (Exod. 20:2–3, 5). "You shall worship no other god, for the Lord, *whose name is Jealous, is a jealous God*" (34:14).

Here our attributes of simplicity, impassibility, and immutability become relevant once again. Unlike the human emotion, divine jealousy is not a mood in God. Jealousy is not the result of a mood swing for him, coming and going, fluctuating one moment to the next. No, this God's very name *is* Jealous. God does not *become* jealous, as if he cared about his glory more passionately at one moment than another. He is jealous for his glory always. It is the essence of his identity.

It is also why he acts the way he does. Ask yourself, Why is it that God puts Egypt through such a drawn-out affliction, sending plagues one by one (ten total) on Pharaoh and his people? It might appear it is merely because Pharaoh is so stubborn. But that is a surface-level answer. Given what we learned about God's omnipotence in chapter 10, God is not a God who can be thwarted. He could have liberated his people the first time Moses told Pharaoh to let them go, if he had wanted.

Even before Moses goes to Pharaoh, way back at the burning bush encounter, God tells Moses ahead of time that he will harden Pharaoh's heart so that Pharaoh will refuse to release the Israelites. "And the Lord said to Moses, 'When you go back to Egypt, see that you do before Pharaoh all the miracles that I have put in your power. But I will harden his heart, so that he will not let the people go'" (Exod. 4:21; cf. 7:13; 9:12; 10:1; 11:10; 14:4, 8). Hardening Pharaoh's heart so that God must send one incredible plague after another—God does all that on purpose. But why? God himself says why during the eighth plague: "Then the Lord said to Moses, 'Go in to Pharaoh, for I have hardened his heart and the heart of his servants, that I may show these signs of mine among them, and that you may tell in the hearing of your son and of your grandson how I have dealt harshly with the Egyptians and what signs I have done among them, that you may know that I am the Lord'" (Exod. 10:1–2). It's as if the Lord hardens Pharaoh's heart so that he can demonstrate his incomparable power over against the strongest ruler on earth in order to showcase the greatness of his glorious might, not just to the Egyptians but to the watching world. As Israel leaves Egypt and heads to the land of Canaan, the nations tremble in fear because they know that this is the God who has crushed Pharaoh. As Moses sings after crossing the Red Sea: "The peoples have heard; they tremble" (Exod. 15:14). God wants the whole world to "know that [he is] the LORD."

A Consuming Fire, a Loving Husband

Israel is chosen to be God's special people, to display to the nations what covenant blessing through covenant fidelity looks like. Israel's relationship with God is described as a marriage (Hos. 2). When Israel proves unfaithful to her husband, perversely abandoning the covenant to whore after foreign divinities, God shows jealousy for his people, both in his discipline and in his loving, gracious pursuit of a stubborn, wayward, and adulterous bride.

It's not as if Israel is not warned ahead of time. Repeatedly Moses instructs Israel to *remember*. "Take care, lest you forget the covenant of the LORD your God, which he made with you, and make a carved image, the form of anything that the LORD your God has forbidden you. For the LORD your God is a consuming fire, a jealous God" (Deut. 4:23–24). Remembering may be one of the most common themes in the Old Testament; Israel is to constantly recall *who* the Lord is: a consuming fire. Doing so will keep her faithful to the covenant so she does not experience the fire that licks up everything in its wake.

God's jealousy, however, is not restricted to wrath. At other times his jealousy is manifested in loving pursuit. The book of Hosea compares God's relationship with Israel to a marriage with a prostitute. God instructs the prophet Hosea to marry Gomer, a "wife of whoredom" (1:2), a visible picture of his people's unfaithfulness and covenant infidelity. Throughout the book God pronounces his judgment against Israel's spiritual adultery (i.e., idolatry), comparing himself not only to a lion that devours but to a bear robbed of her cubs (13:7–8).[8]

The prophet Ezekiel uses the imagery of marriage as well, but in even more provocative terms. Israel is compared to a baby girl left to die in the streets, wallowing in her blood, on the day she is born (Ezek. 16:5). As she is drowning in her blood, the Lord sees her and says, "Live!" (16:6). When she is grown, he makes her his bride, entering into a covenant with her so that she will belong to him and enjoy the endless gifts of his kingdom (16:8). But instead she becomes a "harlot" or "whore," not only prostituting herself but doing so without charge (16:15–34). She has not only committed adultery with one lover but become a professional prostitute, offering herself to many lovers, turning herself into a "commodity to be sold."[9]

What has gone wrong? She has trusted in her own beauty rather than in the Lord (16:15). She has forgotten where she came from and who redeemed her. She lives for vainglory rather than God's glory. As one author has said, the "gift replaces the giver."[10] So the Lord gives her over to her lovers, exposing her nakedness for all to see (16:37), sending her into exile until she realizes that her own beauty has become an abomination (16:35–37). "I will judge you as women who commit adultery . . . and bring upon you the blood of wrath and jealousy," says the Lord (16:38).

While God's jealousy often results in wrath, his jealousy also ensures compassion, steadfast love, and mercy. In Hosea it is because God is a jealous God that he loves his bride with cleansing mercy, guaranteeing the continuation of his covenant promises. Although Israel "went after her lovers and forgot me, declares the LORD" (Hos. 2:13), as her husband God will "allure her" and "speak tenderly to her" (2:14). Then "you will call me 'My Husband,' and no longer will you call me 'My Baal'" (2:16). With a covenant established, "I will betroth you to me forever" (2:19a). The jealousy that leads to compassionate, loving pursuit will produce a marriage characterized by the attributes of God himself: "I will betroth you to me in righteousness and in justice, in steadfast love and in mercy. I will betroth you to me in faithfulness" (2:19b–20). Later in the book, the imagery shifts from God as husband to God as parent. Nevertheless, the emphasis on a jealousy accompanied by compassion, love, and forgiving mercy remains. God is described as a patient parent who has cared for his son, even though his son has disowned the family name (11:1–9).

Whether examples of judgment or mercy, these metaphors are meant to capture God's jealousy for a people, a people that is to be loyal to him, pure and holy, set apart to worship the one, true, and only God. "But I am the LORD your God from the land of Egypt; you know no God but me, and besides me there is no savior" (13:4).[11] But we should not assume that God's loving pursuit of his unfaithful bride is merely for Israel's sake. As much as his jealousy is for Israel's good—turning her away from idols and the path of destruction so that she will enjoy covenant blessing—it is primarily for God's own name's sake, lest his own glory be profaned among the nations. God's own honor being at stake, his jealousy becomes the "cause" of his "loving pursuit of his rebellious people when they go astray."[12]

Trinitarian Glory and the Jealousy of Our Savior

One chronic virus that seems to infect the church in almost every century is the tendency to think the God of the Old Testament is a God of wrath while the God of the New Testament is a God of love. First off, that caricature can be dispelled simply by looking to the countless places in the Old Testament where God's jealousy is expressed through his persistent love for a bride that will not remain faithful. But the caricature is also dismantled whenever we look at the life of Jesus. The one-sided picture of Jesus as meek and mild does not do justice to the many times Jesus is outraged, often at the Pharisees, because of the corruption he sees within the human heart. His outrage—his holy anger—is rooted in divine jealousy.

In the Gospel of John, Jesus talks repeatedly about the glory between him and the Father. Since the Word "became flesh and dwelt among us," the disciples were privileged to have "seen his glory, glory as of the only Son from the Father, full of grace and truth" (1:14). Jesus "manifested his glory" not only with his first miracle at Cana in Galilee (2:11) but every time a lame person walked. As Jesus says prior to raising Lazarus from the grave, "This illness does not lead to death. It is for the glory of God, so that the Son of God may be glorified through it" (11:4). At other times, Jesus specifies that he does "not receive glory from people" (5:41), nor is he one who "seeks his own glory" (7:18); instead, he says, "It is my Father who glorifies me" (8:54), a point made visible when Lazarus walks out of that tomb. Even in the midst of suffering, as Jesus prepares to lay down his life and drink the cup of divine wrath, he prays, "And now, Father, glorify me in your own presence with the glory that I had with you before the world existed" (17:5; cf. 12:12–28). But his prayer is not only for himself; he prays, "Father, I desire that they also, whom you have given me, may be with me where I am, to see my glory that you have given me because you loved me before the foundation of the world" (17:24).

The pricelessness of this divine glory is what moves Jesus to be jealous whenever he sees that glory dragged through the mud. For example, when Jesus travels to Jerusalem for the Passover, he enters the temple only to find money-changers and animal sellers. "And making a whip of cords, he drove them all out of the temple. . . . And he poured out the coins of the money-changers and overturned their tables" (2:15). Jesus is furious: "Take these things away; do not make my Father's house a house of trade" (2:16). Witnessing the righteous indignation of Christ, his disciples remember Psalm 69:9: "Zeal for your house will consume me" (John 2:17). While zeal and jealousy are not identical—someone can be zealous without godly jealousy—it is always the case that godly jealousy is accompanied by zeal in some form, jealousy being an expression of zeal.[13] As Jesus throws over tables and cracks his whip to drive the animals out of the temple, it is plain that Jesus is characterized by a divine jealousy that will not tolerate people who make light of God's holy presence. Jesus's jealousy is an intolerant love.

Should a Perfectly Supreme Being Receive All Glory?

At the start of this book, and throughout, we have claimed, with Anselm's help, that God is someone than whom none greater can be conceived.[14] All attributes, we have argued, stem from this one truth. If God is the supreme being, the being of greatest perfection, then any limitation to his being is impossible. A supreme being must be an infinite being, and an infinite being must be independent, simple, immutable, impassible, eternal, omnipresent, omnipotent, omniscient, all-wise, holy, and loving. But where does God's glory fit into this picture?

If God is the supreme, perfect being, someone than whom none greater can be conceived, then he is the only one in the universe who has the right to elevate himself, and his own glory, above all else. If he is the *summum bonum*, the highest good, then he does not look to someone or something else for fulfillment. Instead he looks to his own self, for that is where perfection itself is to be found. Should he not value himself above all else, he would not be a righteous God. A righteous being values that which is most valuable; a righteous being loves that which is most lovely.[15] However, God need not look outside himself; he himself is the object of his own love, glory, and happiness because he himself is that being which is most valuable, lovely, and worthy of adoration.[16] He is, after all, the "Being of beings, infinitely the greatest and best of beings," says Jonathan Edwards.[17]

If we, as creatures, think of ourselves all the time, and are primarily concerned for our own reputation, believing ourselves to be the one everyone else should praise, we are, without a doubt, selfish. Acting that way might even get the response, "Who do you think you are? God?" And that response would be deserved. After all, we are not little gods, as if the universe revolves around us. Instead, we have been made *for* God, our Creator. As those created in his image, we were put here on earth to mirror him, draw attention to him, and reflect his glory. In a world that is hopelessly narcissistic, humanity's purpose on earth in the biblical worldview is about as countercultural as it gets. While the world encourages its members to look inward and be vainglorious, egotistical, and self-centered, Christianity frames human existence in the perpendicular direction—that is, vertically: you are not a god but made by God, and your purpose in life is to live for his glory.

That purpose, contrary to what many opponents of Christianity claim, is not antithetical to our own happiness. As we saw in chapter 8, the opening question of the Westminster Shorter Catechism asks, "What is the chief end of man?" And it answers, "Man's chief end is to *glorify* God, and *to enjoy him forever.*" John Piper has famously tweaked that answer to: "Man's chief end is to glorify God *by* enjoying him forever."[18] I doubt the Puritans who wrote this catechism would have disagreed. Piper has made a substantial case that our greatest joy and pleasure in life will be obtained only through glorifying God. While the world will say a life glorifying God is a killjoy—"Where's the fun in that!"—the Bible says a life glorifying God is where the greatest joy is to be found. Hence Piper's well-known statement, "God is most glorified in us when we are most satisfied in him."[19]

All that to say, our very existence as image bearers centers on the greatest, most perfect being there is: God. Idolatry occurs every time we fail to see him as supreme. "Isn't that selfish of God?"

you ask. It would be if he were not the most glorious being there is, if he were not someone than whom none greater can be conceived. But since he is the most glorious being there is, to point us to something or someone else instead would be the most selfish thing he could do. It would also be the most *unloving* thing he could do. If he is the most perfect, supreme, glorious being, then he is where the greatest joy in life is to be found. If God did not draw attention to himself as the supreme being, then we would not experience the greatest joy there is in life. So, as it turns out, God's commanding that he receive all glory is the most caring, loving thing he could ever do for us, because only then will we find ourselves truly satisfied in life. A selfish God, ironically enough, is a God who is perfectly supreme yet does not insist that we center our lives on him and live our lives to his glory. — Worshiping God if to our benefit

Godly Jealousy and the Christian Life

If we exist to glorify our Creator, then jealousy should characterize us, his image bearers, as well. While our jealousy is not the same as God's jealousy—we are jealous for his glory, not ours, while he is jealous for his own glory—jealousy is a communicable attribute, and one that is to define the Christian in every way.

That is easier said than done, especially when the culture we live in tempts us with other gods or persecutes us for not worshiping the gods they idolize. When the pressure is on, will we remain jealous for our God? Or will we give in and compromise? That is the dilemma before God's prophet Elijah in 1 Kings 18. Persecution is fierce; Jezebel has "cut off the prophets of the LORD" (1 Kings 18:4a). Times are so desperate that Obadiah, who fears the Lord greatly (18:3)—more than he fears Jezebel—takes a hundred prophets and hides them "by fifties in a cave" (18:4b). To follow God, rather than Baal, is to put one's own neck on the chopping block.

When Elijah challenges the prophets of Baal on Mount Carmel, notice that Elijah rebukes the Israelites looking on. "How long will you go limping between two different opinions? If the Lord is God, follow him; but if Baal, then follow him" (18:21a). The Lord is jealous for his name and for his people; he will not tolerate a people who limp back and forth between true worship and idolatry. God's warning to the church of Laodicea in the book of Revelation could equally be applied to Israel during the days of Elijah: "I know your works: you are neither cold nor hot. Would that you were either cold or hot! So, because you are lukewarm, and neither hot nor cold, I will spit you out of my mouth" (3:15–16). That Israel has lost her godly jealousy is obvious in her response to Elijah: "And the people did not answer him a word" (1 Kings 18:21b). Israel's silence is loud and clear: Elijah is all alone. "I, even I only, am left a prophet of the Lord, but Baal's prophets are 450 men" (18:22).

Elijah knows, however, that he is not alone. Remember, false gods can be seen, made by human hands, but they cannot be heard. No matter what stunts the prophets of Baal perform, silence follows. No fire from heaven comes down to consume the offering. But when Elijah calls on the God who cannot be seen, Elijah's intercession is heard and "the fire of the Lord" comes down and consumes the burnt offering (18:38). Notice Elijah's petition: "Answer me, O Lord, answer me, *that this people may know that you, O Lord, are God*" (18:37). Elijah understands divine jealousy. He knows God is jealous for his name and will act, as he has with Israel under the threat of Pharaoh, to show all people that he alone is the Lord. Later in the story, as Elijah flees from Jezebel, Elijah says to the Lord, "I have been very jealous for the Lord, the God of hosts." Everyone else, he says, has "forsaken your covenant, . . . and I, even I only, am left" (19:10).

Here is the jealousy that should characterize every Christian. Throughout this book we have stared and marveled at God's glory in all its various perfections. But keep in mind, that means nothing at all if we, like Israel, are called on to be jealous for God and his covenant, and yet we do not "answer . . . a word." A Christian without godly jealousy needs a serious identity check. To have Baal on the left and God on the right, and remain silent, limping between the two, is to invite God himself to spit you out of his mouth. It is to welcome the wrath of the God who is a consuming fire.

That warning is applicable to the church as a whole. Frustrated with false apostles creeping into the church and leading Christians to embrace a false gospel, Paul, in the spirit of Elijah, says to the Corinthian church, "I feel a divine jealousy for you, since I betrothed you to one husband, to present you as a pure virgin to Christ. But I am afraid that as the serpent deceived Eve by his cunning, your thoughts will be led astray from a sincere and pure devotion to Christ" (2 Cor. 11:2–3).

A "sincere and pure devotion to Christ"—that is the type of godly jealousy that is to define every Christian and every church. We need more leaders like the apostle Paul, leaders who are so devoted to a right understanding of who God is that they "feel a divine jealousy" for God's people and, like Phinehas and Elijah, have the courage to stand up and say something.

Our Phinehas

As we conclude, isn't it fascinating that when Phinehas thrusts that adulterous, idolatrous couple through, filled as he is with divine jealousy for God's glory and the purity of God's people, we read immediately that the "plague on the people of Israel was stopped" (Num. 25:8)? Atonement is made in that moment, and God's wrath is appeased (25:11).

Phinehas is but a little messiah, a shadow, a type of the true Savior. Knowing the wickedness of God's people, Jesus runs to the cross and stops the plague (Luke 9:51–56). Except this time, the violence that appeases the wrath that should come upon God's people is taken by the one filled with divine jealousy himself, the Son of God in the flesh. Jesus slays no one with a spear—he tells Peter, "Put your sword back into its place" (Matt. 26:52). Instead, he steps forward and offers up himself to be thrust through. So effective is his atonement that he cries out, "It is finished" (John 19:30). So satisfying is his payment for sin that the tomb is found empty on the third day.

Christ is risen and victorious, and all the world will know that Jealous is his name.

Glossary

The following glossary is meant to help the reader track the argument throughout this book. Since the attributes of God are all interconnected with one another, this glossary will help the reader understand references to the various attributes before they are addressed at length. These definitions are brief and are not meant to be exhaustive.

absolute power Refers to God's ability to do all things, including those things that are possible for God but that God, for any variety of reasons, chooses not to do. *Compare to* ORDINATE POWER.

accidental Describes something that is not essential to something or someone else. *Compare to* ESSENCE.

ad extra Describes God's external works in relation to the created order, including creation, providence, and redemption. *See also* AD INTRA.

ad intra Describes God's internal works in relation to himself, apart from the created order; such works are eternal and immutable. *See also* AD EXTRA.

analogical Describes something or someone that shares likenesses and continuity with that which it resembles. There is neither total continuity nor total discontinuity, but a similarity between the two. In relation to God, the creature's knowledge of God and language for God is analogical (rather than univocal or equivocal). *Compare to* EQUIVOCAL; UNIVOCAL.

anthropomorphic Refers to the use of categories and language of the finite, human world to describe God. This language is not meant to be taken literally but is figurative.

anthropopathic Refers to the use of human emotions and passions to describe God. This language is not meant to be taken literally but is figurative.

apophatic theology A method that describes God by saying what he is *not* (e.g., God does not change; he is immutable). *See also* VIA NEGATIONIS; *contrast with* CATAPHATIC THEOLOGY.

appropriations While the external works of the Trinity are undivided (*opera Trinitatis ad extra sunt indivisa*), one person of the Trinity may take a focal role and a special role; a distinct work can be appropriated by a particular person. For example, it is the Son who becomes incarnate, and it is the Spirit who perfects the redemption accomplished by the Son.

archetype The original. In theology, God is the archetype; the creature made in his image is the ectype (the imitation or copy or image). *Compare to* ECTYPE.

aseity (*a se*) God is independent of the created order, self-sufficient, and self-existent. Put positively, he is life in and of himself.

cataphatic theology A method that describes God by saying what he is; a positive affirmation of God. For example, God is love; God is holy. *See also* APOPHATIC THEOLOGY.

Chalcedon, Council of An official church council that met in AD 451 to clarify and establish an orthodox understanding of the person of Christ, particularly his two natures.

classical theism The majority position of the patristic, medieval, and Reformation periods. Classical theism is defined by divine attributes like simplicity, aseity, timeless eternity, and so on, and phrases like "pure act." It is sometimes called "perfect being theology," drawing upon Anselm's argument that God is someone than whom none greater can be conceived; he is the perfect being. Representatives include Augustine, Anselm, Aquinas, and many others. *See also* PURE ACT (*ACTUS PURUS*) / PURE ACTUALITY (*PURUS ACTUA*).

communicable attributes Those divine attributes that are true of God and also reflected in his image bearers in some partial way.

communicatio idiomatum A communication of proper qualities or attributes in the incarnate Son of God. Some Lutherans argued this communication is between the two *natures* of Christ. The Reformed tradition argued that the communication is not at the level of nature but at the level of *person*.

composite *See* COMPOUND.

compound A finite thing (or person) that is made up of parts; to be composite. God is not a compound or composite being; he is not made up of parts. God is simple. *See also* SIMPLICITY.

economic Trinity The triune God in relation to the created order; refers to the external works of the Triune God in creation, providence, and redemption. *See also* AD EXTRA; IMMANENT TRINITY.

ectype A copy of the archetype. In theology, the creature is the ectype and God is the archetype. *Compare to* ARCHETYPE.

equivocal Something or someone is totally different from something or someone else; there is no relation (e.g., it is cool outside vs. somebody has a cool style). If applied to knowledge of God, we would know nothing true of God. *Compare to* ANALOGICAL; UNIVOCAL.

esse In relation to God it refers to God as the supreme being.

essence Refers to the being of God; his whatness. God's essence (substance; being) is not one thing and his existence another thing, but they are one and the same. God's essence is his attributes and his attributes are his essence. In reference to the Trinity, God is one essence, three persons. *See also* ESSE; *compare to* ACCIDENTAL.

eternal/eternity *See* TIMELESS ETERNITY.

eternal generation and spiration *See* ETERNAL RELATIONS OF ORIGIN.

eternal personal modes of subsistence *See* ETERNAL RELATIONS OF ORIGIN.

eternal relations of origin Refers to the way Father, Son, and Spirit relate to one another in eternity: the Father is unbegotten (paternity), the Son is eternally begotten from the Father (filiation; eternal generation), and the Holy Spirit is eternally spirated from the Father and the Son (spiration; eternal spiration/procession). These eternal relations of origin are the metaphysical basis for the external/economic missions of the Trinity. Sometimes the phrase "eternal personal modes of subsistence" is used instead to be more precise: the one, simple essence of God eternally subsists in three persons: Father, Son, and Spirit.

extra Calvinisticum Although the Word becomes incarnate, the person of the Son cannot be contained or circumscribed by his human nature; due to his divinity, he continues to exist and operate outside, or beyond, his flesh as well. Even during the incarnation, for example, the Son continues to uphold the universe by the word of his power (Heb. 1:3; Col. 1:15–17). Therefore, although mysterious, the person of the Son is actively and concurrently engaged in and through both natures. The *extra Calvinisticum* is not original with John Calvin but can be found in the works of patristic and medieval fathers.

filiation *See* ETERNAL RELATIONS OF ORIGIN.

holiness Describes God's utter transcendence as the one who is *a se* (aseity), independent of the world, as well as his ethical purity, righteousness, and justice. *See also* ASEITY (*A SE*).

immanent Trinity The triune God in and of himself in eternity, apart from the created order. *Compare to* ECONOMIC TRINITY.

immensity There is no diffusion of God's essence; he is boundless, not contained by space. God is immeasurable. *See also* INFINITUDE; OMNIPRESENCE.

immutability God does not change in any way.

impassibility God does not experience emotional change in any way; he does not suffer. God does not merely choose to be impassible; impassibility is intrinsic to his very being. Impassibility is a necessary implication of immutability. *See also* IMMUTABILITY.

incommunicable attributes Those divine attributes that are true of God but *not* true of the creature (e.g., infinitude, aseity, simplicity, etc.). *Compare to* COMMUNICABLE ATTRIBUTES.

incomprehensibility The finite creature cannot comprehend the infinite essence of God. The creature can know God as he has revealed himself in his *works* but cannot know God's infinite *essence* in all its glory and mystery. The creature may know God truly but not exhaustively or comprehensively. *See also* APOPHATIC THEOLOGY; *VIA NEGATIONIS*.

incorporeal Nonphysical. God has no body; God is not material. *See also* INFINITUDE.

infinitude God cannot be measured; his being is boundless.

inseparable operations In his external works of creation, providence, and redemption, the Triune God is undivided. In every work or operation of God the three persons work inseparably. The external works of the Trinity are undivided (*opera Trinitatis ad extra sunt indivisa*). The unity of the three persons in the external works of the Trinity (economic Trinity) stems from the unity of being/essence of the triune God in eternity (immanent Trinity). *See also* APPROPRIATIONS; ECONOMIC TRINITY; IMMANENT TRINITY.

jealousy Refers to God's jealous love for his own glory and his covenant people's devotion to him; not to be confused with sinful types of human jealousy.

modalism A heresy that denies the Triune God is three distinct persons. It is also called "Sabellianism" and "modalistic monarchianism."

modalistic monarchianism *See* MODALISM.

modus significandi Refers to how a term is applied to something or someone. Thomas Aquinas argued that the *res significata* does not change in any way, but the *modus significandi* can change. *Compare to* RES SIGNIFICATA.

monopolytheism God is not a different *type* of being but merely a bigger being than his creatures. This God is not that different from the many gods of ancient religions (polytheism), gods who are a lot like the human beings that worshiped them—mutable and controlled by passions. The only difference is that the monopolytheistic God is one (mono-) instead of many (poly-). Monopolytheism is also called "theistic personalism," "theistic" referring to God but "personalism" referring to the way this God is defined primarily by the way he is a person like human beings are persons. *Compare to* POLYTHEISM.

monotheism The belief in one God. *Compare to* POLYTHEISM.

moral will God's moral commands revealed to humankind concerning right and wrong, good and evil. It is also called his "perceptive" or "revealed" will. *Compare to* SOVEREIGN WILL.

mutable Describes something or someone that changes. *Compare to* IMMUTABILITY.

Nicaea, Council of An official church council that met in AD 325 and condemned Arianism, the movement and view that denied the Son's divine equality with the Father in eternity.

omnipotence God is all-powerful.

omnipresence God is everywhere present simultaneously with his whole being.

omnisapience God is all-wise.

omniscience God is all-knowing.

ontology The study of something's or someone's essence, nature, being, or existence.

open theism A view that denies God knows the future; it denies God has exhaustive foreknowledge.

opera Trinitatis ad extra sunt indivisa The external works of the Trinity are undivided. *See also* INSEPARABLE OPERATIONS.

ordinate power Refers to what God has ordained, decreed, and willed to do. *Compare to* ABSOLUTE POWER.

panentheism A view that God is distinct from the world but nevertheless depends on the world either for his existence or fulfillment, or both. While God and the world are not synonymous (pantheism), nevertheless, God is in the world and the world is in God. Panentheism is affirmed by the view known as process theology. *Compare to* PANTHEISM.

pantheism A view that God and the world are synonymous. God is the world and the world is God. *Compare to* PANENTHEISM.

passible A finite creature who undergoes emotional change; someone who suffers. *Compare to* IMPASSIBILITY.

passive potency Describes something in need of being activated and fulfilled; something that still must meet its potential and reach perfection. Classical theism denies that God is characterized by passive potency. *Compare to* PURE ACT (*ACTUS PURUS*) / PURE ACTUALITY (*PURUS ACTUA*).

paternity *See* ETERNAL RELATIONS OF ORIGIN.

perfect being *See* CLASSICAL THEISM.

polytheism The belief that there is not just one God but many gods.

potency *See* PASSIVE POTENCY.

power *See* ABSOLUTE POWER; ORDINATE POWER.

propitiation Out of love for his people, the Father sent his Son to become incarnate and substitute himself for the sinner in order to pay the penalty for the sinner's transgressions—namely, the wrath of God. Scripture says Christ is the propitiation for our sins (Rom. 3:25; Heb. 2:17; 1 John 2:2; 4:10).

pulchrum Used to refer to God as the supreme beauty.

pure act (*actus purus*) / pure actuality (*purus actua*) There is not anything in God that must be activated to reach its potential, as if God needs to become something more than he is already or become more perfect than he is eternally. Instead, he is maximally alive, fully actualized, absolute life in and of himself, and therefore incapable of change or improvement as the perfect being. God is pure act, able to change and affect others, he has no passive potency, as if he could be affected and changed by others. Pure act is tied to attributes like infinitude, aseity, simplicity, immutability, timeless eternity, and so on. *Compare to* PASSIVE POTENCY.

quiddity Something's or someone's essence.

remunerative justice God distributes rewards (remunerates) for obedience to his holy law; stems from God's covenantal love and grace. *Compare to* RETRIBUTIVE JUSTICE.

res significata The object being identified is in view; one thing is being signified. In relation to God, *res significata* refers to the attribute that is being signified. This phrase is used by Thomas Aquinas. *Compare to* MODUS SIGNIFICANDI.

retributive justice God distributes punishment (retributes, penalizes) for breaking his holy law; stems from God's holiness, righteousness, and justice in the form of divine wrath. Retributive justice is key to propitiation. *See also* PROPITIATION; *compare to* REMUNERATIVE JUSTICE.

Sabellianism *See* MODALISM.

simplicity God is not made up of parts; he is not composite or a compounded being. Consequently, it is not theologically precise to say God possesses attributes; rather, he *is* his attributes. His essence is his attributes and his attributes are his essence; all that is in God simply is God. *Compare to* COMPOUND.

social trinitarianism While there are different types of social trinitarianism, at its core it is the belief that the Trinity is defined not primarily by eternal relations of origin (eternal generation and eternal spiration) but instead by certain social aspects such as love or wills. Social trinitarianism has been adopted by a variety of modern theologians. *See also* ETERNAL RELATIONS OF ORIGIN.

sovereign will God's immutable, independent, and efficacious decree in eternity concerning all things; secret to the council of God. It is also called his "decretive" or "secret" will. *Compare to* MORAL WILL.

spiration *See* ETERNAL RELATIONS OF ORIGIN.

subsistence Typically used of the Trinity to say the one, simple divine essence eternally subsists in three personal modes of subsistence: Father, Son, and Spirit. In short, God's essence subsists in three persons. *See also* ETERNAL RELATIONS OF ORIGIN.

summum bonum The highest good.

supereminent A communicable attribute seen in the creature is true of God but in infinite measure. Since his being is boundless, any communicable attribute in the creature can only be true of God in a limitless manner, for the Creator is a different type of being than the creature. *See also* INFINITUDE.

theistic personalism *See* MONOPOLYTHEISM.

timeless eternity God is not a being who is bound by the limitations of time. There is no duration of God's essence. *See also* INFINITUDE.

tritheism There is not one God but three gods. Tritheism undermines the unity of the Trinity, denying that one essence wholly subsists in three persons.

ubiquity *See* IMMENSITY; OMNIPRESENCE.

univocal Something has the same, identical meaning as something else. If applied to knowledge of God, this would mean we can know God as he is in himself, in his essence. We would know something just as God knows it. Classical theism rejects univocal knowledge of an infinite God. *Compare to* ANALOGICAL; EQUIVOCAL.

unmoved mover God is the only being who is not moved by another being. A first being who is unmoved is necessary to explain the movement of all other moved beings and objects. *See also* IMMUTABILITY; TIMELESS ETERNITY.

verum In relation to God it refers to God as the supreme truth.

via negationis The way of negation. Since God is infinite and the creature is finite, the creature comes to know God the most by understanding what he is *not*. This method is appropriate, says classical theism, since there is far more discontinuity than continuity between the Creator's essence/being and the creature's essence/being. *See also* APOPHATIC THEOLOGY.

Notes

Preface

1. Calvin, *Institutes* 2.12.1.

Introduction

1. Calvin, *Institutes* 1.1.3.
2. Calvin, *Institutes* 1.1.3.
3. Augustine, *Confessions* 1.4 (4) (pp. 4–5). Cf. Charnock, *Existence and Attributes of God*, 1:200.
4. Augustine elaborates in similar fashion elsewhere: see Augustine, *Trinity* 5.2.
5. Anselm, *Proslogion* 2 (*Major Works*, 87).
6. Hogg ("Anselm of Canterbury," 17) has pointed out, "The nature and being of God were not separable qualities" for Anselm. "Proving that God existed meant that one could simultaneously establish the nature of God (what God is like)."
7. Naturally, answering that question will lead us to answer another question: What must God be like to do the very things the Bible says he does?
8. Tozer, *Knowledge of the Holy*, 9.
9. Augustine, *Confessions* 1.1 (1) (p. 3).
10. Helm, *Eternal God*, 195.

Chapter 1 Can We Know the Essence of God?

1. Cf. Kenneth L. Harris's comments in the *ESV Study Bible* on these verses.
2. Weinandy, *Does God Suffer?*, 33.
3. Bavinck, *Reformed Dogmatics*, 2:36.
4. Augustine, *Lectures on the Gospel of John*, tractate 38; as quoted in Bavinck, *Reformed Dogmatics*, 2:48.
5. Aquinas, *Summa Theologiae* 1a.12.7.
6. Bavinck, *Reformed Dogmatics*, 2:36.
7. Bavinck, *Reformed Dogmatics*, 2:36.
8. Bavinck, *Reformed Dogmatics*, 2:39.
9. *Merriam-Webster*, s.v. "quidditative (*adj.*)," accessed August 20, 2018, https://www.merriam-webster.com/dictionary/quidditative.

10. Anselm uses the word "ineffable" throughout his *Monologion* and *Proslogion*. E.g., Anselm, *Proslogion* 17 (*Major Works*, 97).

11. *Merriam-Webster*, s.v. "ineffable (*adj.*)," accessed August 20, 2018, https://www.merriam-webster.com/dictionary/ineffable.

12. Anselm, *Proslogion* 1 (*Major Works*, 87).

13. Weinandy, *Does God Suffer?*, 33.

14. Bavinck, *Reformed Dogmatics*, 2:44.

15. Bavinck, *Reformed Dogmatics*, 2:51.

16. Bavinck, *Reformed Dogmatics*, 2:44.

17. Bavinck, *Reformed Dogmatics*, 2:47.

18. Bavinck, *Reformed Dogmatics*, 2:47.

19. *Merriam-Webster*, s.v. "antinomy (*n.*)," accessed August 20, 2018, https://www.merriam-webster.com/dictionary/antinomy.

20. *Merriam-Webster*, s.v. "insoluble (*adj.*)," accessed August 20, 2018, https://www.merriam-webster.com/dictionary/insoluble.

21. Bavinck, *Reformed Dogmatics*, 2:47.

22. Bavinck, *Reformed Dogmatics*, 2:49.

23. Bavinck, *Reformed Dogmatics*, 2:49.

24. Bavinck, *Reformed Dogmatics*, 2:39.

25. Augustine, *Trinity* 5.1 (trans. Hill, p. 189).

26. Calvin, *Institutes* 1.5.9.

27. Bavinck, *Reformed Dogmatics*, 2:48.

28. First stanza of Smith, "Immortal, Invisible."

Chapter 2 Can We Think God's Thoughts after Him?

1. Bavinck, *Reformed Dogmatics*, 2:30.

2. Origen, *Homilies on Jeremiah* 18.6.4 (pp. 198–99). For an overview of the fathers on accommodation, see Sheridan, *Language for God*.

3. Calvin, *Institutes* 1.13.1.

4. Calvin, *Institutes* 1.13.1.

5. Bavinck, *Reformed Dogmatics*, 2:49.

6. Bavinck, *Reformed Dogmatics*, 2:51.

7. For a full treatment of divine revelation, specifically how God has spoken to us through Scripture, see M. Barrett, *God's Word Alone*.

8. Bavinck, *Reformed Dogmatics*, 2:159.

9. For an extensive treatment of these categories, see Aquinas, *Summa Theologiae* 1a.13.5–7.

10. Aquinas, *Summa Theologiae* 1a.13.10.

11. It is the difference between *theologia* and *oikonomia*, the former being who God is in himself and the latter being what God does, specifically in the accomplishment of his redemptive plan. Cf. Sheridan, *Language for God*, 27.

12. Rogers, *Perfect Being Theology*, 17.

13. Rogers, *Perfect Being Theology*, 17.

14. Rogers, *Perfect Being Theology*, 17.

15. This illustration of a dog comes from Rogers, *Perfect Being Theology*, 17. However, I am running with it and elaborating on it in various ways.

16. Rogers, *Perfect Being Theology*, 17.

17. Bavinck, *Reformed Dogmatics*, 2:130.

18. Hart, *Experience of God*, 132. "Supereminent" is a term from scholastic theology.

19. Augustine, *Confessions* 11.4 (6) (p. 224).

20. Rogers, *Perfect Being Theology*, 17, uses the word "sameness," but I worry that could cause confusion, sounding univocal.

21. Aquinas, *Summa Theologiae* 1a.13.2.

22. For more on this distinction, see Hart, *Experience of God*, 142.

23. Rogers, *Perfect Being Theology*, 17.

24. Bavinck, *Reformed Dogmatics*, 2:130.

25. Calvin (*Institutes* 1.13.1) says we should even be fearful of doing so: "Surely, his infinity ought to make us afraid to try to measure him by our own senses."

26. Lewis, *Weight of Glory*, 134.

27. Lewis, *Weight of Glory*, 134.

28. "Scripture does not contain a few scattered anthropomorphisms but is anthropomorphic through and through" (Bavinck, *Reformed Dogmatics*, 2:99).

29. Aquinas, *Summa Theologiae* 1a.3.1.

30. Aquinas, *Summa Theologiae* 1a.3.1.

31. Aquinas (*Summa Theologiae* 1a.3.1) has another purpose in mind: "One approaches God, and one draws away from him, not by bodily movement, since he is everywhere, but by movement of the heart. In this context, 'approaching' and 'drawing away' are metaphors that picture being moved in spirit as if it were like being moved in space."

32. Bavinck, *Reformed Dogmatics*, 2:130.

33. Bavinck, *Reformed Dogmatics*, 2:130.

34. Tertullian, *Against Marcion* 2.16 (p. 310); quoted in Weinandy, *Does God Suffer?*, 102.

35. Tozer, *Knowledge of the Holy*, 9.

36. Charnock, *Existence and Attributes of God*, 1:201.

Chapter 3 Is God the Perfect Being?

1. Hart, *Experience of God*, 88.

2. Hart, *Experience of God*, 127 (cf. 130).

3. Muller, *Divine Essence and Attributes*, 330; cf. Dolezal, *All That Is in God*, 48.

4. Hart, *Experience of God*, 109.

5. Aquinas, *Summa Theologiae* 1a.7.3.

6. Aquinas, *Summa Theologiae* 1a.7.3.

7. Anselm, *Proslogion* 2 (*Major Works*, 87).

8. Hart, *Experience of God*, 122.

9. Augustine, *On Free Choice of the Will* 1 (p. 4).

10. Others have used the language of "plentitude of being." See Dolezal, *God without Parts*, 77.

11. Rogers, *Perfect Being Theology*, 11.

12. À Brakel, *Christian's Reasonable Service*, 1:96.

13. Rogers, *Perfect Being Theology*, 11 (cf. 13).

14. Rogers, *Perfect Being Theology*, 11.

15. Rogers, *Perfect Being Theology*, 15. Helm, *Eternal God*, 11, makes a similar point.

16. Bavinck, *Doctrine of God*, 154, 157.

17. Charnock, *Existence and Attributes of God*, 1:383.

18. Notice, even our language here—"infinite measure"—defies itself, for something that is infinite has no measure. Even our attempts to speak of an infinite God are trapped by the finitude of our grammar.

19. See John B. Polhill's commentary on Acts 19:19 in the *ESV Study Bible*.

20. Harman, "Singing and Living Justification," forthcoming.

21. Anselm, *Monologion* 4 (*Major Works*, 15).

22. Rogers, *Perfect Being Theology*, 2.

Chapter 4 Does God Depend on You?

1. I have worded the definition of aseity this way so as to pay heed to John Webster's warning that we should primarily define aseity not in "negative terms, as the mere absence of origination from or dependence upon an external cause" but in positive terms—that is, "God's life" is "*from* and therefore *in* himself" (Webster, *God without Measure*, 19).

2. One would be mistaken to conclude that, if God has no external cause, then he must cause himself. Self-causation would contradict divine simplicity, eternity, and immutability, as well as his own perfection. See Webster, *God without Measure*, 23; Charnock, *Existence and Attributes of God*, 1:187.

3. Webster, *God without Measure*, 27.

4. Anselm, *On the Fall of the Devil* 1 (*Major Works*, 194).

5. Augustine, *Confessions* 11.4 (6) (p. 224).

6. Edwards, *Discourse on the Trinity*, 113.

7. To clarify, that phrase "personal modes of subsisting" is one way the church has talked about the eternal relations of origin (eternal generation and spiration). It is not to be confused with the trinitarian heresy known as "modalism," which denies that the modes of subsistence are personal—that is, three distinct persons. Hence, the word "personal" is key. To see how the Reformed tradition has used this language ("mode of subsistence"), consult Muller, "*modus subsistendi*," in *Dictionary of Latin and Greek Theological Terms*, 222. Also, in the phrase "eternal relations of origin" the word "relations" does not mean "relationship" as the word is used today. Rather, by "relations" we have in mind the eternal *origin* of the three persons.

8. There is a long-standing debate as to whether the eternal generation of the Son consists of a generated *essence* or a generated *person*. Patristics line up on each side, and John Calvin is controversial for his affirmation of the latter, seeking to guard the Son as he who is *autotheos*. On this debate, see Ellis, *Calvin, Classical Trinitarianism & the Aseity of the Son*; M. Barrett, "Balancing *Sola Scriptura* and Catholic Trinitarianism."

9. Webster, *God without Measure*, 25.

10. Bavinck, *Reformed Dogmatics*, 2:239.

11. In my answer I am using some of the phrases (self-divine, self-wise, self-virtuous, self-excellent, etc.) that Bavinck does and following his lead, though at

times I am elaborating and incorporating the input of others, such as Anselm. See Bavinck, *Reformed Dogmatics*, 2:151.

12. Anselm, *Monologion* 16 (*Major Works*, 29).
13. Anselm, *Monologion* 4 (*Major Works*, 15).
14. Bavinck, *Reformed Dogmatics*, 2:151.
15. Anselm, *Monologion* 6 (*Major Works*, 18).
16. Calvin, *Institutes* 1.2.1.
17. Anselm, *Monologion* 7 (*Major Works*, 20).
18. Horton, *Christian Faith*, 235.

Chapter 5 Is God Made Up of Parts?

1. Augustine, *City of God* 11.10. Also see Augustine, *Trinity* 7.10.
2. Augustine, *Trinity* 6.7 (trans. McKenna); as quoted in Bavinck, *Reformed Dogmatics*, 2:118. Also see Turretin, *Institutes*, 1:187–89.
3. Anselm, *Proslogion* 18 (*Major Works*, 98).
4. Aquinas, *Summa Theologiae* 1a.3.7 (cf. 1a.3.1, where Aquinas explains why there are no accidents in God, his chief reason being that accidents assume potential). To clarify, God is not only free from all and any composition, he is totally incapable of any composition. See Turretin, *Institutes*, 1:191.
5. Irenaeus, *Against Heresies* 2.13.3 (p. 374); emphasis added.
6. Cf. Duby, *Divine Simplicity*, 88.
7. Aquinas, *Summa contra Gentiles* 1.18.3–5 (p. 103).
8. Anselm, *Monologion* 17 (*Major Works*, 30).
9. Bavinck, *Reformed Dogmatics*, 2:173.
10. Aquinas, *Summa Theologiae* 1a.3.7.
11. Rogers, *Perfect Being Theology*, 25.
12. Aquinas, *Summa Theologiae* 1a.3.7 (cf. 1a.3.8 on God being the first efficient cause of things).
13. Charnock, *Existence and Attributes of God*, 1:333.
14. Hart, *Experience of God*, 92.
15. Rogers, *Perfect Being Theology*, 25.
16. Rogers, *Perfect Being Theology*, 25.
17. Hart, *Experience of God*, 92.
18. Rogers, *Perfect Being Theology*, 25.
19. Rogers, *Perfect Being Theology*, 26.
20. Rogers, *Perfect Being Theology*, 27.
21. Swinnock, *Incomparableness of God*, 4:423–24.
22. Augustine, *Trinity* 6.4 (trans. McKenna); Augustine, *City of God* 12.18; as quoted in Bavinck, *Reformed Dogmatics*, 2:127.
23. Augustine, *Homily* 341 §8; as quoted in Bavinck, *Reformed Dogmatics*, 2:126.
24. *Encyclopaedia Britannica*, s.v. "refraction," accessed August 20, 2018, https://www.britannica.com/science/refraction.
25. It is an imperfect illustration or metaphor. "Prisms exist apart from light, whereas finite essences are always dependent on the being they receive and, so to speak, modulate" (Hart, *Experience of God*, 133).
26. Dolezal, *All That Is in God*, 76.

27. Dolezal, *All That Is in God*, 76.

28. Bavinck, *Reformed Dogmatics*, 2:127.

29. Anselm, *Monologion* 17 (*Major Works*, 30). Cf. Bavinck, *Reformed Dogmatics*, 2:128.

30. Hart, *Experience of God*, 126.

31. Aquinas, *Summa Theologiae* 1a.13.4.

32. The illustration of a child and coins comes from Bavinck, though I have given it a life (and story) of its own. See Bavinck, *Reformed Dogmatics*, 2:176. Bavinck takes these illustrations from Augustine, Moses Maimonides, and Basil.

33. Bavinck, *Reformed Dogmatics*, 2:127.

34. Aquinas, *Summa Theologiae* 1a.3.3. For a helpful treatment of this point, see Dolezal, *All That Is in God*, 77.

35. E.g., Craig, "Toward a Tenable Social Trinitarianism," 95–99; Moreland and Craig, *Philosophical Foundations*, 580–94.

36. Turretin, *Institutes*, 1:193.

37. Duby (*Divine Simplicity*, 214) helpfully adds a qualifier: "Yet each has or really is the divine essence (with its attributes) *in his own peculiar manner.*"

38. À Brakel, *Christian's Reasonable Service*, 1:141.

39. To go deeper on eternal relations of origin, see Sanders, *The Deep Things of God* and *The Triune God*.

40. Turretin, *Institutes*, 1:193.

41. The eternal relations of origin are the basis for the way the three persons work in salvation history. The missions of the three persons in history stem from their eternal and personal modes of subsistence in eternity. However, one should not assume that the immanent Trinity is to be collapsed into the economic Trinity. Rather, the immanent is the metaphysical basis for the economic and remains distinct.

42. Gregory of Nyssa, *Quod Non Sint Tres Dii*, 45:125–28.

43. See Muller, *The Triunity of God*, 267–74.

44. John Owen highlights both divine appropriation and inseparable operations in the same sentence: "Whereas *the order of operation* among the distinct persons depends on the *order of their subsistence* in the blessed Trinity, in every great work of God, the *concluding, completing, perfecting acts* are ascribed unto the Holy Ghost." Owen, *Works*, 3:94.

45. This point is made by John of Damascus, *Expositio de Fide Orthodoxa*, 94:828–29. Cf. Duby, *Divine Simplicity*, 217.

46. Duby, *Divine Simplicity*, 214–15.

47. Augustine, *City of God* 11.10.

48. Ironically, the real challenge is for the individual who denies simplicity. Such a denial leaves one curious as to how monotheism can still be maintained. See Dolezal, *All That Is in God*, 105; Swain, "Divine Trinity," 102–3.

49. Duby, *Divine Simplicity*, 233.

50. Hart, *Experience of God*, 128 (cf. 134).

51. Hart, *Experience of God*, 128.

Chapter 6 Does God Change?

1. These words are repeated almost verbatim in Ps. 18:2, 31 (cf. 30:3).

2. Also see Deut. 32:4, 18, 30, 31, 37; 1 Sam. 2:2.

3. Charnock, *Existence and Attributes of God*, 1:318.

4. Charnock, *Existence and Attributes of God*, 1:318.

5. Though he does not introduce the concept of perfection, Charnock appeals to power as well (something I learned after writing this book). Cf. Charnock, *Existence and Attributes of God*, 1:334.

6. Rogers, *Perfect Being Theology*, 28.

7. Aquinas, *Summa Theologiae* 1a.9.1; as quoted in Rogers, *Perfect Being Theology*, 47.

8. Rogers, *Perfect Being Theology*, 47.

9. Rogers, *Perfect Being Theology*, 28.

10. Weinandy, *Does God Suffer?*, 38, 123.

11. Rogers, *Perfect Being Theology*, 28. Regarding Aquinas, Rogers has in mind *Summa Theologiae* 1a.3.4; 1a.4.1.

12. See Aquinas, *Summa contra Gentiles* 1.16 (*Opera Omnia*, 13:44–45); Aquinas, *Summa Theologiae* 1a.2.3 (*Opera Omnia*, 4:31); 1a.3.1 (*Opera Omnia*, 4:35–6); 1a.3.2, corp. (*Opera Omnia*, 4:37); 1a.3.3, corp. (*Opera Omnia*, 4:39–40). Cf. Duby, *Divine Simplicity*, 12. Also see Turretin, *Institutes*, 1:188; Rennie, "Theology of the Doctrine of Divine Impassibility: (I)," 289; Rennie, "Analogy and the Doctrine of Divine Impassibility."

13. Rennie, "Theology of the Doctrine of Divine Impassibility: (I)," 288.

14. On "pure active potency," see Feser, *Scholastic Metaphysics*, 39; Rennie, "Theology of the Doctrine of Divine Impassibility: (I)," 288.

15. Aquinas, *Summa Theologiae* 1a.3.1.

16. Aquinas, *Summa Theologiae* 1a.2.3.

17. Dolezal, "Strong Impassibility," forthcoming.

18. Aquinas, *Summa Theologiae* 1a.9.1; as quoted in Weinandy, *Does God Suffer?*, 38, 123.

19. Weinandy, *Does God Suffer?*, 38, 123.

20. Bavinck, *Reformed Dogmatics*, 2:156, 157, 211.

21. Aquinas, *Summa Theologiae* 1a.9.1; as quoted in Weinandy, *Does God Suffer?*, 38, 123.

22. Charnock, *Existence and Attributes of God*, 1:318.

23. Sproul, *Enjoying God*, 166.

24. Bavinck, *Reformed Dogmatics*, 2:156.

25. Bavinck, *Reformed Dogmatics*, 2:173.

26. Charnock, *Existence and Attributes of God*, 1:332.

27. Charnock, *Existence and Attributes of God*, 1:332.

28. Cf. Heb. 1:11–12, which applies this to Christ.

29. Charnock, *Existence and Attributes of God*, 1:318.

30. Charnock, *Existence and Attributes of God*, 1:326.

31. I am indebted here to Charnock, *Existence and Attributes of God*, 1:353.

32. At other points in Scripture God is said to "forget" the sins of those forgiven. That does not mean that he literally does not have knowledge of those sins, which would mean he is no longer all-knowing. Rather, this is anthropopathic language, familiar to our human experience, to say God will not hold our sins against us in the future; he has forgiven us.

33. Charnock, *Existence and Attributes of God*, 1:353.

34. Edwards, *Charity and Its Fruits*, 215–16.

35. Bavinck, *Reformed Dogmatics*, 2:211; Rennie, "Theology of the Doctrine of Divine Impassibility: (II)," 307–10.

36. Bavinck, *Reformed Dogmatics*, 2:158.

37. See Barth, *Church Dogmatics*, 2.1:494; as referenced by Weinandy, *Does God Suffer?*, 123.

38. Weinandy, *Does God Change?*, 79.

39. Weinandy, *Does God Change?*, 124.

40. Bavinck, *Reformed Dogmatics*, 2:158.

41. The idea for this illustration comes from Bavinck, *Reformed Dogmatics*, 2:159.

42. For other examples, see Ps. 106:44–45; Isa. 38:1–6; Jer. 18:7–10; 26:3, 13, 19; Joel 2:13–14; Amos 7:3–6.

43. A similar passage is Num. 23:19.

44. Duby, *Divine Simplicity*, 137.

45. Duby, *Divine Simplicity*, 137.

46. Augustine, *Trinity* 5.2 (trans. Hill, p. 190).

47. Dolezal (*All That Is in God*, 18) makes a key qualification: "This clearly indicates that immutability signifies more than simply God's covenant faithfulness since the assurance of His covenant faithfulness is itself staked on His unchangeable being." Contra Bruce Ware and Scott Oliphint who modify immutability.

48. Space will not permit me to explore how it is the Son can be immutable yet become incarnate. Nevertheless, see Muller, "Incarnation, Immutability, and the Case for Classical Theism," 22–40; Weinandy, *Does God Change?*

Chapter 7 Does God Have Emotions?

1. Parker, "Greek Religion," 249.

2. Parker, "Greek Religion," 250.

3. Parker, "Greek Religion," 255.

4. For more information, see *The Rape of Europa*, The National Gallery website, accessed September 28, 2018, https://www.nationalgallery.org.uk/paintings/paolo-veronese-the-rape-of-europa.

5. Horton, *Pilgrim Theology*, 80.

6. Weinandy, *Does God Suffer?*, 37–39.

7. Weinandy, *Does God Suffer?*, 38–39 (numbers added).

8. Weinandy, *Does God Suffer?*, 38, 111.

9. Helm, "Impossibility of Divine Passibility," 138.

10. Helm, "Impossibility of Divine Passibility," 138.

11. This point distinguishes my view from other views that hold to some version of impassibility but in very modified forms, believing God only to be impassible where, when, and if he chooses. Also, one implication that follows from my view is that God's sovereignty stems from his immutable, impassible nature, not vice versa. See Dolezal, "Still Impassible," 141.

12. Weinandy, *Does God Suffer?*, 38, 111. Elsewhere he defines "impassible" as "that divine attribute whereby God is said not to experience inner emotional changes, whether enacted freely from within or effected by his relationship to and interaction with human beings and the created order" (Weinandy, "Impassibility of God," 7:357).

13. Helm, "Impossibility of Divine Passibility," 123. As Dolezal ("Strong Impassibility," forthcoming) says, "He is so dynamic, so active that no change can make him more active. He is act pure and simple."

14. Gavrilyuk ("God's Impassible Suffering in the Flesh," 139) blames the misunderstanding on the fact that most assume impassibility is not a metaphysical term but a psychological one, conveying emotional apathy.

15. Weinandy's entire book *Does God Suffer?* is, in one sense, an effort to correct such a caricature.

16. Weinandy, *Does God Suffer?*, 38.

17. Dolezal, "Strong Impassibility," forthcoming.

18. Dolezal, "Strong Impassibility," forthcoming.

19. Weinandy, *Does God Suffer?*, 38, 111.

20. Weinandy, *Does God Suffer?*, 37.

21. Elie Wiesel, *Night*, quoted in Moltmann, *Crucified God*, 410.

22. Moltmann, *Crucified God*, 410.

23. Moltmann, *Crucified God*, 417.

24. Moltmann, *Crucified God*, 370, 400, 406.

25. Moltmann, *Crucified God*, 406–7.

26. Moltmann, *Crucified God*, 407.

27. Moltmann, *Crucified God*, 409; he is quoting Kuhn, *Gottes Selbsterniedrigung in der Theologie der Rabbinen*, 89–90.

28. Moltmann, *Crucified God*, 362.

29. Moltmann, *Crucified God*, 368.

30. Moltmann, *Crucified God*, 375.

31. Moltmann, *Crucified God*, 404.

32. Moltmann, *Crucified God*, 411 (cf. 310).

33. In a fascinating study of culture, Weinandy ("Does God Suffer?," 2) calls this the "prevailing social and cultural milieu."

34. My original inspiration for this illustration comes from Gavrilyuk, *Suffering of the Impassible God*, 10, though that is not to say Gavrilyuk and I hold the same position.

35. Gavrilyuk, *Suffering of the Impassible God*, 10.

36. Gavrilyuk, *Suffering of the Impassible God*, 11.

37. Augustine, *Confessions* 3.2 (3) (p. 37).

38. Helm, "Impossibility of Divine Passibility," 120.

39. Helm, "Impossibility of Divine Passibility," 120 (cf. 121).

40. Helm, "Impossibility of Divine Passibility," 122.

41. Helm, "Impossibility of Divine Passibility," 125.

42. Weinandy, *Does God Suffer?*, 161.

43. Weinandy, *Does God Suffer?*, 161.

44. Calvin, *Institutes* 1.13.1. See also chapter 2, "Baby Talk," above.

45. Ussher, *Body of Divinitie*, 34.

46. Weinandy, "Does God Suffer?," 7.

47. Calvin, *Covenant Enforced*, 250.

48. This point is superbly expressed by Helm, "Impossibility of Divine Passibility," 134.

49. Rennie, "Analogy and the Doctrine of Divine Impassibility," 65. A similar point is made by Weinandy, *Does God Suffer?*, 100.

50. Anselm, *Proslogion* 7 (*Major Works*, 90).

51. Dixon, "Theology, Anti-Theology and Atheology," 307. Also see his much larger study, *From Passions to Emotions*.

52. Moltmann reads the Reformed interpretation of the *communicatio idiomatum* critically. See Moltmann, *Crucified God*, 640–41.

53. Moltmann, *Crucified God*, 307.

54. Moltmann, *Crucified God*, 333.

55. "Chalcedonian Decree."

56. Moltmann, *Crucified God*, 336.

57. I am quoting Moltmann, *Crucified God*, 337 (cf. 310–11).

58. "Symbol of Chalcedon," 2:62.

59. Weinandy, *Does God Suffer?*, 200.

60. Weinandy, *Does God Suffer?*, 200. Consider other ways Weinandy puts this point: The "person of the Son of God is truly born, grieves, suffers and dies, not as God, but as man for that is now the new manner in which the Son of God actually exists."

61. Weinandy, *Does God Suffer?*, 202, 206.

62. Gregory of Nazianzus, *To Cledonius the Priest against Apollinarius*, 7:439.

63. Some manuscripts use "the church of the Lord" instead of "the church of God" in Acts 20:28 (cf. ESV text note). Yet even that phrase assumes no mere man has been crucified, as evidenced in 1 Cor. 2:8.

64. Weinandy, *Does God Suffer?*, 204–5.

65. Weinandy, *Does God Suffer?*, 206.

66. Aquinas, *Summa Theologiae* 3.10.1

67. Weinandy, *Does God Suffer?*, 206.

68. Weinandy, *Does God Suffer?*, 206.

69. This point is insightfully made by Dodds, *Unchanging God of Love*, 207–8. Also see Dolezal, "Strong Impassibility."

Chapter 8 Is God in Time?

1. Augustine, *Confessions* 11.10 (12) (p. 228).

2. Augustine, *Confessions* 11.12 (14) (p. 229).

3. Augustine, *Confessions* 11.12 (14) (p. 229).

4. Augustine, *Confessions* 11.12 (14) (p. 229).

5. Augustine, *Confessions* 11.12 (14) (p. 229). Cf. Rogers, *Perfect Being Theology*, 48, who also recognizes this section of the *Confessions*, except she makes the point that such an objection also strikes at the heart of a perfect being. She believes, however, that Augustine redeems God's perfection.

6. Bavinck, *Reformed Dogmatics*, 2:160.

7. These references are listed in Bavinck, *Reformed Dogmatics*, 2:161.

8. Also consider Isa. 48:12: "I am he; I am the first, and I am the last."

9. Augustine, *Confessions* 11.11 (13) (p. 229). Also see, Turretin, *Institutes*, 1:202–4.

10. Bavinck, *Reformed Dogmatics*, 2:162.

11. Aquinas, *Summa Theologiae* 1a.10.1.

12. Bavinck, *Reformed Dogmatics*, 2:163.

13. Augustine, *Confessions* 11.11 (13) (p. 228).

14. Rogers, *Perfect Being Theology*, 55–56.
15. Bavinck, *Reformed Dogmatics*, 2:162.
16. Anselm, *Monologion* 22 (*Major Works*, 39).
17. Aquinas, *Summa Theologiae* 1a.10.1 (Aquinas acknowledges he is taking this phrase, "instantaneous whole," from Boethius). On why Scripture uses temporal language to refer to God, see Aquinas, *Summa Theologiae* 1a.10.1.
18. Aquinas, *Summa Theologiae* 1a.10.4.
19. Anselm, *Monologion* 24 (*Major Works*, 40–41).
20. Augustine, *Confessions* 11.14 (17) (p. 230).
21. E.g., Turretin, *Institutes*, 1:203.
22. Rogers, *Perfect Being Theology*, 56. Rogers uses the phrase "time-free," and she defaults to Helm (*Eternal God*, 36), who has used this phrase for some time to avoid many of the misconceptions we are addressing.
23. Tertullian, *Against Marcion* 1.8 (p. 276); quoted in Weinandy, *Does God Suffer?*, 103.
24. Rogers, *Perfect Being Theology*, 57.
25. Rogers, *Perfect Being Theology*, 63.
26. Aquinas, *Summa Theologiae* 1a.14.6.
27. Helm, *Eternal God*, 17.
28. Charnock, *Existence and Attributes of God*, 1:287 (cf. 307); emphasis added.
29. Charnock, *Existence and Attributes of God*, 1:280.
30. Charnock, *Existence and Attributes of God*, 1:287.
31. Anselm, *Monologion* 28 (*Major Works*, 44).
32. Charnock, *Existence and Attributes of God*, 1:289.
33. Charnock, *Existence and Attributes of God*, 1:283.
34. Anselm, *Monologion* 21 (*Major Works*, 36).
35. Anselm, *Monologion* 21 (*Major Works*, 36).
36. Charnock, *Existence and Attributes of God*, 1:279–80.
37. Charnock, *Existence and Attributes of God*, 1:280.
38. Charnock, *Existence and Attributes of God*, 1:284.
39. Charnock, *Existence and Attributes of God*, 1:284.
40. Anselm, *Monologion* 21 (*Major Works*, 37).
41. Charnock, *Existence and Attributes of God*, 1:283.
42. Boethius, *Consolation of Philosophy* 5, prose 6 (p. 132).
43. Charnock, *Existence and Attributes of God*, 1:288.
44. Rogers, *Perfect Being Theology*, 62.
45. Helm, *Eternal God*, 21–22. Cf. Rogers, *Perfect Being Theology*, 64.
46. On the being and will of God being identical, see Aquinas, *Summa contra gentiles*, book 1, chapter 82 (pp. 260–63).
47. Hanby, *No God, No Science?*, 322.
48. Helm, *Eternal God*, 21–22; Rogers, *Perfect Being Theology*, 64.
49. Augustine, *Trinity* 5.2 (trans. Hill, p. 190).
50. Augustine, *Confessions* 1.4 (4) (p. 5). Cf. Charnock, *Existence and Attributes of God*, 1:200.
51. Charnock, *Existence and Attributes of God*, 1:296.
52. Charnock, *Existence and Attributes of God*, 1:296.
53. See T. Desmond Alexander's comments in the *ESV Study Bible*.

54. See Waltke and Houston, *Psalms as Christian Worship*, 509.

55. Charnock, *Existence and Attributes of God*, 1:294.

56. Charnock, *Existence and Attributes of God*, 1:297.

57. Augustine, *Confessions* 1.1 (1) (p. 3).

58. This phrase is found throughout his book *Desiring God* (e.g., p. 10).

59. Piper, *Desiring God*, 18.

60. Lewis, *Weight of Glory*, 26.

61. Charnock, *Existence and Attributes of God*, 1:298.

62. Charnock, *Existence and Attributes of God*, 1:298.

63. Charnock, *Existence and Attributes of God*, 1:298.

64. Charnock, *Existence and Attributes of God*, 1:299.

65. Charnock, *Existence and Attributes of God*, 1:304.

Chapter 9 Is God Bound by Space?

1. Bavinck, *Reformed Dogmatics*, 2:166.

2. Charnock, *Existence and Attributes of God*, 1:368.

3. Charnock, *Existence and Attributes of God*, 1:367.

4. This phrase comes from Rogers, *Perfect Being Theology*, 59.

5. Bavinck, *Reformed Dogmatics*, 2:166.

6. Charnock, *Existence and Attributes of God*, 1:380.

7. Bavinck, *Reformed Dogmatics*, 2:167.

8. Charnock, *Existence and Attributes of God*, 1:368.

9. Bavinck, *Reformed Dogmatics*, 2:167.

10. The phrase "spatially divisible" is from Helm, *Eternal God*, 53.

11. Aquinas, *Summa Theologiae* 1a.8.2.

12. Charnock, *Existence and Attributes of God*, 1:375.

13. Anselm, *Monologion* 20 (*Major Works*, 34). Cf. *Monologion* 21 (*Major Works*, 35).

14. Charnock, *Existence and Attributes of God*, 1:374–75.

15. Charnock, *Existence and Attributes of God*, 1:367.

16. Charnock, *Existence and Attributes of God*, 1:369.

17. Charnock, *Existence and Attributes of God*, 1:374.

18. Charnock, *Existence and Attributes of God*, 1:389.

19. Charnock, *Existence and Attributes of God*, 1:374.

20. Charnock, *Existence and Attributes of God*, 1:383.

21. Charnock, *Existence and Attributes of God*, 1:381.

22. Charnock, *Existence and Attributes of God*, 1:381.

23. Charnock, *Existence and Attributes of God*, 1:381.

24. Charnock, *Existence and Attributes of God*, 1:383.

25. Charnock, *Existence and Attributes of God*, 1:394.

26. Charnock, *Existence and Attributes of God*, 1:394.

27. Charnock, *Existence and Attributes of God*, 1:385.

28. My emphasis here falls on the *works* or *operations* of God. As Turretin (*Institutes*, 1:201) explains, "When God is said to ascend or descend . . . it is not said with respect to his essence, but only to the absence or presence of his diverse operations."

29. Turretin, *Institutes*, 1:200.

30. Charnock, *Existence and Attributes of God*, 1:387.

31. Charnock, *Existence and Attributes of God*, 1:387.

32. I draw the basics of this illustration from Charnock, though I have colored them in considerably to elaborate upon his illustration. Charnock, *Existence and Attributes of God*, 1:329.

33. Charnock, *Existence and Attributes of God*, 1:329.

34. Charnock, *Existence and Attributes of God*, 1:369.

35. Charnock, *Existence and Attributes of God*, 1:369.

36. E.g., moralistic therapeutic deism. To learn what MTD is, see Horton, *Christless Christianity*.

37. There are exceptions; some deists do make room for providence but nevertheless preclude supernatural intervention and involvement. Many deists deny the supernatural in Jesus's ministry.

38. Paul is quoting Epimenides of Crete, who lived in the seventh century BC.

39. Aquinas is quoting Gregory in *Summa Theologiae* 1a.8.3. (Note 9 explains that this is quoted from the *Glossa ordinaria* on Song of Songs 5:17, which attributes the statement to Gregory, but without reference.)

40. Charnock, *Existence and Attributes of God*, 1:405. Aquinas makes a similar distinction (*Summa Theologiae* 1a.8.3).

41. Packer, *Keep in Step with the Spirit*, 43.

42. Peterson, *Possessed by God*, 28.

43. Bavinck, *Reformed Dogmatics*, 2:169–70.

44. Augustine, *Expositions on the Psalms*, on Ps. 94; as quoted in Bavinck, *Reformed Dogmatics*, 2:170.

45. Bavinck, *Reformed Dogmatics*, 2:170.

46. Augustine, *Expositions on the Psalms*, on Ps. 34; as quoted in Bavinck, *Reformed Dogmatics*, 2:170.

47. Augustine, *Expositions on the Psalms*, on Ps. 74; as quoted in Bavinck, *Reformed Dogmatics*, 2:170.

48. To flesh this out, see Charnock, *Existence and Attributes of God*, 1:399.

Chapter 10 Is God All-Powerful, All-Knowing, and All-Wise?

1. Charnock, *Existence and Attributes of God*, 2:17.

2. Charnock (*Existence and Attributes of God*, 2:17) puts this point more technically: omnipotence is "nothing but the Divine essence efficacious *ad extra.*"

3. Bavinck, *Reformed Dogmatics*, 2:235.

4. See Bavinck, *Reformed Dogmatics*, 2:212, 237, 249.

5. Bavinck, *Reformed Dogmatics*, 2:247.

6. Charnock, *Existence and Attributes of God*, 2:12.

7. These latter two come from Aquinas, *Summa Theologiae* 1a.7.2.

8. Anselm, *Proslogion* 7 (*Major Works*, 90).

9. Rogers, *Perfect Being Theology*, 31.

10. Bavinck, *Reformed Dogmatics*, 2:192.

11. Augustine, *Trinity* 15.4.22 (trans. Hill, p. 414).

12. John of Damascus, *Orthodox Faith* 2.2, p. 205.

13. Rogers, *Perfect Being Theology*, 31.

14. Augustine, *Trinity* 15.13; 6.10; as quoted in Aquinas, *Summa Theologiae* 1a.14.8. Charnock, *Existence and Attributes of God*, 1:324, says something very similar.

15. To explore the debate over middle knowledge (Molinism) would move us beyond the introductory level of this book, but it should at least be noted that I reject Molinism because it does just this—namely, conditions God's knowledge upon something or someone outside himself, even if it be other possible worlds. For that reason, I am not convinced it escapes some of the same issues and challenges faced by open theism or Arminianism, which likewise condition God's knowledge and his ability to act on that knowledge upon human libertarian freedom, a freedom that can always do otherwise and is never necessitated. For a critique of Molinism, see Blocher, "'Middle Knowledge': Solution or Seduction?"

16. To see God's comprehensive, exhaustive, and meticulous omniscience, see 2 Kings 13:19; Job 37:16; Pss. 139:1–4, 16; 147:5; Isa. 5:1–7 (cf. Deut. 31:16–21); 41:21–29; 42:8–9; 43:8–13; 44:6–8; 44:24–28; 45:1–7; 45:18–25; 46:8–11; 48:3–8; Pss. 44:21; 94:11; 139:1–6, 17–18; Dan. 11:2, 4, 5–35; Isa. 40:12–14; 42:9; 44:7–8; Jer. 1:4–5; 38:17–20; John 13:19–21 (cf. Isa. 43:10); 13:38 with 18:19–27; 21:18–19; Rom. 11:33–36; Heb. 4:13. Omniscience is attributed to Jesus as well: John 6:64, 70–71 (cf. Matt. 26:21–25); 13:19; 13:38 (cf. 18:19–28); 14:29; 16:4; 21:18–19; Luke 22:31–32.

17. Bavinck, *Reformed Dogmatics*, 2:198; Sproul, *Enjoying God*, 127.

18. Bavinck, *Reformed Dogmatics*, 2:200.

19. "For that reason his knowledge is undivided, simple, unchangeable, eternal. He knows all things instantaneously, simultaneously, from eternity; all things are eternally present to his mind's eye" (Bavinck, *Reformed Dogmatics*, 2:196). Here Bavinck appeals to Irenaeus, Augustine, Lombard, Aquinas, Zanchius, and Polanus. Also consult Turretin, *Institutes*, 1:207, who says God knows all things "by his essence"; he knows all things "undividedly, because he knows all things intuitively and noetically, not discursively and dianoetically."

20. Augustine, *Confessions* 11.1 (1) (p. 221).

21. Charnock, *Existence and Attributes of God*, 1:285.

22. Rogers, *Perfect Being Theology*, 31.

23. Anselm, *On the Incarnation of the Word* 7 (*Major Works*, 247).

24. As is the case here, I have occasionally added italics to Scripture quotations for emphasis.

25. Thomas E. McComiskey, "*bārā*'," in Botterweck and Ringgren, eds., *Theological Dictionary of the Old Testament*, 1:127–28. I owe this observation to Ware, *God's Greater Glory*, 71–72.

26. Ware, *God's Greater Glory*, 72. Cf. G. Herbert Livingston, "*rā'a'*," in Botterweck and Ringgren, *Theological Dictionary of the Old Testament*, 2:854–57.

27. Other passages that say the same include Lam. 3:37–38 and Eccles. 7:13–14.

28. Bavinck, *Reformed Dogmatics*, 2:241.

29. Turretin, *Institutes*, 1:515.

30. This distinction is one assumed throughout Scripture, but it is also one affirmed from Augustine to the Reformers. On this distinction in the will of God, see Bavinck, *Reformed Dogmatics*, 2:241–45.

31. Bavinck, *Reformed Dogmatics*, 2:243. See Pss. 33:11; 115:3; Dan. 4:25, 35; Isa. 46:10; Matt. 11:26; Rom. 9:8; Eph. 1:4; Rev. 4:11.

32. Bavinck, *Reformed Dogmatics*, 2:244.

33. There are a multitude of reasons God might ordain evil. See Bavink, *Reformed Dogmatics*, 2:591–620.

34. Letter to Bishop Mandell Creighton, April 5, 1887. Quoted in Dalberg-Acton, *Historical Essays and Studies*, 504.

35. Bavinck, *Reformed Dogmatics*, 2:240.

36. Bavinck, *Reformed Dogmatics*, 2:240.

37. Schaeffer, *No Little People*, 5.

38. Rogers, *Perfect Being Theology*, 9.

Chapter 11 Can God Be Both Holy and Loving?

1. Garrett, *Exodus*, 207.

2. Garrett, *Exodus*, 207 and 212. I don't necessarily agree with Garrett that to "ask his 'name' is to miss the point completely, because he is not one of the gods at all." While Moses does ask God's name, God is taking the initiative in appearing to Moses and revealing his plan. Furthermore, God is not shy throughout the Exodus story line, as well as the story line of the Old Testament, to reveal his name or names. In Exod. 3 he certainly does want Moses and Israel to know him by this particular name as well.

3. Hamilton, *Exodus*, 66.

4. See Frame, *Doctrine of God*, for a treatment of this theme.

5. See Sproul, *Enjoying God*, 138.

6. See Brian E. Kelly's comments on 2 Chron. 26:16 in the *ESV Study Bible*.

7. Kelly (comments in the *ESV Study Bible*) thinks Uzziah is moving beyond political authority to claim spiritual authority as well.

8. Oswalt, *Isaiah*, 177.

9. Oswalt, *Isaiah*, 177.

10. For both interpretations, see Num. 21:6; Isa. 14:29; 30:6. Fire "is everywhere associated with God's holiness (Exod. 3:1–6; 13:21; 19:18; Lev. 10:1–2; Num. 11:1–2; 1 Kings 18:24; Isa. 6:6–7), so that it would be entirely appropriate for those who declare that holiness (v. 3) to be 'fiery' in their appearance" (Oswalt, *Isaiah*, 180–81).

11. Oswalt, *Isaiah*, 181.

12. For another example, see Rev. 4:8.

13. Carson, *Difficult Doctrine of the Love of God*, 16–21.

14. Turretin, *Institutes*, 1:237.

15. On this point, see Bavinck, *Reformed Dogmatics*, 2:224.

16. Emphasis added.

Chapter 12 Should God Be Jealous for His Own Glory?

1. You may remember from chapter 7 the story of Balaam in Num. 22–24. Balaam speaks the word of the Lord, but he is a reluctant, even disobedient and ungodly, man. We are told in Rev. 2:14 that it was Balaam that "taught Balak to put a stumbling block before the sons of Israel, so that they might eat food sacrificed to idols and practice sexual immorality." So even though Balaam delivers prophecies that bless Israel, contrary to what Balak wants out of Balaam, nevertheless, in

the end Balaam finds another way to undercut Israel—namely, through sending seductive women to entice Israel into idolatry and immorality.

2. See Gordon J. Wenham's comments on this disgraceful type of death in the *ESV Study Bible*.

3. Exod. 20:5; 34:14; Num. 25:11; Deut. 4:24; 5:9; 6:15; 29:20; 31:16–17; 32:16, 21; Josh. 24:19; 2 Kings 19:31; Pss. 78:58; 79:5; Isa. 9:7; 26:11; 37:32; 42:13; 59:17; 63:15; Ezek. 5:13; 8:3–5; 16:38, 42; 23:25; 36:5–6; 39:25; Joel 2:18; Nah. 1:2; Zeph. 1:18; 3:8; Zech. 1:14–15; 8:2; John 2:17; 1 Cor. 10:22; 2 Cor. 11:2; James 4:5.

4. To further explore the difference, see Thoennes, *Godly Jealousy*, 13–15. Thoennes makes further distinctions; e.g., zeal and jealousy are not identical either, the former being a broader category than the latter.

5. Thoennes, *Godly Jealousy*, 13.

6. The subtitle of Thoennes's book is "A Theology of Intolerant Love."

7. Thoennes, *Godly Jealousy*, 22.

8. Isa. 1:21; 54:5–6; 57:3; 57:8; Jer. 2:2, 23–25; 3:20; 31:32; Ezek. 16:1–43.

9. Thoennes, *Godly Jealousy*, 64, though he is drawing from Block, *Ezekiel*, 1:465.

10. Zimmerli, *Ezekiel*, 1:342; cf. Thoennes, *Godly Jealousy*, 107.

11. The consequences of rejecting the Lord are plain: Israel "stirred him to jealousy with strange gods" and "provoked him to anger" (Deut. 32:16). "They have made me jealous with what is no god; they have provoked me to anger with their idols," says the Lord (32:21; cf. 6:13–16).

12. Thoennes, *Godly Jealousy*, 23.

13. Thoennes, *Godly Jealousy*, 12.

14. Anselm, *Proslogion 2* (*Major Works*, 87).

15. Thoennes, *Godly Jealousy*, 64.

16. For more on this point, see Rennie, "Theology of the Doctrine of Divine Impassibility: (II)," 307.

17. And, therefore, "True virtue must chiefly consist in love to God" (Edwards, *Nature of True Virtue*, 550).

18. Piper, *Desiring God*, 18.

19. This is a statement found throughout Piper, *Desiring God* (e.g., p. 10).

Bibliography

à Brakel, Wilhelmus. *The Christian's Reasonable Service.* Vol. 1, *God, Man, and Christ.* Grand Rapids: Reformation Heritage Press, 2012.

Anselm of Canterbury. *The Major Works.* Edited by Brian Davies and G. R. Evans. Oxford: Oxford University Press, 1998.

Aquinas, Thomas. *Opera Omnia.* Leonine ed. Rome: Typographia Polyglotta, 1882–.

———. *Summa contra Gentiles, Book One: God.* Translated by Anton C. Pegis. Notre Dame, IN: University of Notre Dame Press, 1955.

———. *Summa Theologiae, Questions on God.* Edited by Brian Davies and Brian Leftow. Cambridge Texts in the History of Philosophy. Cambridge: Cambridge University Press, 2006.

Augustine of Hippo. *The City of God.* Edited by G. R. Evans. Translated by Henry Bettenson. New York: Penguin, 1972.

———. *The Confessions.* Translated by Henry Chadwick. Oxford: Oxford University Press, 1991.

———. *On Free Choice of the Will.* Translated by Thomas Williams. Indianapolis: Hackett, 1993.

———. *The Trinity.* Edited by John E. Rotelle. Translated by Edmund Hill. The Works of Saint Augustine 5. Hyde Park, NY: New City, 1991.

———. *The Trinity.* Translated by Stephen McKenna. Fathers of the Church 45. Washington, DC: Catholic University of America Press, 1963.

Baines, Ronald S., Richard C. Barcellos, James P. Butler, Stefan T. Lindblad, and James M. Renihan, eds. *Confessing the Impassible God: The Biblical, Classical, and Confessional Doctrine of Divine Impassibility.* Palmdale, CA: RBAP, 2015.

Barrett, Jordan. *Divine Simplicity: A Biblical and Trinitarian Account.* Emerging Scholars. Minneapolis: Fortress, 2017.

Barrett, Matthew. "Balancing *Sola Scriptura* and Catholic Trinitarianism: John Calvin, Nicene Complexity, and the Necessary Tension of Dogmatics." *Midwestern Journal of Theology* 16, no. 2 (Fall 2017): 45–78.

———. *God's Word Alone: The Authority of Scripture.* Grand Rapids: Zondervan, 2016.

Barth, Karl. *Church Dogmatics.* Vol. 2.1, *The Doctrine of God.* 1957. Reprint, Peabody, MA: Hendrickson, 2010.

Bavinck, Herman. *The Doctrine of God.* Edinburgh: Banner of Truth, 1978.

———. *Reformed Dogmatics.* Vol. 2, *God and Creation.* Grand Rapids: Baker Academic, 2006.

Berkhof, Louis. *Systematic Theology.* 1959. Reprint, Edinburgh: Banner of Truth, 2003.

Blocher, Henri A. G. "'Middle Knowledge': Solution or Seduction?" *Unio cum Christo* 4, no. 1 (2018): 29–46.

Block, Daniel. *The Book of Ezekiel.* 2 vols. New International Commentary on the Old Testament. Grand Rapids: Eerdmans, 1997–98.

Boethius. *The Consolation of Philosophy.* Translated by Victor Watts. London: Penguin, 1999.

Botterweck, G. Johannes, and Helmer Ringgren, eds. *Theological Dictionary of the Old Testament.* Translated by John T. Willis et al. 15 vols. Grand Rapids: Eerdmans, 1974–2006.

Boyer, Steven D., and Christopher Hall. *The Mystery of God: Theology for Knowing the Unknowable.* Grand Rapids: Baker Academic, 2012.

Bray, Gerald. *The Doctrine of God.* Contours of Christian Theology. Downers Grove, IL: InterVarsity, 1993.

Calvin, John. *The Covenant Enforced: Sermons on Deuteronomy 27 and 28.* Edited by James B. Jordan. Tyler, TX: Institute for Christian Economics, 1990.

———. *Institutes of the Christian Religion.* Edited by John T. McNeill. Translated by Ford Lewis Battles. 2 vols. The Library of Christian Classics. 1960. Reprint, Louisville: Westminster John Knox, 2006.

———. *The Secret Providence of God*. Edited by Paul Helm. Wheaton: Crossway, 2010.

Carson, D. A. *The Difficult Doctrine of the Love of God*. Wheaton: Crossway, 2000.

———. *Divine Sovereignty and Human Responsibility: Biblical Perspectives in Tension*. Eugene, OR: Wipf and Stock, 2002.

———. *How Long, O Lord? Reflections on Suffering and Evil*. 2nd ed. Grand Rapids: Baker Academic, 2006.

Carter, Craig A. *Interpreting Scripture with the Great Tradition: Recovering the Genius of Premodern Exegesis*. Grand Rapids: Baker Books, 2018.

"The Chalcedonian Decree." In *Christology of the Later Fathers*, edited by Edward R. Hardy, Library of Christian Classics, 373. Louisville: Westminster John Knox, 1954.

Charnock, Stephen. *Discourses upon the Existence and Attributes of God*. 2 vols. 1874. Reprint, Grand Rapids: Baker, 1996.

———. *The Works of Stephen Charnock*. Volumes 1 and 2. Edinburgh: Banner of Truth, 1986, 2010.

Craig, William Lane. "Toward a Tenable Social Trinitarianism." In *Philosophical and Theological Essays on the Trinity*, edited by Thomas McCall and Michael C. Rea, 89–99. Oxford: Oxford University Press, 2009.

Dalberg-Acton, John. *Historical Essays and Studies*. Edited by J. N. Figgis and R. V. Laurence. London: Macmillan, 1907.

Dixon, Thomas. *From Passions to Emotions: The Creation of a Secular Psychological Category*. Cambridge: Cambridge University Press, 2006.

———. "Theology, Anti-Theology and Atheology: From Christian Passions to Secular Emotions." *Modern Theology* 15, no. 3 (1999): 297–330.

Dodds, Michael J. *The Unchanging God of Love: Thomas Aquinas and Contemporary Theology on Divine Immutability*. Washington, DC: Catholic University of America Press, 2008.

Dolezal, James E. *All That Is in God: Evangelical Theology and the Challenge of Classical Christian Theism*. Grand Rapids: Reformation Heritage Books, 2017.

———. *God without Parts: Divine Simplicity and the Metaphysics of God's Absoluteness*. Eugene, OR: Pickwick, 2011.

———. "Still Impassible: Confessing God without Passions." *Journal of the Institute of Reformed Baptist Studies* 1 (2014): 125–51.

———. "Strong Impassibility." In *Divine Impassibility: Four Views of God's Emotions and Suffering*, edited by Robert Matz and A. Chadwick Thornhill. Downers Grove, IL: IVP Academic, 2019.

Dorner, Isaak A. *Divine Immutability: A Critical Reconsideration.* Translated by Robert R. Williams and Claude Welch. Fortress Texts in Modern Theology. Minneapolis: Fortress, 1994. First published in German in 1856–58.

Duby, Steven J. *Divine Simplicity: A Dogmatic Account.* T&T Clark Studies in Systematic Theology. New York: Bloomsbury T&T Clark, 2016.

Edwards, Jonathan. *Charity and Its Fruits.* Carlisle, PA: Banner of Truth Trust, 1969.

———. *Discourse on the Trinity.* In *The Works of Jonathan Edwards*, vol. 21, *Writings on the Trinity, Grace, and Faith.* New Haven: Yale University Press, 2003.

———. *The End for Which God Created the World.* In John Piper, *God's Passion for His Glory: Living the Vision of Jonathan Edwards*, 117–252. Wheaton: Crossway, 1998.

———. *The Nature of True Virtue.* In *The Works of Jonathan Edwards*, vol. 8, *Ethical Writings*, ed. Paul Ramsey, 537–627. New Haven: Yale University Press, 1989.

Ellis, Brannon. *Calvin, Classical Trinitarianism & the Aseity of the Son.* Oxford: Oxford University Press, 2012.

The ESV Study Bible. Wheaton: Crossway, 2008.

Feinberg, John S. *No One Like Him: The Doctrine of God.* Foundations of Evangelical Theology. Wheaton: Crossway, 2001.

Feser, Edward. *Scholastic Metaphysics.* Germany: Editiones Scholasticae, 2014.

Frame, John M. *The Doctrine of God.* Phillipsburg, NJ: P&R, 2002.

Garrett, Duane A. *A Commentary on Exodus.* Kregel Exegetical Library. Grand Rapids: Kregel Academic, 2014.

Gavrilyuk, Paul L. "God's Impassible Suffering in the Flesh: The Promise of Paradoxical Christology." In *Divine Impassibility and the Mystery of Human Suffering*, edited by James F. Keating and Thomas Joseph White, 127–49. Grand Rapids: Eerdmans, 2009.

————. *The Suffering of the Impassible God: The Dialectics of Patristic Thought*. Oxford Early Christian Studies. Oxford: Oxford University Press, 2004.

Gill, John. *A Body of Doctrinal Divinity*. Atlanta: Turner Lassetter, 1957.

Gregory of Nazianzus. *Theological Orations*. In *Nicene and Post-Nicene Fathers*, second series, edited by Philip Schaff and Henry Wace, 7:203–434. Peabody, MA: Hendrickson, 2012.

————. *To Cledonius the Priest against Apollinarius*. In *Nicene and Post-Nicene Fathers*, second series, edited by Philip Schaff and Henry Wace, 7:439–43. Peabody, MA: Hendrickson, 2012.

Gregory of Nyssa. *Quod Non Sint Tres Dii, ad Ablabium*. In *Patrologia Graeca*, edited by Jacques-Paul Migne, vol. 45. Paris, 1863.

Gunton, Colin E. *Act and Being: Towards a Theology of the Divine Attributes*. London: SCM, 2002.

Hamilton, Victor P. *Exodus: An Exegetical Commentary*. Grand Rapids: Baker Academic, 2011.

Hanby, Michael. *No God, No Science? Theology, Cosmology, Biology*. Oxford: Wiley-Blackwell, 2013.

Harman, Allan. "Singing and Living Justification by Faith Alone: The Psalms and the Wisdom Literature." In *The Doctrine on Which the Church Stands or Falls*, edited by Matthew Barrett. Wheaton: Crossway, forthcoming.

Hart, David Bentley. *The Experience of God: Being, Consciousness, Bliss*. New Haven: Yale University Press, 2013.

Helm, Paul. *Eternal God*. Oxford: Clarendon, 1988.

————. "The Impossibility of Divine Passibility." In *The Power and Weakness of God: Impassibility and Orthodoxy; Papers Presented at the Third Edinburgh Conference in Christian Dogmatics, 1989*, edited by Nigel M. de S. Cameron, 119–40. Edinburgh: Rutherford, 1990.

Henry, Carl F. H. *God Who Stands and Stays*. Vol. 5, *God, Revelation and Authority*. Wheaton: Crossway, 1999.

Hodge, Charles. *Systematic Theology*. Vol. 1. Grand Rapids: Eerdmans, 1986.

Hogg, David S. "Anselm of Canterbury (1033–1109)." In *The Dictionary of Historical Theology*, edited by Trevor A. Hart, 16–18. Grand Rapids: Eerdmans, 2000.

Horton, Michael. *The Christian Faith: A Systematic Theology for Pilgrims on the Way*. Grand Rapids: Zondervan, 2011.

———. *Christless Christianity: The Alternative Gospel of the American Church*. Grand Rapids: Baker Books, 2008.

———. *Pilgrim Theology*. Grand Rapids: Zondervan, 2013.

Huffman, Douglas S., and Eric L. Johnson, eds. *God under Fire: Modern Scholarship Reinvents God*. Grand Rapids: Zondervan, 2000.

Irenaeus. *Against Heresies*. In *Ante-Nicene Fathers*, edited by Alexander Roberts and James Donaldson, 1:315–567. Peabody, MA: Hendrickson, 2012.

John Chrysostom. *On the Incomprehensible Nature of God*. Translated by Paul W. Harkins. Washington, DC: Catholic University of America Press, 2010.

John of Damascus. *Expositio de Fide Orthodoxa*. In *Patrologia Graeca*, edited by Jacques-Paul Migne, vol. 94. Paris, 1863.

———. *Exposition of the Orthodox Faith*. Translated by S. D. F. Salmond. In *Nicene and Post-Nicene Fathers*, second series, edited by Philip Schaff and Henry Wace, 9:1–101. Peabody, MA: Hendrickson, 2012.

———. *The Orthodox Faith*. In *Writings*, translated by Frederic H. Chase Jr., 165–406. Washington, DC: Catholic University of America Press, 1958.

Kuhn, P. *Gottes Selbsterniedrigung in der Theologie der Rabbinen*. Munich: Kösel, 1968.

Leigh, Edward. *A Systeme or Body of Divinity*. London, n.d.

Lewis, C. S. *The Problem of Pain*. New York: Macmillan, 1959.

———. *The Weight of Glory*. New York: HarperCollins, 2001.

Lister, J. Ryan. *The Presence of God: Its Place in the Storyline of Scripture and the Story of Our Lives*. Wheaton: Crossway, 2015.

Lister, Rob. *God Is Impassible and Impassioned: Toward a Theology of Divine Emotion*. Wheaton: Crossway, 2013.

Littlejohn, Bradford. *God of Our Fathers: Classical Theism for the Contemporary Church*. Moscow, ID: The Davenant Institute, 2018.

Long, D. Stephen. *The Perfectly Simple Triune God: Aquinas and His Legacy*. Minneapolis: Fortress, 2016.

McCormack, Bruce L., ed. *Engaging the Doctrine of God: Contemporary Protestant Perspectives*. Grand Rapids: Baker Academic, 2008.

McGinnis, Andrew M. *The Son of God beyond the Flesh: A Historical and Theological Study of the* extra Calvinisticum. New York: Bloomsbury T&T Clark, 2014.

Molina, Luis de. *On Divine Foreknowledge: Part IV of the "Concordia."* Translated by Alfred J. Freddoso. Cornell Classics in Philosophy. Reprint, New York: Cornell University Press, 2004.

Moltmann, Jürgen. *The Crucified God: The Cross of Christ as the Foundation and Criticism of Christian Theology.* 40th anniv. ed. Minneapolis: Fortress, 2015.

———. *The Trinity and the Kingdom: The Doctrine of God.* Minneapolis: Fortress, 1993.

Moreland, J. P., and William Lane Craig. *Philosophical Foundations for a Christian Worldview.* Downers Grove, IL: InterVarsity, 2003.

Mozley, J. K. *The Impassibility of God: A Survey of Christian Thought.* Cambridge: Cambridge University Press, 1926.

Muller, Richard A. *Dictionary of Latin and Greek Theological Terms: Drawn Principally from Protestant Scholastic Theology.* 2nd ed. Grand Rapids: Baker Academic, 2017.

———. *The Divine Essence and Attributes.* Vol. 3, *Post-Reformation Reformed Dogmatics: The Rise and Development of Reformed Orthodoxy, ca. 1520 to ca. 1725.* Grand Rapids: Baker Academic, 2003.

———. "Incarnation, Immutability, and the Case for Classical Theism." *Westminster Theological Journal* 45 (1983): 22–40.

———. *The Triunity of God.* Vol. 4 of *Post-Reformation Reformed Dogmatics: The Rise and Development of Reformed Orthodoxy, ca. 1520 to ca. 1725.* Grand Rapids: Baker Academic, 2003.

Nash, Ronald H. *The Concept of God: An Exploration of Contemporary Difficulties with the Attributes of God.* Grand Rapids: Zondervan, 1983.

Ockham, William. *Predestination, God's Foreknowledge, and Future Contingents.* Translated by Marilyn McCord Adams and Morman Kretzmann. 2nd ed. Indianapolis: Hackett, 1983.

Oden, Thomas C. *The Living God.* Vol. 1, *Systematic Theology.* San Francisco: HarperSanFrancisco, 1987.

Oliphint, K. Scott. *God with Us: Divine Condescension and the Attributes of God.* Wheaton: Crossway, 2012.

———. *The Majesty of Mystery: Celebrating the Glory of an Incomprehensible God.* Bellingham, WA: Lexham, 2016.

Origen. *De Principiis*. In *Ante-Nicene Fathers*, edited by Alexander Roberts and James Donaldson, 4:239–382. Peabody, MA: Hendrickson, 2012.

———. *Homilies on Jeremiah; Homily on 1 Kings 28*. Translated by John Clark Smith. Fathers of the Church 97. Washington, DC: Catholic University of America Press, 1998.

Oswalt, John N. *The Book of Isaiah: Chapters 1–39*. New International Commentary on the Old Testament. Grand Rapids: Eerdmans, 1986.

Owen, John. *The Works of John Owen*. Edited by William H. Goold. Vol. 2, *Of Communion with God the Father, Son, and Holy Ghost*. Edinburgh: Banner of Truth, 1965.

———. *The Works of John Owen*. Edited by William H. Goold. Vol. 3, *Discourse Concerning the Holy Spirit*. 1850–53. Reprint, Edinburgh: Banner of Truth Trust, 2009.

———. *The Works of John Owen*. Edited by William H. Goold. Vol. 12, *Vindicae Evangelicae*. 1850–53. Reprint, Edinburgh: Banner of Truth Trust, 1999.

Packer, J. I. *Keep in Step with the Spirit: Finding Fullness in Our Walk with God*. Rev. ed. Grand Rapids: Baker Books, 2005.

———. *Knowing God*. Downers Grove, IL: InterVarsity, 1973.

———. *Puritan Portraits*. Fearn, Ross-shire: Christian Focus, 2012.

Parker, Robert. "Greek Religion." In *The Oxford Illustrated History of Greece and the Hellenistic World*, edited by John Boardman, Jasper Griffin, and Oswyn Murray, 248–68. Oxford: Oxford University Press, 1988.

Peterson, David. *Possessed by God: A New Testament Theology of Sanctification and Holiness*. Downers Grove, IL: InterVarsity, 1995.

Pink, Arthur W. *The Attributes of God*. Grand Rapids: Baker, 1975.

Piper, John. *Desiring God: Meditations of a Christian Hedonist*. Colorado Springs: Multnomah, 2011.

———. *The Pleasures of God: Meditations on God's Delight in Being God*. Rev. ed. Sisters, OR: Multnomah, 2000.

Placher, William C. *The Domestication of Transcendence: How Modern Thinking about God Went Wrong*. Louisville: Westminster John Knox, 1998.

Raddle-Gallwitz, Andrew. *Basil of Caesarea, Gregory of Nyssa, and the Transformation of Divine Simplicity*. Oxford Early Christian Studies. Oxford: Oxford University Press, 2009.

Renihan, Samuel. *God without Passions: A Primer; A Practical and Pastoral Study of Divine Impassibility.* Palmdale, CA: RBAP, 2015.

———, ed. *God without Passions: A Reader.* Palmdale, CA: RBAP, 2015.

Rennie, Charles J. "Analogy and the Doctrine of Divine Impassibility." In Baines et al., *Confessing the Impassible God*, 47–80.

———. "A Theology of the Doctrine of Divine Impassibility: (I) Impassibility and the Essence and Attributes of God." In Baines et al., *Confessing the Impassible God*, 279–304.

———. "A Theology of the Doctrine of Divine Impassibility: (II) Impassibility and the Divine Affections." In Baines et al., *Confessing the Impassible God*, 305–36.

Rogers, Katherin A. *Perfect Being Theology.* Reason and Religion. Edinburgh: Edinburgh University Press, 2000.

Sanders, Fred. *The Deep Things of God: How the Trinity Changes Everything.* Wheaton: Crossway, 2010.

———. *The Triune God.* New Studies in Dogmatics. Grand Rapids: Zondervan, 2016.

Sanlon, Peter. *Simply God: Recovering the Classical Trinity.* Nottingham, England: Inter-Varsity, 2014.

Schaeffer, Francis A. *No Little People.* In *The Complete Works of Francis A. Schaeffer*, 3:3–194. Wheaton: Crossway, 2003.

Shedd, William G. T. *Dogmatic Theology.* Edited by Alan W. Gomes. 3rd ed. Phillipsburg, NJ: P&R, 2003.

Sheridan, Mark. *Language for God in Patristic Tradition: Wrestling with Biblical Anthropomorphism.* Downers Grove, IL: IVP Academic, 2005.

Smith, William Chalmers. "Immortal, Invisible." In *Hymns for Praise and Worship*, no. 21. Nappanee, IN: Evangel, 1984.

Sonderegger, Katherine. *Systematic Theology.* Vol. 1, *The Doctrine of God.* Minneapolis: Fortress, 2015.

Sproul, R. C. *Enjoying God: Finding Hope in the Attributes of God.* Grand Rapids: Baker Books, 2017.

Swain, Scott R. "Divine Trinity." In *Christian Dogmatics: Reformed Theology for the Church Catholic*, edited by Michael Allen and Scott R. Swain, 78–106. Grand Rapids: Baker Academic, 2016.

Swinnock, George. *The Incomparableness of God.* Vol. 4 of *The Works of George Swinnock.* Edinburgh: Banner of Truth, 1992.

"The Symbol of Chalcedon." In *The Creeds of Christendom*, edited by Philip Schaff, 2:62–63. Reprint, Grand Rapids: Baker Books, 2007.

Tertullian. *Against Marcion.* In *Ante-Nicene Fathers*, edited by Alexander Roberts and James Donaldson, 3:271–475. Peabody, MA: Hendrickson, 2012.

Thoennes, K. Erik. *Godly Jealousy: A Theology of Intolerant Love.* Fearn, Ross-shire: Mentor, 2005.

Tozer, A. W. *The Attributes of God.* Vol. 1, *A Journey into the Father's Heart.* Camp Hill, PA: Christian Publications, 1997.

———. *The Attributes of God.* Vol. 2, *Deeper into the Father's Heart.* Camp Hill, PA: Christian Publications, 2001.

———. *The Knowledge of the Holy.* San Francisco: HarperSanFrancisco, 1961.

Turretin, Francis. *Institutes of Elenctic Theology.* Edited by James T. Dennison Jr. Translated by George Giger. Vol. 1, *First through Tenth Topics.* Phillipsburg, NJ: 1992.

Ussher, James. *A Body of Divinitie, or the Summe and Substance of Christian Religion.* London: M.F., 1645.

Vanhoozer, Kevin J. *Remythologizing Theology: Divine Action, Passion, and Authorship.* Cambridge Studies in Christian Doctrine. Cambridge: Cambridge University Press, 2010.

Vos, Geerhardus. *Reformed Dogmatics.* Translated by Richard B. Gaffin Jr. Vol. 1, *Theology Proper.* Bellingham, WA: Lexham, 2012–14.

Waltke, Bruce K., and James M. Houston. *The Psalms as Christian Worship: A Historical Commentary.* Grand Rapids: Eerdmans, 2010.

Ware, Bruce, ed. *Four Views on the Doctrine of God.* Nashville: B&H, 2008.

———. *God's Greater Glory: The Exalted God of Scripture and the Christian Faith.* Wheaton: Crossway, 2004.

———. *God's Lesser Glory: The Diminished God of Open Theism.* Wheaton: Crossway, 2000.

Watson, Thomas. *A Body of Divinity.* Reprint, Edinburgh: Banner of Truth, 2012.

Webster, John. *Confessing God: Essays in Christian Dogmatics II.* New York: Bloomsbury T&T Clark, 2016.

—————. *God without Measure: Working Papers in Christian Theology.* Vol. 1, *God and the Works of God.* New York: Bloomsbury T&T Clark, 2016.

Weinandy, Thomas G. *Does God Change? The Word's Becoming in the Incarnation.* Studies in Historical Theology 4. Still River, MA: St. Bede's Press, 2002.

—————. "Does God Suffer?" *First Things* 117 (November 2001): 35–41.

—————. *Does God Suffer?* Notre Dame, IN: University of Notre Dame Press, 2000.

—————. "Impassibility of God." In *New Catholic Encyclopedia*, edited by Thomas Carson and Joann Cerrito, 7:357–60. 2nd ed. Detroit: Thomson Gale, 2003.

Williams, Garry J. *His Love Endures Forever: Reflections on the Immeasurable Love of God.* Wheaton: Crossway, 2016.

Zimmerli, Walther. *Ezekiel.* Hermeneia. 2 vols. Philadelphia: Fortress, 1979–83.

CREDO

MAGAZINE AND PODCAST

Credo is an online magazine published quarterly with articles, interviews, and columns on today's most important theological issues. Our desire is to see biblically grounded, Christ-exalting reformation and transformation in the church today.

Listen to **Matthew Barrett** talk with today's top theologians about doctrines that matter.